The Swords of Shakespeare

To Monika
in gratitude for her unfailing support.
To my daughters, Anna and Lea,
for their patience with a preoccupied father.
And to the late Timothy Robert, who first encouraged my desire to write.

"They are worthy to inlay heaven with stars"
CYMBELINE V, v.

The Swords of Shakespeare

An Illustrated Guide to Stage Combat Choreography in the Plays of Shakespeare

J. D. MARTINEZ

McFarland & Company, Inc., Publishers
Jefferson, North Carolina, and London

> *The present work is a reprint of the library bound edition of* The Swords of Shakespeare: An Illustrated Guide to Stage Combat Choreography in the Plays of Shakespeare, *first published in 1996 by McFarland.*

ACKNOWLEDGMENTS: It is a great pleasure to list the names of those individuals who have had a direct influence on my work: Inez Galvan, Margaret Meyer, Henry Marshall, Hugh Cruttwell, David Boushey, Erik Fredrickson, Andrew Fracher, Patrick Crean, Albert Gordon, Thomas Ziegler, David Leong, Allen Suddeth, J. R. Beardsley, Christopher Villa, Richard Raether, B. H. Barry, Jarlath Conroy, Charles McGaw, James Roose-Evans, Joe Mantegna, Meshach Taylor, Stuart Gordon, Linda McCullom, Richard Gradkowski, Dale Kirby, Albert Gordon, Thomas Ziegler, John Elrod, Liam O'Brien, Colleen Kelly, Susan Eviston, Normand Beauregard, Reid Gilbert, David Knight, Doris Helton, Maury Erickson, John Ficca, Delia Ford, Brad Waller, James O'Connor, Elizabeth Weaver, Edward Rozinsky, Rod Casteel, Mark Olsen, Dan Carter, Charles Conwell, James Finney, Willis Middleton, Mark Guinn, Payson Burt, Robert Walsh, David Woolley, Doug Mumaw, Susan Chrietzberg, Robin McFarquhar, Jack Young, Don Baker, Barry Mines, Troy Hill, Charles Currier, Lewis Shaw, Michael Johnson.

LIBRARY OF CONGRESS CATALOGUING-IN-PUBLICATION DATA

Martinez, J. D., 1949–
The swords of Shakespeare : an illustrated guide to stage combat choreography in the plays of Shakespeare / J. D. Martinez.
p. cm.
Includes bibliographical references and index.
ISBN 978-0-7864-7609-1
softcover : acid free paper ∞

1. Shakespeare, William, 1564–1616—Dramatic production. 2. Shakespeare, William, 1564–1616—Knowledge—Military art and science. 3. Stage fencing. 4. Swordplay in literature. 5. Stage fighting. I. Title.
PR3091.M23 2013   792'.9—dc20   95-18168

BRITISH LIBRARY CATALOGUING DATA ARE AVAILABLE

© 1996 J. D. Martinez. All rights reserved

No part of this book may be reproduced or transmitted in any form or by any means, electronic or mechanical, including photocopying or recording, or by any information storage and retrieval system, without permission in writing from the publisher.

On the cover: Knights sword fighting on stage (both iStock/Thinkstock)

Manufactured in the United States of America

McFarland & Company, Inc., Publishers
Box 611, Jefferson, North Carolina 28640
www.mcfarlandpub.com

TABLE OF CONTENTS

Acknowledgments	iv
Introduction	1
Principles of Stage Fight Choreography	3
Ancient History vs. Modern Practice	7
Safety and Training	11
A Brief History of Elizabethan Swordplay	19
THE CHOREOGRAPHY	**27**
Henry IV, Part 1	29
Douglas vs. Blunt	29
Douglas vs. King Henry	32
Douglas vs. Prince Henry	37
Hotspur vs. Prince Henry	41
Henry IV, Part 2	51
Falstaff vs. Pistol	51
Henry VI, Part 1	54
Charles vs. Joan De Pucelle	54
Talbot vs. Joan De Pucelle	60
Henry VI, Part 2	70
Horner vs. Peter	70
Cade vs. Iden	75
Clifford vs. York	82
Richard vs. Somerset	86
Henry VI, Part 3	92
Richard vs. Clifford	92
Richard III	99
Richard vs. Richmond	99
Romeo and Juliet	109
Benvolio vs. Tybalt	111
Mercutio vs. Tybalt	120
Romeo vs. Tybalt	129
Paris vs. Romeo	134
Hamlet	139
Hamlet vs. Laertes	139
Troilus and Cressida	162
Ajax vs. Hector	163
Troilus vs. Diomedes	168
Troilus vs. Ajax and Diomedes	174
Achilles vs. Hector	180
Menelaus vs. Paris	184
Othello	191
Montano vs. Cassio	191
King Lear	199
Cornwall and Regan vs. Servant	199
Kent vs. Edmund	203
Oswald vs. Edgar	207
Edgar vs. Edmund	213
Macbeth	220
Macbeth vs. Young Siward	220
Macbeth vs. Macduff	224

Coriolanus	230	*Glossary*	263
Coriolanus vs. Aufidius	230	*Appendix I. The Society of American Fight Directors*	265
Cymbeline	239		
Cloten vs. Guiderius	239	*Appendix II. Suppliers of Stage Weapons*	266
Jachicmo vs. Posthumus	245		
The Two Noble Kinsmen	254	*Bibliography*	267
Palamon vs. Arcite	254	*Index*	271

INTRODUCTION

Romeo and Juliet, *Hamlet*, *Macbeth*, *Richard III*, and many other of Shakespeare's plays have at least one thing in common; they all require swordfighting.

Shakespeare was an actor before he was a playwright. As an actor in one of London's most prestigious theatre companies he would have been able to speak eloquently, dance gracefully, and swordfight expertly—it was expected. As an actor he knew that his audience appreciated good swordplay and could easily distinguish a master from a novice.

Later, as a playwright, Shakespeare gave his audiences the thrilling spectacle of an action-packed display of arms in more than a third of his plays. His audiences flooded into the Globe or Blackfriars theatres anticipating expert swordsmanship. They were not disappointed. In fact, at least one famous Elizabethan actor (Richard Tarleton) was known to be a "London Master of Defence"—a title that required many years of formal training with the popular weapons of the day.

What did the stage fights look like? What did Shakespeare intend when he included a stage fight in his famous tragedies and early history plays? How can one hope to recapture the excitement of Elizabethan swordplay as Shakespeare must have witnessed it?

Fortunately, there are a few existing manuscripts which record the training methods of the ancient Masters of Defence who were teaching swordplay not just in London but throughout Europe during Shakespeare's lifetime. It is to these masters that we turn for inspiration. In addition, Shakespeare himself left many tantalizing clues within his dialogue that allude to a way in which the dramatic scenes of violence might be staged. And finally, there are a group of highly trained professionals in the United States, Fight Masters of the Society of American Fight Directors, who have learned how to use the historic weapons of Elizabethan England and to teach these ancient secrets to others.

The Swords of Shakespeare is intended to be used as a guide for anyone interested in how the armed conflicts in the plays of Shakespeare are presented upon the stage. This book links the training of the ancient Masters of Defence with modern techniques used by professional stage combat choreographers.

All of the principal duels (both tragic and comic) in Shakespeare's plays are outlined and explained. The logic underlying each of the violent conflicts is discussed, together with textual references, to place them within the context of the play.

Sample choreography, fully illustrated,

is offered as an example of what can be done by actors and actresses who have been adequately trained by a Certified Teacher or Fight Master of the Society of American Fight Directors. Thousands of actors have been taught successfully to perform thrilling stage fights utilizing techniques similar to those presented in this book.

Draw thy sword,
That if my speech offend a noble heart,
Thy arm may do thee justice;
　　　　Kɪɴɢ Hᴇɴʀʏ ᴛʜᴇ Fɪꜰᴛʜ
　　　　V, iii

PRINCIPLES OF STAGE FIGHT CHOREOGRAPHY

A stage fight choreographer (entitled Fight Master by the Society of American Fight Directors—SAFD) is a highly specialized theatre artist who assumes primary responsibility for the safety of the performers entrusted to him. Beyond all other creative considerations, the professional stage fight choreographer places safety first.

The stage fight choreographer is skilled in the arts of acting, directing and stage movement. Formal training often includes classes in theatre history, dramatic literature and criticism, dance, mime, acrobatics, physiology, lighting design, stage setting and property design, stage effects and explosives, as well as stage firearm maintenance and handling. In addition, professional stage fight choreographers have taken courses in First Aid.

The Fight Master is a specialist working with a team of theatre specialists and must be an effective communicator who genuinely enjoys working with others for the good of the entire dramatic production.

Beyond the general qualifications and theatre training common to professional theatre artists, Fight Masters in the SAFD share a singular body of knowledge about the art and craft of stage fight choreography. This unique information is initially acquired by taking classes from Fight Masters and Certified Teachers of the Society of American Fight Directors. Some of this special knowledge is also gained through private study of historical weapons training and defense, and experience in choreographing professional stage fights. There is no substitute for experience.

Stage fight choreography is a vast subject that reflects upon the entire history of civilized man. It is helpful to understand some of the practicalities underlying a stage fight choreographer's creative choices, to enjoy all the more the brilliance of Shakespeare's scenes of dramatic conflict as they are presented upon the stage.

A dramatically effective and safely choreographed stage fight will appear to an untrained audience member as a logical sequence of violent actions which tells a clear story. The combatants will seem to be reacting spontaneously to events as they unfold in the conflict.

A balance will also be maintained between a thrilling theatrical impression of desperate violence and an audience's trust that the actors are in control. There is nothing more detrimental to an audience member's "suspension of disbelief" than fear for an actor's safety.

It is the *image* of violence that stage fight directors seek: a "poeticized" version of the violent conflict, which not only horrifies an audience but also helps to clarify the choices the characters make.

The responses of characters in the thick of battle should advance the plot. Each character in a play will fight in his or her own unique fashion. How a particular character will fight is composed of that character's attitude toward violence, combative skills, physical type, physical and psychological condition when the fight occurs, type of weapon(s) used, and the quality of the opponent.

The storyline of the fight will be dictated by the temperament of the characters involved and most importantly, by the dramatic purpose for the conflict within the play. The outcome of the fight (who wins and who loses) is only part of the issue. *How* and *why* one character triumphs over another must also serve the basic themes of the play.

The most important factors shaping a choreographer's choices when initially choreographing a stage fight are the actor-combatants themselves. What are their limitations and strengths? How are they interpreting their characters? Is the director of the play incorporating an actor's idiosyncratic tendencies into the very fabric of the play? Is the character being interpreted to fit the needs of the performer? Thus, the creative decisions based upon the chosen cast of actors are taken into account when a choreographer begins to look at the overall *strategy* of a fight.

Strategy, which is a carefully worked out plan of action, provides a logical storyline that an audience can follow. A flamboyant series of spectacularly violent actions will not capture an audience member's imagination. Only the logic of strategy creates coherent sequences of action which can lead an audience to understand *why* the "winner" has "won," and *how* he has won the conflict.

Strategy supports the logical sequence of events within a stage fight and is comprised of a few basic principles or guidelines which inform all types of stage fights. The following are a few of the more important strategic principles that stage fight choreographers consider before creating a stage fight.

Powerful drama is economical. There is no time to waste in a play and the same is true for a good stage fight. Let us assume that the characters in a presented stage fight are skilled warriors. Seasoned combatants would adhere to the notion of economy.

Skilled warriors would eliminate all unnecessary movements and seek to achieve the maximum effect with minimum effort. The combatant's objective is almost always to avoid personal injury. A character is trying to minimize the worst that can happen to himself while maximizing the worst that can happen to his opponent. Therefore, the combatant is seeking the most vulnerable body target available. For dramatic effect, choreographers vary the targets to capitalize on the element of surprise.

Intrinsic strategy in a stage fight is often displayed through the use of relative *spatial advantages*. Such advantages come in two forms, defensive and offensive.

Defensive spatial advantage relates to the ability to retreat from an attack or from a counter-attack. Trapping an opponent against an obstacle takes advantage of an opponent's inability to retreat. We have often seen this tactic used in film fights. Offensive spatial advantage arises when a character commands all reasonable offensive spaces or fencing "measure" (measure is defined as striking distance on the offensive, and outside of striking distance on the defensive).

The methods of gaining ground—of increasing and decreasing the measure in combat—were very important to the ancient Masters of Defence. Salvator Fabris, an Italian fencing master of the seventeenth century, wrote of *misura larga* and *misura stretta*. Misura larga, or a wide measure, made it possible to strike the enemy by advancing one step. Misura stretta, or close measure, made it possible to strike the adversary by extending the arm without moving the body.

In addition, the ancient masters gave great importance to gaining the high ground. For the stage fight choreographer, this means taking advantage of steps, chairs, tables, levels, etc.

How a combatant arranges his arms and legs relative to his opponent, either for protection or to invite a response, encompasses the idea of *stance*. Invariably, the ancient systems of defense employed a wide stance; in keeping with their prevalent nonlinear forms of swordplay. The ancient masters often would refer to stances as *wards*.

Wards could be defensive positions or invitational positions, depending upon weapons used or combat circumstances. Much of the flavor of a particular period style is conveyed through the choice of these historic wards.

Another essential element for good choreography is the notion of *position*. There are always vulnerable targets available. A character who is portrayed as a skilled combatant uses the strengths of his position against the weaknesses in his opponent's position. This means that the aggressor might move around an opponent to take advantage of uneven ground, obstacles, etc., in order to gain an advantageous position of strength. The skilled combatant assumes a position which would enhance the exposure of an opponent's vulnerability.

Positional advantages can also be gained when an adversary presents an improper ward, or makes an uneconomical blocking motion (parry), embarks upon a premature attack, or has sloppy balance. Gaining an advantageous position of strength in combat has historically relied upon four basic principles: *time*, *space*, *stance*, and *physique*.

Time relies a great deal on a combatant's natural rhythm and speed. Time was one of the first principles understood by the ancient Masters of Defence.

To take advantage of time it is necessary to reduce the motions of the weapon and the body to their minimum in both number of movements performed to accomplish an attack or defense, and the extent of each movement. The purpose was to discern the best possible moment for a parry and attack, and to counterpoise those motions, so as to thwart the adversary's counter-motions.

Time, as taught by the ancients, was inseparable from the execution of particular techniques or *botte secrete* (secret attacks). For example, Marco Docciolini, an Italian fencing master and a contemporary of Shakespeare, states, "It is necessary that in taking a 'time' thou shouldst remove thy body from 'the line'; and that thou shouldst seize thy 'time' whenever thy adversary displaces his point from the line of thy body."

Expanding on this ancient concept that each movement or technique commands its own increment of time has a direct relationship to the various tempos built into a stage fight. The choreographer strings together particular techniques which take advantage of various time-lengths. The fight can then be theatrically manipulated by the selection and sequence of techniques.

To support the differences between characters in a stage fight a choreographer will consider various physical advantages displayed by his actors and by the physical types outlined by the playwright. Physical advantages come in the form of greater strength, size, speed, coordination, endurance, or agility.

Combinations of these strengths in an opponent dictates balancing tactics. Since most fighters fit into one broad category or another, a choreographer will take care to choose a battle plan tailored to the physical type of his actors.

If a combatant is taller and stronger than his opponent he will avoid wasteful attacks, maintain a wide fighting measure, and use direct frontal attacks. He would not allow his opponent's mobility to draw him off balance. He would limit the opponent's mobility by closing off his opponent's defensive space by using powerful counter-attacks. If an opponent succeeds in getting in close, the combatant would push him away or resort to either wrestling techniques or disarming techniques.

If a combatant is taller and weaker, he would stay well out of range and use a mobile defense coupled with rapid attacks. He would wait for an opening, make leading attacks quickly and accurately, vary attacks from frontal to flank and use mobile footwork. He would not allow the opponent to limit his mobility. He would use counter-attacks to stop his opponent from fighting. Whenever the opponent does succeed in getting in close, he would push him away and begin anew. He would not allow his opponent to get in close and use wrestling techniques.

If the combatant is shorter and stronger, he would stay well out of range until ready to attack. He would avoid wasteful attacks. He might draw an attack, and then *slip* (a slip is a footwork technique for allowing an attack to pass by harmlessly by jumping or stepping diagonally). He would slip attacks, or counter-attack, in order to get in close. He would try to capture a limb and disarm or wrestle with his opponent. He would use an unending forward-moving offense, vary attacks with emphasis on indirect attacks and make unexpected charges. He wouldn't allow the opponent's mobility to draw him off balance. He would close off the opponent's defensive space.

If a combatant is shorter and weaker, he would stay well out of range; he would not initiate attacks. His attacks would complement his defense and he would attack quickly and accurately. He would use mobile footwork to draw the opponent off balance. He might sidestep counter-attacks quickly, always being aware of his defensive space, and he would not allow the opponent to limit his mobility. He certainly would not try to wrestle or disarm his opponent.

A choreographer can dramatize a character's mistakes by violating these basic principles of physical advantage. In this way the audience is led to witness how a character may be defeated at the hand of his opponent. The choreographer can also use these basic principles to justify to an audience how a seemingly disadvantaged combatant can manage to win a fight.

Taken separately, the concepts of economy, stance, position, spatial advantage, and physical advantage are not automatic blueprints for a successful stage fight. The stage fight choreographer manipulates these elements with an eye toward the larger picture. The choreographer is creating cohesive images. He must use his creative imagination to give the dry tactical elements of personal warfare a theatrical flow and shape.

The stage fight choreographer may weave the defensive and offensive positions together by imagining them as linear, angular, or circular. He may visualize the interwoven offensive and defensive positions as geometric patterns occupying high, middle and low levels.

The choreographer sometimes imagines tactics as words in a sentence. Like words in a sentence, tactics lend color, and nuance, but are always subordinate to the overall idea of the conflict.

He sees the tactics as actions which advance the plot, or storyline, of the fight. The skillful choreographer remembers that the audience must be able to "read" the dramatic intentions behind the tactics in a fight.

In order for a fight to be dramatic and not merely an empty display of motion and counter-motion, the audience must be led to anticipate an action, to understand the action as it is performed, and to have time to appreciate the effect of the action after it has occurred. In other words, the story being told by the interchange between combatants must have a beginning, middle and end. It should also include one or more climaxes.

Occasionally the stage fight choreographer imagines the offensive and defensive movements as directed energy. This directed energy, or "dynamic energy," is created by manipulating the direction of lines of force, by the amount of force used to complete a movement, and by controlling the resistance of a moving object against gravity.

By varying the quality of the dynamic energy of the moving bodies and of the various weapons used in the stage fight, the choreographer creates excitement. For example, some possibilities when moving weapons through space are: pushing, pulling, resisting, yielding, shaking, slashing, sliding, gliding, swinging, swaying, bouncing, stretching, bobbing, striking, collapsing, etc.

It is often helpful for the choreographer to imagine the actors' bodies moving upon the stage setting and leaving behind a continuous track, as in a blurred slow motion film. In this way he can visualize how the three dimensional space on stage is being filled. This visualization of movements in space can then be manipulated into variegated patterns which criss-cross up and down, side to side, and so on. The choreographer never forgets, however, that all of these movements are anchored by either going out, coming in, or moving around a target.

Finally, the stage fight choreographer should be sensitive to the sounds of conflict that the audience will hear. He must listen to the music of the entire fight, as though it were being played in his inner ear. He might imagine hearing breathing, groans, shouts, feet pounding and scraping on the floor, the clash and clangor of weapons in varied rhythms, moments of silence punctuating the din, the sounds of pivoting, hopping and leaping, the impact of bodies being punched, kicked, slapped, rolled on the floor, and dialogue, musical instrumentation, and audience exclamations.

By forming a strategy of combat and then choosing from his palette of historical techniques while adding imaginative elements, the stage fight choreographer will create a rough draft on paper of a visualized stage fight. He will alter his initial blueprint for the fight many times, taking into account the needs of his director, actors and designers. The ultimate result can be a thrilling and evocative scene of conflict which tells a logical story that enhances the message of the play.

Ancient History vs. Modern Practice

The art of stage fighting is more closely related to theatrical tradition and performance theory than it is to the history and practice of self defense. The theatre director, stage fight choreographer and actor-combatant are dedicated to creating a theatrical illusion. They are not attempting to replicate the dangerous systems of self defense taught with such deadly effect in the Elizabethan era, or in any other age.

Nor are wise theatre practitioners overly concerned with historical accuracy. If a theatrical production set in a particular historic period and in a specific geographic locale is being presented, then an effort to be faithful to the epoch is indeed consistent with creative integrity. However, a slavish dedication to absolute authenticity often does not serve to enhance the texture of a dramatic action. It is far more effective, as Shakespeare put it, "to hold the mirror up to nature; to show virtue her own feature, scorn her own image, and the very age and body of the time his form and pressure"—*Hamlet*, Act III, Scene ii.

It is more effective to gain the attention of a modern Western audience (whose sensibilities and attention span have been influenced by the cacophony of images from the electronic mass media) by carefully choosing the most vibrant qualities of an event than it is to be accurate in every historical detail. Therefore, the rich legacy left by the Masters of Defence who practiced in Shakespeare's time serves principally as an historic array of techniques from which the choreographer carefully borrows to furnish a theatrical effect. More important than picking and choosing from among the multitude of historic combat techniques proffered by the ancient Masters of Defence is the process of "weeding out" unsafe techniques that are applicable only to actual combat situations or that may be too difficult for the average actor to master. Among the more obvious of these questionable historic combat techniques are a simultaneous attack and defense; targeting the face; completing an attack by actually thrusting into or cutting the body; various crippling and grappling maneuvers.

It may be argued that all of the techniques taught by the masters of earlier times, if not adapted for stage practice, are potentially dangerous. Obviously the objectives of the ancient masters in teaching these fighting skills were very different from the benign theatrical motives of today.

Scholars and theatre critics whose love of history outweighs their passion for the theatrical event, understandably become irate at any apparent disregard among theatre practitioners for verisimilitude. Without wishing to protect the dilettante, I must nevertheless defend the creative theatre artist whose primary aim is to engage an audience in the most emotionally affecting manner possible. This mission, at times, demands a re-examination and not-so-subtle transmutation of historic authenticity. After all, history is an interpretation of events. It is subjective; not scientific. Making an "informed guess" is the best any of us can do.

When the question of ancient history versus modern practice comes up, it is best to trust the Fight Master who has had many years of practical experience staging battles in period plays. The Fight Master will at least produce an exciting night in the theatre. Surely the audience member who has purchased a ticket in pleasant anticipation and is then thrillingly transported by a novel stage fight will admire the choreographer's goal to "play the play" above that of maintaining a fustian opinion on a point of historical accuracy.

For the past couple of decades there has been an important effort by a number of the members of the Society of American Fight Directors to rediscover the actual systems of swordplay advocated by masters practicing in the Medieval, Renaissance, Elizabethan, Jacobean and Georgian periods of English history. Concurrently, the use of accurate facsimile weaponry in period plays has also seen a most dramatic increase in the United States, because of a greater demand for and knowledge of historic swordplay.

Never before in the history of stage fighting have we had a more widespread appreciation for the historic methods of our ancestors. The inaccuracies, or deviations, from traditional technique and strategy in swordplay are not the result of a contemptuous disregard for what has come before, but are rather the product of theatrical choices made to adjust to the practicalities and limitations of the modern stage.

When a specific technique (or training practice) is extracted from historical source material it is adapted in a number of ways to better serve the special requirements of the modern stage. In the first place, a chosen historic technique cannot be overly difficult to master. Usually, only enough rehearsal time is allotted for actors to quickly memorize and practice all of the stage fights in a production (remembering that five seconds of a choreographed stage fight requires approximately one hour of rehearsal time). Secondly, an historic technique is most effective if it is visually dramatic and lends period "color" to a fight.

The most important theatrical transformation to be made upon an actual self defense technique is to include elements of safety within the adapted technique itself. To illustrate the process of restructuring actual historic techniques of self defense into safe stage practice let us examine, for example, an offensive movement that was popular during Queen Elizabeth's reign.

An exciting sword fighting technique of the sixteenth century was a very quick snapping cut, controlled from the wrist. This cut could be executed with the "false" or "reverse" edge of the blade. This "reverse cut" was often directed at the face or at the tendons behind the knee. It is very dangerous to actually direct an attack to the face, or even to cross the path of the face. Should a defender's responses be slow, an accident could easily ensue. If either partner is inaccurate in maintaining a proper stage fighting distance, then a weapon merely crossing in front of the face could do irreparable harm. Therefore, the "reverse cut" is always performed either *below* or *above* the face and head when creating the illusion of a cut to the face.

The snapping "reverse cut" (as taught by sixteenth century masters) was very fast; so fast that its speed must be purposely retarded by first extending the action from the elbow, then from the wrist. By slightly exaggerating the sequential movements of the joints in the sword arm in this manner, the attacker furnishes a clear cue for the partner well in advance of the blade's reaching a target. Incidentally, if an actor elaborates the movements of the sword arm during the "reverse cut," an audience is better able to follow the strategic drama of this very rapid technique.

The other crucial adaptation of the "reverse cut" also relates to the notion of establishing a cue and the proper sequence of events between partners following the cue. If the illusion is to appear to be a cut directed at the face, then the defender reacts away from the "reverse cut" a moment *before* the attacker delivers the cut. In fact, the attacker does not follow through with the "reverse cut" unless the victim has already moved out of harm's way. When the partners become adept at synchronizing their timing the audience is not able to perceive the safety sequence of *cue-reaction-action*.

If the "reverse cut" is to be made to the back of the knee, then the attacker carefully places the "false edge" of the blade against the *outside* of the knee in a simulated cut. When the victim feels the attacker's blade touch the outside of the knee, the victim contracts the muscles of the body and is momentarily immobile. At this point a facial grimace is all that is needed to convey the wound. The attacker then lifts the edge of the blade slightly clear of the leg, and *pulls* the blade away from the victim in a follow-through. The edge of the attacker's blade does not drag against the victim's leg at any time. The victim does not kneel, nor otherwise initiate any large-scale pain reaction, until the point of the attacker's sword is out of fighting distance and to the outside of the victim's body outline. All of this happens quickly enough to support the violent illusion and to convince an audience.

In a manner consistent with the process outlined above, stage fight choreographers adapt each and every technique borrowed from historical manuals of defense in a myriad of clever ways. The point is to render antique systems of self defense safer, easier to learn, and theatrically effective. Archaic techniques of self defense are indeed a rich source of creative material, but they are useful only if adapted for the theatre.

The Fight Masters and Certified Teachers of the Society of American Fight Directors have continued to strive to unveil the mysteries of swordplay so laboriously discovered by their historical predecessors and to theatricalize those discoveries upon the stage. Through their efforts, and those of the legion of highly trained SAFD Actor-Combatants, modern audiences are favored by intimate living examples of historic swordplay.

Night after night, in scores of theatres around the nation, walloping stage fights are being enacted with an educated eye toward their genesis in history and with a studied concern for the performer's well-being. Day after day, facsimiles of historic weapons are being adapted and improved by modern swordsmiths, whose associates in the theatre are testing their products for balance, durability and design. Year after year, the standards of training and performance continue to rise.

In such a fertile theatrical climate, would not Shakespeare be stimulated once again to illustrate the great conflicts of mankind upon the field of battle? Perhaps we are more prepared than ever before to display the horror of armed conflict upon the stage, which Shakespeare so poignantly displayed in all its variegation. Are not Claudius' ominous forebodings in Hamlet as relevant today as in his fractious age?

> *There's something in his soul*
> *O'er which his melancholy sits on brood:*
> *And I do doubt the hatch and the disclose*
> *Will be some danger.*

SAFETY AND TRAINING

There are several general principles concerning safety and basic training that may be applied to stage fighting with any kind of weapon. The intention here is to introduce the most important aspects of safety and training in a universal context; not to attempt to illustrate specific techniques. The teaching of specific techniques with potentially lethal weapons should only be attempted in a controlled environment with a qualified teacher and alert pupils.

It is in the areas of training and stage safety that modern stage fight choreographers and teachers depart most widely from the practices of the ancient Masters of Defence. It is common for present-day teachers of stage fighting to incorporate into their training sessions a few time honored drills, footwork patterns, or attack and defense combinations that have been used for hundreds of years. Nevertheless, contemporary teachers adapt those historic training methods in order to promote safe cooperation between combatants and to unite systems of defense with performance theory. This positively sets current stage swordplay apart from the sword fighting of the past.

The very first principle of safety is to study with a qualified teacher of stage combat. Because of the complexities and potential for injury, the Society of American Fight Directors recognizes only Fight Masters and Certified Teachers as competent to safely conduct stage combat classes. Many years of training (a minimum of eight years for a Fight Master and five years for a Certified Teacher), rigorous testing, an apprenticeship, and professional experience as a teacher and choreographer are required before one may earn either title.

The second principle of safety is to use only the very best quality stage weapons. There are now a number of respected swordsmiths and manufacturers of stage worthy weaponry in the United States who meet the standards of the Society of American Fight Directors. Valuing safety above all else, no director should ever compromise when obtaining stage worthy weaponry. Someone's life may depend upon the integrity of a stage weapon.

If one is practicing or rehearsing for a play it is essential that an identical weapon is used for both practice and performance. It is folly to practice with a lighter, heavier, or altogether different weapon from the one which the actor will actually be using in performance. Preparing for a performance in stage fighting requires an enormous commitment of time and is a difficult task even in the best of circumstances; the fewer surprises the better, for all concerned.

Remember also that, regardless of quality, stage weapons deteriorate over time—depending upon how often they are used and how roughly they are handled. It is a wise policy to replace the blades on weapons that have been used for practice prior to performance. Replacement blades are less expensive than purchasing a separate weapon for performances. Therefore purchasing stage weaponry that may be disassembled, rather than those that have been welded together, is advantageous.

While on the subject of hardware: the use of fencing masks for initial practice and rehearsal sessions is also advocated. Once the actor-combatants master the basics, the masks may be removed and the combatants may rely on safe training methodologies to avoid injuries to the face. Gloves and soft-soled shoes that afford good traction are also essential equipment.

The actor-combatants must be able to wear the same shoes in training and rehearsal of the stage fight as will be worn in the actual production. It is also important to wear any costume piece that may interfere with the actor's safety on stage during training and rehearsal sessions.

The rehearsal room, or combat studio, is a very special place. A friendly yet disciplined atmosphere must be maintained. The primary elements in developing a disciplined, cooperative and safe working environment are:

1. Establishing protocols for handling swords as combatants move into practice positions,

2. Instituting correct fighting distances if there are a large number of people sharing the space,

3. Organizing logically progressive training techniques,

4. Setting regular rest periods,

5. Formalizing systems for questions and criticisms, and

6. Familiarizing all the students with a loud signal (a coach's whistle) that will instantly stop everyone in the room at the same moment.

Obviously, anyone under the influence of alcohol or drugs must not be permitted to handle a weapon or participate in a combat class. It is also vital that the teacher ascertain a combatant's physical condition. A formal questionnaire of physical history is useful in this context. Sometimes it is wise to have a combatant with a chronic physical or psychological condition obtain a doctor's written permission prior to undertaking the rigors of stage fight training.

"Speed, speed, speed, how youth loves speed!" It has been said to young automobile drivers that "Speed Kills!" In stage fighting uncontrolled speed also equals danger! The first order of business then, when practicing stage combat techniques or when rehearsing a choreographed stage fight, is to practice very, very, slowly. All basic training should proceed in *slow-motion*. The practicing students should appear to the observer as though they were performing a slow-motion dance sequence.

The slow pace of training cannot be over-emphasized or repeated by the teacher often enough. Patrick Crean, former Fight Master to the Stratford Shakespeare Festival in Canada and one of Errol Flynn's fight choreographers and swordfighting doubles, puts it this way: "Thoughts fast, BLADES SLOW."

However, admonishing students to "practice slowly" is not enough. Words alone and constant reminders to "slow down," although helpful, will not in themselves induce a student to learn how to practice slowly. The keys to learning how to practice slowly and safely reside in a careful attention to Partnering, Breath Control, Balance, Tempo, Targeting and Cueing, Sensory Awareness, Fighting Distance, and Intention.

Partnering. In stage combat the attacker is responsible for the safety of the defender! One can create a safer *illusion of violence* by redirecting the emphasis on force and aggression that are the normal facets of violence. For example, the actor who makes a sword-cut at his or her partner is responsible for the safety of the actor who is parrying the sword-cut. If the defender forgets to parry, the attacker does not complete the cut. If the defending partner does not retreat, the attacking partner does not advance. If the defending partner does not duck, the attacking partner does not perform a head slash, and so on. If both partners concentrate on protecting each other when executing offensive techniques, then a higher level of safety is achieved.

A nonviolent working relationship is dependent upon a willingness to correct each other and to accept criticism without anger or hurt feelings. Pretending that a partner is an enemy, as is often required in a stage fight from a play, can sometimes influence an actor's attitude towards a scene partner. Stage combatants sometimes fool themselves into thinking that they are adversaries instead of partners in a theatrical dance. Occasionally tempers flare and one seeks to blame the other for a mistake. Acknowledging and altering these natural aggressive tendencies is essential for obvious safety reasons. Cooperation, not competition, promotes the safest learning environment.

In order to foster cooperation combatants must frequently practice objective criticism. Partners should freely give and receive critical comments. Combatants must learn to love their mistakes and view them as opportunities to improve. There is no such thing as a "perfect" stage fight. One does not seek "perfection." Actors are seeking to communicate to each other with weapons. Stage fighting is a gestural conversation.

A combatant should not seek to be a winner, or to be better than his or her partner. There are no winners or losers among actors. The only "winner" should be the audience.

The secret to sensitive partnering is the simple axiom, *If you help your partner to look good, then you will look good too!* All too often training and good intentions are thrown out the window when it comes time to perform a stage fight in front of an audience. If, during training and rehearsals, the combatants are encouraged to help their partners look good (giving them time to respond, insuring targeted attacks are accurate and consistent, helping each other to memorize choreography, etc.), then when an audience is present the partners will be more inclined to work together for a common effect.

Concern for each other's safety, open communication, and helping one's fellow combatants perform to the best of their potential are the essentials to sensitive partnering. A good working relationship between combatants will diminish the risk of accidental injury and will insure a smooth transition from rehearsal to performance. Of course, there is no substitute for adhering to a rigorous and consistent schedule of rehearsals.

Breath Control. Have you ever watched two people actually fight each other? It is not a pretty sight. To a spectator a real fight most often appears clumsy and crude. If it were not for the fact that someone is getting hurt, a genuine fight might seem comical. The individuals who are fighting seem out of control. One aspect of their lack of control is obvious—their breathing rhythms are erratic.

Pretending to fight often triggers measurable physiological changes in a performer's body that are akin to actual fighting. This phenomenon is linked to the instinctual "fight or flight" syndrome. This syndrome is often coupled with a rapid, almost wild, panting breath.

Vocalizations such as those which indicate pain, effort, emotional responses, or shouted dialogue, or the like during a stage fight can contribute to a disturbance of rhythmic breath and may also induce an instinctual aggressive response. All vocalizations should be carefully rehearsed in conjunction with the choreography. Combatants should not wait to the last moment to add dramatic vocalizations, but rather should incorporate and experiment with them very early in rehearsals.

To counteract instinctual responses to simulated fighting, the combatants must practice linking all movements and choreographic phrases with their abdominal breathing rhythms. The combatants, together with the choreographer, will consciously choose when to inhale or exhale and how and when to vocalize during the stage fight. A good choreographer will build breathing rhythms, as well as moments for catching one's breath, into a fight.

Actor-Combatants should never hold their breath, especially when learning new techniques, nor should they allow their breathing to become completely involuntary and uncontrolled. Breath control requires a great deal of practice, but it is an essential ingredient for safety.

In addition, stage fighting is physically very demanding and requires actors who are reasonably physically fit. Sensible warm-ups and moderate aerobic training are a good idea to insure that the actors do not run out of breath in the middle of a stage fight. Breath control, like other physiological aspects of performance training, must be practiced at each and every rehearsal.

Balance. **Untrained** actors who are stage fighting and normal people who are actually fighting lack balance and appear awkward. More importantly, performers who lose their balance are dangerous—to themselves and to others.

A qualified Fight Master or Teacher can immediately distinguish a stage combatant who is out of control, because invariably the combatant will exhibit imbalances. Balance = control.

Maintaining a fluid, dynamic balance when learning and practicing stage fighting techniques will often help correct problems of extraneous tensions throughout the body, the tendency to hold the breath, and excessive speed. Maintaining an unfailing balance indicates that the combatants are experiencing the proper mix of tension and release in the muscles. All of the techniques therefore must be performed from a position of balance. Each and every technique in stage fighting embodies an inherently effective position of balance for its proper and safe execution. It is the Fight Master's or the Certified Teacher's responsibility and the performers' obligation to identify and foster correct positions of balance throughout the rehearsal and performance process.

Aside from helping to promote safely executed upper body movements, balance is also one of the unifying elements in basic training. Balance is a wonderful unifying element in stage fighting because *balance is dependent upon:*

1. Maintaining a wide stance,
2. Sensitivity to changes of weight,
3. Flexibility in the joints (knee joints in particular),
4. Centering the upper body over the base of support,
5. Breathing rhythmically,
6. Practicing at a controllable tempo, and
7. A psycho-physical preparation prior to each offensive or defensive technique.

Tempo. The combatants should always be provided with a consistent tempo (rate of speed) for practice. "Slow" is a purely subjective word. What the teacher or choreographer requires is that both partners practice at exactly the same tempo.

It is best that the choreographer or teacher establish a slow-motion tempo by using a small drum, metronome, or other regulating device (such as a synthesizer) so that the combatants can hear and follow a prescribed, consistent tempo. Obviously, the fighters cannot watch a baton beat out a tempo, because they need to focus on the tasks at hand. Therefore, tempo is established auditorily.

Once a tempo is established, the combatants themselves may reinforce the tempo by counting aloud while practicing. By linking their movements to a count, both partners adjust to each other and remain kinesthetically in tandem.

When a drill or a choreographic phrase is created with the awareness of tempo and rhythm (the regular succession of motions), speeding up the drill or choreography will be less difficult. In this way, tempo harmonizes with the techniques themselves and the combatants become masters of their timing. If they personally reinforce the chosen tempo with each cut and parry, students will recognize the changing rhythms of a fight and will be less likely to go spinning off into the various speed-traps so prevalent with the inexperienced.

Each stage fighting technique has an intrinsic tempo for its correct execution that is based upon the practicalities of Time, Weight and Force. The challenge for the Fight Master or Certified Teacher and the Actor-Combatant is to discover and reinforce a particular technique's intrinsic tempo. The rhythms which contribute to an exciting and logical stage fight are dependent upon a variety of appropriate tempos associated with technique.

Targeting and Cueing. Knowing what you are going to do *before* you do it and being scrupulous in the accuracy of what you do are the initial concerns in Targeting. In stage fighting, one is seeking a target that is safe for the combatants and yet appears theatrically vulnerable to an audience. For example, there is no point in attacking a shield, it cannot be hurt. On the other hand, striking at the face is foolish—even if that might excite the audience.

Action follows thought. The target must be accurately sighted by the attacker before the attacker begins even to swing towards the target. Regardless of speed, the thought, i.e., intention behind the attack, must precede the attack. Therefore, a combatant can only fight as quickly as he or she can think ahead.

It may be obvious, yet it is important to note that the smaller the target, the greater the need for accuracy. If an attacker is very specific as to the target, then there is a better chance that he or she will be accurate in striking that target. To this end, Colleen Kelly, an SAFD Certified Teacher, places colored adhesive dots on the requisite target areas to aid in specificity. This teaching tool is very effective early in rehearsals or training sessions and eliminates any guesswork on the part of the attacker. In the final analysis, accuracy in targeting is simply a matter of extensive practice. All hand-eye coordination activities require constant drill.

Since a solid defense is as important as an accurate attack, it helps the defender to be given a subtle advance warning by the attacker as to which target will be attacked next. This is called Cueing. By strongly focusing on the chosen target just prior to the attack, a cue is given by the attacker. It is quite easy to read your partner's eye-focus and discern your partner's target from that focus. The attacker's eye-focus on a target also helps subconsciously to direct the audience's attention; aiding them in dramatically "reading" the strategy of the fight.

Don't mistake the combatant's *eye-focus* on a target with the safety feature of *eye-contact* preceding an attack. Eye-contact is a way that combatant's communicate to each other that they are mutually ready to perform another phrase in the fight or begin a technique. Eye-contact precedes an attacker's eye-focus on a target.

Another aspect of cueing, which aids in telegraphing to the defender the attacker's intentions, is the development of a uniform method of linking a specific preparatory movement and angle of approach with the attack itself. For example, if the attacker is to perform a head cut, then the angle of approach toward the target is perfectly vertical and not skewed over either shoulder. Likewise, the angle of approach of a thrust towards the center chest is unmistakably horizontal to the floor. Allen Suddeth, SAFD Fight Master, often teaches a slight pulling back of the sword as a cue prior to a thrust. Regardless of individual fighting styles, each weapon has its own particular family of targets and each target should also have an attendant precise preparation which foreshadows the attack upon that target.

By linking these concerns of forethought, cueing, and angle of approach with an insistence upon adhering to very specific targets, the combatants are coerced into practicing slowly and carefully. If any of the elements of targeting are sloppy or missing, then the combatants are forbidden to speed up the tempo until the problems are corrected.

Sensory Awareness. Well trained Actor-Combatants are acutely aware of the physical properties of the weapon(s) they are using. Every weapon has been designed and built for a particular function. The form of a weapon follows its function. Each weapon is unique in that it has a specific weight, length, balance point, grip, guard, edge(s) and tip. The physical properties of a weapon, as well as its form and function, inform the manner of its use.

Prior to imitating a teacher or choreographer with a new weapon, the wise actor will spend sufficient time becoming kinesthetically connected with the new weapon. Even with a familiar weapon and before facing a partner at a training or rehearsal session, an actor should examine the weapon for flaws and become refamiliarized with the particular "feel" of the weapon.

A quick and effective method for establishing a sensory awareness with a weapon is to move it in a free-form manner with eyes closed in a large safe space. Closing one's eyes eliminates external distractions and assists a combatant in focusing on internal, kinesthetic stimuli. When once again sighted, the combatant should continue to remain sensitive to the discoveries made while blind.

It is not enough to externally imitate the teacher or choreographer. It is the performer's obligation to *kinesthetically absorb* stage fighting techniques. Once a choreographic phrase or training combination is memorized, the combatant should practice his or her part of the phrase *apart from a partner* (with eyes closed) to rediscover how the sequence of techniques internally affect footwork, balance, tension, breath control, and so on.

Another principal method for developing a sensory awareness with various stage weapons is to use a weapon in a manner consistent with its original design, i.e., cut, thrust into, or hit something that is resistant. Bales of straw, wrapped wooden poles, or covered hanging weights are quite effective for target practice. A combatant who has practiced thrusting into a bale of straw, or has learned to cut into a wooden pole at the most effective angle, or has attempted to strike a moving target, is more adept at replicating the illusions of stage fighting and more aware of the way in which a particular weapon should be swung or extended towards a target. One should, however, always remember that learning how to accurately *miss a target* is more important in stage fighting than learning how to hit one.

Fighting Distance. It stands to reason that one would need to be closer to injure an adversary with a knife than if one had a sword, because the knife is shorter than the sword (supposing for this example that the knife was not going to be thrown). Naturally, if a combatant is taller and has longer arms, then the fighting distance is again adjusted. This simple logic is at the heart of fighting distance in stage combat.

It is also reasonable to suggest that individual tactics require specific fighting distances. For example, yanking an opponent's dagger out of his or her grasp would require the attacker to get in closer than would be necessary for a thrusting attack with a sword. Each technique, therefore, presupposes an appropriate change of distance between combatants.

Maintaining a proper distance (in relation to the length of weapons used, the physiology of the combatants, and the chosen technique) is perhaps the most important element of safety in stage fighting. More injuries have occurred in stage fighting from inaccurate fighting distance than from all other reasons combined.

Fighting distance is principally controlled by accurate footwork. Footwork drills should be included in every practice session. A rigid, even authoritarian, attitude toward accurate footwork and fighting distance at each training, rehearsal and performance session should never be compromised.

Complementing the practice of altering distance from a partner because of the length of a particular weapon, technique, or actor's physique, is the notion of "theatrical distance." Theatrical distance from a partner is predicated upon creating the most visually effective distance for showing a technique (or hiding it from) an audience.

If there is to be a stage wounding or a kill, then the technique is often "masked" or hidden by closing the fighting distance and obscuring—from the point of view of the audience—a weapon's contact with the victim's body. Although it is a fight director's responsibility to place combatants in the best angle for an audience to view a chosen moment, altering the fighting distance remains an important aspect of visually revealing or hiding techniques in a fight.

Finally, an audience's "suspension of disbelief" requires that they be able to clearly witness an attack and believe that the attacker is trying to harm the opponent without getting hurt in return. Besides being unsafe, if the combatants are fighting too close together the fight becomes visually muddled and destroys the illusion that the combatants are afraid of being hurt by each other's weapons. Actors should be accurate in their fighting distance not only for serious safety reasons, but also because it helps them to look good on stage.

Intention. Konstantin Stanislavsky, the great Russian stage director and acting teacher, believed that even the simplest action on stage should be accompanied by a specific motivation. Simply put:

there should be a reason supporting every action on stage. Actors must know *why* they are doing something. Knowing why one is doing something will then influence *what* one is doing. Combining *why* and *what* reveals for an audience a character's intentions and influences the quality of the dramatic action.

Since a stage fighting scene in a play is similar in principle (from a characterization point of view) to any other scene in a play, it is important to consistently link training in stage fighting techniques with the theatrically strategic reasons supporting each technique. It is counterproductive, when preparing to perform a role in a play within a stage fighting scene, for an actor to mindlessly perform drills without connecting intention to action.

Each and every time a cut, thrust, piece of footwork, or the like is practiced, the actor should link the action in his or her mind with an intention supporting that action. This may be as simple as recognizing that the target is exposed prior to attempting to execute a cut, or it may be as complex as a "triple intention attack," where the first two movements are merely preparatory to creating the opportunity for the success of the third action.

Ultimately, it is the actor's responsibility to train himself to think before acting. Not only will the final stage fight be more consistent with the actor's chosen character traits expressed throughout the play, but the individual techniques themselves will be safer and more dramatic.

A BRIEF HISTORY OF SHAKESPEAREAN SWORDPLAY

Historians organize their documented research, their personal prejudices and interpretations into a form convenient for themselves. They attempt to fashion the enormity of history into a manageable series of lists, or an entertaining story, or a tool for supporting a particular point of view.

An historian's interpretation of past events will naturally influence a reader's conclusions. When an historian is a devoted enthusiast of competitive sport fencing, for example, a reader could be led to the conclusion that the history of swordplay is one of a steady refinement of swordfighting techniques culminating in the perfection of the competitive foil! Attractive as that notion may be to many, the history of swordplay is not quite a "march of progress" climaxing in the modern sport. It is probable, however, that the modern competitive weapons of foil, epée and sabre, together with their techniques, are derivative of early sword types and methods of swordplay. Because fencing for sport is derivational of the swordfighting styles of the eighteenth century, many modern fencers mistakenly believe that all types of swords and swordplay were spawned by an orderly evolutionary process.

The history of swordplay is not a progressive amalgamation of swordfighting techniques maturing from the broadsword to the "perfection" of the small sword, as so many historians fondly profess. In fact, the basic principles and strategies of swordplay have changed very little over the centuries. What did evolve was a wide array of distinctly brilliant forms of combat tailored intimately to the properties of particular types of swords. When a sword with unique properties of weight, shape and balance was fashioned for a particular martial need, the expert swordsmen of the age selected tried and true swordfighting techniques and adapted them to the new weapon. A wholly distinct type of swordfighting was painstakingly created over many years by the trial and error of hundreds if not thousands of practitioners. Finally, highly effective methods of swordplay emerged that were organically linked to a specific type of sword.

The history of swordplay is primarily a function of the history of the weapons themselves. Swordsmiths were by nature innovators and have been producing a wide array of swords and other edged weapons in an unbroken stream from prehistoric times to the present day. Historically, as new types of swords and variations on existing weaponry were introduced by swordsmiths, in order to satisfy their customer's various needs, the new weapons became popular with particular segments of the population. However, the older swords continued to be used coincidently with the newly introduced weaponry. The broadsword and the dagger, for example, are two of the most ancient of edged weapons that were never abandoned.

A common misapprehension is that any sword introduced at a later time was a refinement of any previously introduced weapon—and here "refinement" is defined as "becoming free of what is crude or uncouth." Following this erroneous assumption, many have come to believe that the swordfighting techniques devised for each subsequently introduced weapon were an improvement upon the techniques designed for an earlier weapon. The same peculiar logic would support the statement that the use of the pistol is a refinement of the use of the rifle. In fact, rifle and pistol are very different weapons and require very different kinds of training and technique. The rifle and pistol were devised to perform very different duties; neither weapon is superior nor inferior to the other.

That men learned from their mistakes and passed on a more perfect use of a particular type of weapon to their students is certainly correct. It is also obvious to anyone who examines and uses various examples of distinctive sword types that characteristic swords were altered to reflect an individual fighter's style; such adaptations continue today via a dialogue between seasoned swordfighters and their swordsmiths. Therefore, refinement within a class of weapon was a natural process; as was the ongoing improvement of material and the manufacture of swords in general.

It is incorrect to say that the techniques used for a particular class of weapon (or the weapon itself) were inferior to the techniques devised for subsequently introduced weapons. For example, to assume that sixteenth century short sword technique was crude, and that small sword fighting was refined, is to be blinded by prejudice. Or to say that the small sword was more effective than the rapier and dagger when defending one's life can only be professed by someone who has never faced an opponent in a combat situation with the weapons in question. It is germane to point out that the simple staff or quarterstaff was a very formidable sixteenth century weapon (also one of the most ancient weapons known to man). There are a number of historical anecdotes citing the victory of a staff wielder over several swordsmen! It was this simple weapon's elaborated style of fighting and its unique properties that furnished its advantage.

For the stage combat choreographer as historian, research into unique systems of training and defense is of primary importance. Fighting styles and training techniques were derived from the experiences garnered by swordsmen in actual combat over long periods of time with a particular type of weapon. The changes in weight, balance, cross section of the blade, durability, accessibility of a particular type of weapon, and the vagaries of popular fashion, induced changes in training systems, theory and combat strategies. As swords of different type crossed paths in street fights, in duels of honor or on the field of battle, the systems of defense and offense went through further adaptations.

Each of the weapons used during the Elizabethan and Jacobean periods had its own unique developmental history. Consequently, each of the weapons paraded across the Shakespearean stage had skilled proponents who demonstrated intricate strategies and styles of technique.

To visualize how the expert combatants in Shakespeare's plays may have looked, it will be helpful to briefly survey the swordsmen, weapons and fighting styles of the sixteenth and early seventeenth centuries that are alluded to in Shakespeare's plays.

Whatever one's opinion about how Shakespeare spent his "lost years," 1585–1592, when he arrived in London to begin his apprenticeship as an actor his training would not have been complete until he had learned to become an expert swordsmen with the fashionable weapons of the day. The young William had a choice of masters from whom to study. (It might be more to the point to ascertain from whom Richard Burbage studied swordfighting, as it was he who performed several of the principal swordfighting roles.) Both English born and foreign masters kept schools in London.

The Corporation of the London Masters of Defence had a history of renting the London area playhouses for the purposes of publicly testing their students for advancement. Perhaps they even had a monopoly on presenting their public displays in the playhouses—in researching this book, no record of a foreign master "playing a prize" (a public display of skill) at an Elizabethan London playhouse was uncovered. This suggests an intimate financial connection between the London fight masters and the theatre companies. It would be of benefit for the theatre managers to steer new apprentices to the fencing teachers who patronized the playhouses. Therefore, it is probable that Shakespeare (and Burbage) studied swordplay from a recognized master who was favored by the theatre community. (It is also possible that either took lessons from a member of an acting company, such as the famous comedic actor Richard Tarleton, who was "allowed" a master in 1587.)

It was frowned upon for anyone to teach the mysteries of swordplay who was not "allowed master" by the London Masters of Defence. It was dangerous to defy the traditional masters. Foreigners who taught swordplay in the capital were compelled to seek protection from powerful noblemen at court.

In spite of obstacles and hostility from the established English masters, by the middle 1580s the Hispano-Italian and the French rapier and dagger styles of swordfighting were unquestionably à la mode among the noble patrons of the theatre. It would behoove an ambitious player to become familiar with the current fashions, whatever they might be. It is known that several Italian masters kept very modish schools convenient to the playhouses. One could surmise that there may have been French and, in spite of tensions between the two countries, Spanish teachers of swordplay doing business in the capital. Shakespeare may have extended himself by studying with one of the foreign masters.

Several of the weapons which were being taught in the London fencing schools, both English and foreign, were represented in Shakespeare's plays and suggest his expertise in their use. They are the staff, long sword, short sword, rapier, target, buckler, dagger, and poniard. Although not mentioned in his plays, the bastard sword, which was a common weapon taught by the sixteenth century London Masters of Defence, can also be included. By the 1580s, the application of these weapons had developed into a fine art through a long and rich history of use in England and on the continent.

The staff was a weapon to be feared for its deadly powers in the hands of a skilled practitioner. The staff, the tips of which would be shod in iron or bone, was a weapon of the common man and varied in length. Both ends of the weapon were used for offense and defense. Striking and thrusting were taught. Some sixteenth century masters maintained that the long sword and the staff techniques were identical. The technique for the Staff was the basis for the systems of defense devised for the myriad pole arms used by guards, civilian peace keepers and foot soldiers.

Adherents of the Medieval hand-and-a-half (bastard sword) and the two-handed long sword were still to be seen throughout Queen Elizabeth's reign. Shakespeare mentions the long sword in *Romeo and Juliet* and in *The Merry Wives of Windsor*. In both instances he ridicules the long sword as the weapon of an old man; an outmoded weapon belonging to a bygone era. Nevertheless, proficiency in the long sword was required in order to rise to the rank of Master of Defence in the late 1580s (also required, as recorded in the Minute Book of the London Masters of Defence, were the bastard sword, the pike, backe sword, short sword and dagger, and the rapier and dagger). Shakespeare mentions the "backsword" in *Henry VI, Part 2*. He is more respectful when he adverts to sword and dagger or rapier and dagger in his plays.

The long sword was an offensive and defensive weapon. It was developed to counter the armored knight on horseback and because it was thought to be effective when defending oneself against several opponents at once, it was a popular weapon for the defense of the standard bearer or, "aunciet," in battle. The weapon was wielded by very powerful men and was used for both thrust and parry. Despite its size, the long sword enjoyed a well defined, swift manner of swordplay. All parts of the weapon—blade, cross hilts and pummel—were used for offense and defense. There was even a technique advocated by Hans Thalhoffer in 1443 for tripping an opponent with the long sword. The long sword was mostly a military, not a civilian, weapon. However there is mention in a sixteenth century fencing manual that, "it is accoustomed to be carried in the Citie, as well by night as by day"—Giacomo Di Grassi, 1594. How appropriate for Old Capulet to call for his "long sword, ho!" in response to his civil brawl with the Montagues in *Romeo and Juliet*.

The backsword (mentioned once in *Henry IV, Part 2* in reference to Falstaff) was a single edged weapon used almost exclusively for cutting; not to be confused with the weapon made of a stick and a wicker basket hilt, pursued as a sport in Elizabethan England. The fighting techniques of the backsword, very popular with the common people, curiously devolved into the single-stick sport of the gentry in the eighteenth century. In Shakespeare's time every English fight master taught the weapon to his beginning students.

The bastard sword was a versatile weapon which could be wielded with one hand, or with two hands. The bastard sword most often was used in conjunction with either a shield, a dagger, or a gauntlet made of steel plate, chain mail, or leather. This was a cut and thrust weapon, whose technique was very similar to the long sword's when plied with two hands. The bastard sword, when used with a defensive weapon, was akin to the methods of the Elizabethan short sword. The bastard sword would be an obvious choice for an Elizabethan actor when called upon to perform a medieval battle in one of Shakespeare's history plays.

The evolution of the single-handed sword, as Shakespeare knew it, from its heavier Medieval version, was largely complete by the first half of the sixteenth century. It had become a very serviceable, straight, double edged weapon sporting a variety of hilts and guards, with a pointed tip and flattened blade.

Upon examination of early examples of this type of sword in England, it is apparent that it was already being used with great accuracy in the 1300s, not only as a cutting weapon but as a thrusting weapon as well. In *Cut and Thrust*, Eduard Wagner points out, "The blade also underwent certain changes in the constant struggle against the stronger armour, which was beginning to be made so as to withstand the cuts for which the broader sword blade (up to 6cm) had been mainly designed. Hence the contestants had to seek out the less well-protected parts of the opponent's armor and use the most suitable moment for attack. This method of fighting demanded greater cunning, agility, and, of course, training. To hit a small target open to the danger of attack for merely a brief moment, the most suitable action was the thrust...."

The English Masters of Defence who championed the sixteenth century short sword recognized the versatility of this cut and thrust weapon. By the time that Shakespeare considered its use as an apprentice actor, the properties of this weapon had been studied and refined for hundreds of years in England. The methods of training with the typical English short sword were effectively standardized. A standardization of training systems evinces an acute level of sophistication.

The sixteenth century short sword, advocated by the English masters, was light enough to swing very rapidly and was used primarily as an offensive weapon. Together with a defensive weapon held in the other hand (target, buckler, dagger, gauntlet, etc.), the English Masters of Defence taught an active, aggressive and strategic style of combat. They advocated using the weapon for both cutting and thrusting and taught ways of integrating pummel and hilt techniques as well.

The sixteenth century short sword was an eminently practical weapon, useful for both military and civilian altercations. Recognizing the uncertainties of a real-world fight, the Masters of Defence promoted techniques for using the pummel and cross hilts offensively when fighting in close. They coached students in how to defend themselves with this stout sword against a wide array of various weapons. They also taught a variety of cutting actions utilizing both edges of the blade. Thrusting at the most vulnerable targets—the face, armpits, belly and groin—led to complex exchanges of parry and attack. Although the short sword was used principally as an offensive weapon, it was understood that combining a deflecting with an attacking movement was effective at times.

Footwork was elaborate, incorporating movements forward and back, side to side, or circling the opponent. Seeking advantages in the high ground or keeping one's back to the sun, maintaining various fighting distances, leaping and running were also taught.

The split-second timing of movements to correspond with an opponent's movements became an explicit tool for success. This led to intricate strategies for leading one's opponent into attacking apparently open targets. Improvements in the principle of timing also ushered in sophisticated feinting movements which were coupled with corresponding counter-attacks.

Because the sixteenth century short sword was a no-nonsense weapon, it was ordinary to teach an assortment of disarming and grappling techniques. Body blows with the defensive weapon were certainly commonplace.

The double edged short sword was so appropriate for military campaigns that it was often carried by soldiers for more than two hundred years following Shakespeare's death. In the streets of Shakespeare's London, the sturdy

English short sword was ubiquitous and remained a weapon of the common man in spite of changes in fashion.

The target, a small shield equiped with a forearm strap and a handle, was a distinctive form of the larger medieval shield. Not only was it used to stop and deflect an opponent's sword, the edge and surface of the target was sometimes used to strike at an opponent. The target was more popular as a military than a civilian weapon and Shakespeare mentions the target in mostly military contexts.

An even smaller shield than the target was the buckler, a very popular civilian weapon. It was held by a single handle mounted in back. The buckler was light and quick. Held stiffly away from the body or obliquely to the side, it offered excellent protection. A few examples of extant bucklers have a large spike protruding from the center front, suggesting a very active offensive role for this normally defensive weapon.

Some have argued that the buckler was not very effective against a thrusting weapon. It was, however, used extensively in conjunction with the rapier—a thrusting weapon—for many decades. (Experience affirms the validity of the buckler as a fitting defensive companion to the rapier.) The buckler fell out of favor in the final decade of the sixteenth century among the nobility, not because it was an inferior defensive weapon against the rapier, but rather because of a taste for something new and fashionable. Changes in fashion often do not reflect practicalities.

Sword and buckler play mirrored similar complexities shared by all sixteenth century two-weapon techniques. It was possible to both defend oneself and to launch a counterattack at the same moment. Masters also taught their students to use both weapons for defense or for simultaneous attacks. The buckler provided an efficient defense against heavier weapons and was light enough to quickly counter a sharp thrust from a rapier or dagger. In close fighting, the buckler could be used like an iron fist.

The most complex and picturesque style of swordplay ever devised was that for the late sixteenth century rapier and dagger. The elaborate foot and hand movements were perfected to such a degree that it required a great deal of practice to master them. The principles governing the several systems of defense tailored to the rapier and dagger were profound and cleverly enunciated in Italian, Spanish, German, French and English manuals of defense.

Because of earlier feudal traditions in England and on the continent, particular civilian weapons came to be associated with a social class. In Elizabethan England, the rapier and dagger were the weapons of the nobility and upper merchant class; while the short sword and buckler were the weapons of servants and common people. The aristocracy were enamored with not only the sense of refinement inherent in rapier play, but also with the attendant code of ethics taught by the foreign Masters of Defence who introduced these exotic weapons to the English court.

To witness an expert swordsman maneuver the rapier and dagger is to immediately realize that this combination of weapons is both elegant and deadly. Elizabethan audiences (as well as modern audiences) relished the opportunity to watch accomplished Actor-Combatants perform an intricate and ferocious rapier and dagger fight upon the stage. This, in no little way, has contributed to the enduring popularity of *Romeo and Juliet*.

Although the London Masters of Defence were jealous of the foreigners who taught rapier and dagger under the protection of powerful patrons, and most likely resisted the new fangled weapons at first, nevertheless, by the early 1560s they were including the rapier and dagger in their public challenges performed before the queen at Whitehall. By 1578, rapier and dagger was included in their public proficiency tests. Shakespeare could, if he were in a patriotic vein, study rapier and dagger swordplay with an English Master of Defence.

The rapier was a thrust and cut weapon, i.e., the thrust was principally advocated, but the weapon had sharp edges and cuts were taught in particular circumstances. The dagger was defensive. The dagger was used offensively only when fighting distance permitted, or when one was attempting an attack upon the blade in order to create an opening or to disarm an opponent.

Footwork was essential to attack and defense. Since the rapier was primarily a thrusting weapon, fighting distance, regulated by a variety of prescribed foot movements, became a crucial safety issue. Certain attacking and defensive techniques were predicated upon ascertaining appropriate degrees of fighting distance. Every extant manual of defense outlining the systems of rapier and dagger swordplay stresses the importance of accurate footwork.

A daunting number of combinations of attack and defense were created for the rapier and dagger. Deceiving one's opponent with quick feinting actions, shifting of defensive positions, complex systems of counterattack and intricate footwork, all added to the deadly mystique of rapier and dagger swordplay.

Swordfighting with rapier and dagger began to simulate the sophistication of a dangerous chess match. A man's strategy and cool deliberation in the heat of combat were as significant as physical skill. It is little wonder that this combination of weaponry, that required such erudition in its use and embodied such poetry in its "philosophy," became so popular among the more educated and wealthy in England. Although Shakespeare abhorred abusive violence and ridiculed the hypocritical rapier enthusiasts of his age, there is little doubt that he admired the elegance that Richard Burbage must have displayed in Hamlet's final duel.

The weapons described above and others of every description were on prominent display in Shakespeare's England. The unremitting wars and civil demands kept the armorers busy. Armed men, many of whom were extremely skilled, strode the streets of London. The birthright, even the obligation, to bear arms was a cherished tradition. In open fields surrounding London, in courtyards, in numerous "schools of fence," and upon the stage, displays of martial skill were a daily occurrence. At fairs and holiday gatherings, swordplay for sport was counted on to be part of the festivities. This omnipresent high-spirited environment produced an audience eager for the dramatization of famous battles and poignant duels. Living in such an energetic atmosphere, what playwright of genius could resist putting a sword into an actor's hand and sending him out upon the stage to illuminate the tragedy and heroism, or the cowardice and folly of his age?

THE CHOREOGRAPHY

Shakespeare did not write gratuitous scenes of violence into his plays. Unlike several other playwrights of the period, he did not simply bow to his audience's desire for histrionic sensationalism (*Titus Andronicus* is no exception to this statement). Shakespeare included scenes of violence in order to reveal his characters' personalities, to advance the plot of the play, or to illuminate a dramatic theme.

In light of the care he took in creating these scenes of violent conflict, the choreography in this book has been created with a special regard for the text. The first and foremost consideration is safety. The second is that an actor be able to dramatically portray a consistent character during a stage fight. The play does not stop while the battle is waged.

Each choreographic sample is preceded with a "conceptual framework." This conceptualization provides a dramatic interpretation of the scene within the play. These conceptual frameworks are the result of distillations of textual references, readings from dramatic criticism, assumptions about characterization, examinations of the dramatic situations; Tudor, Elizabethan and Jacobean stage practice; and the knowledge of the history of self defense.

Detailed choreographic choices were then based on each conceptual framework.

Many exciting and conflicting interpretations exist for the following scenes from these famous plays. Do not pretend that these are definitive. The fact that Shakespeare's plays may be equally effective when presented with any of numerous cogent but differing interpretations is one of the marks of his genius. Simple, often clichéd, interpretive choices have been deliberately made. The intention is to illustrate more succinctly how the link between dramaturgic interpretation and dramatic action influences choreographic decisions.

All textual examples have been drawn from *The Riverside Shakespeare* (please see Bibliography).

The illustrated choreographic samples in this book are purposefully simple and highly adaptable to a variety of stage settings. They are short and therefore useful for productions with rehearsal time constraints. The suggested stage fights might be considered somewhat generic. They are, however, closely and logically linked to their conceptual frameworks.

The illustrations accompanying the written choreography are intended merely to aid in visualizing the action. They are not intended to be absolutely accurate in every detail. The illustrations should not be construed as nearly photographic representations of correct stage combat techniques. One should not attempt precisely to imitate postures or positions delineated in the illustrations.

As illustrated, all of the combatants are "right-handed." The combatants hold the offensive weapon (for example, a sword) in the right hand and the defensive weapon (a shield, or a dagger) in the left hand.

The figures are presented to help illustrate the choreographic techniques as clearly as possible. Therefore, figures may be at the left in one sketch and at the right in another—in order to present the most instructive view (not necessarily the best dramatic position from an audience's point of view in the theatre). The captions or choreographic descriptions accompanying the illustrations, together with the relative positions of the offensive weapons, will aid in denoting front or back views.

Despite the uncomplicated nature of this choreography, it would be unwise for anyone to attempt to recreate these suggested stage fights without the guidance of a qualified SAFD Fight Master or Certified Teacher. There are many hidden dangers when learning and performing a stage fight. To ensure an adequate level of safety for the performers, it is best to rely upon the experience of a professional.

Conspicuously absent from the following choreography are mass battle scenes, acts of murder, and group brawls. These types of scenes are too complex to describe in a book of this scope. Also absent are fight scenes spuriously added to Shakespeare's plays because of theatre tradition, such as the Viola/Aguecheek comic duel in *Twelfth Night*.

Several of the following stage fights take place amid great mayhem and with many other combatants present. Such complications have been purposely ignored in an attempt to focus upon those significant stage duels which either include dialogue and thus illuminate character, are essential to the action of the play, or are obviously meant to take place on stage as indicated by textual references.

The term *duel* is used in its broadest sense to mean a combat between two characters. Purists will assiduously point out that the formal duel was a rigidly codified event (much written about in Shakespeare's lifetime) and that any-old-fight would not qualify as a duel proper. It could, though, be argued that, in a thematic sense, every stage fight involving recognizable characters in Shakespeare's plays satisfies some element of the "code duello"—even if treated, at times, farcically.

Thus with imagin'd wing our swift scene flies
In motion of no less celerity
Than that of thought.
KING HENRY THE FIFTH
Chorus

HENRY IV, PART 1

*What honor dost thou seek
Upon my head?*

The battle of Shrewsbury, which concludes *Henry IV, Part 1*, is an ambitious undertaking for any stage fight choreographer. Each encounter heightens the dramatic tension until the forces in conflict, represented in the persons of Hotspur and the Prince of Wales, are thrillingly resolved.

Amid the strident trumpets and drums of war, a series of single and bloody encounters fleshes out this historic battle. In these tumultuous scenes of action and violence, Shakespeare brilliantly concatenates the crucial themes that he has woven throughout his play.

With superb logic and without upsetting the consistencies of character he has established, Shakespeare leads the audience through a series of linked duels. The first of these begins in Act V, Scene iii, between the "noble Scot," Douglas, and Sir Walter Blunt. Douglas is armed with a Scottish basket-hilted sword and shield. Blunt is armed with a single-handed sword and shield (we shall see that the true king is similarly armed).

The scene opens by establishing that the battle proper has begun. We see the King's army cross the stage in full battle armor. Douglas, who is fighting on behalf of Hotspur's rebel forces, has been seeking the King all day. Apparently a number of the King's knights have donned similar armor and emblems in order to confuse the enemy as to the identity of the true King. Hotspur explains this to Douglas in line 25 of Act V, Scene iii.

HOTSPUR.
The King hath many marching in his
    coats.

Douglas vs. Blunt

Following the spectacle of an army crossing the stage with drums and colors and the subsequent "Alarm to the Battle," which begins the battle proper, the first of the noble adversaries confront each other.

BLUNT.
What is thy name, that in battle thus
Thou crossest me? What honor dost thou
    seek
Upon my head?

DOUG.
Know then, my name is Douglas,
And I do haunt thee in the battle thus
Because some tell me that thou art a king.

BLUNT.
They tell thee true.

DOUG.
The Lord of Stafford dear to-day hath brought
Thy likeness, for in stead of thee, King Harry,
This sword hath ended him. So shall it thee,
Unless thou yield thee as my prisoner.

BLUNT.
I was not born a yielder, thou proud Scot,
And thou shalt find a king that will revenge Lord Stafford's death.

[They fight. Douglas kills Blunt.]

Douglas intercepts Blunt and blocks his path menacingly. There is no treachery here, only the chivalrous formalities of war waged among the nobility. Insults and challenges must be exchanged in their proper sequence so that the spoils of war may be honorably won. After the obligatory demand to yield is defiantly denied by Blunt, Douglas attacks without hesitation.

Douglas' powerful attack is met by Blunt, who stands his ground. Blunt deflects Douglas' series of cuts by turning in a tight circle. Douglas continues to launch his attack like a dog snapping at the heel of a bear.

Quickly changing his angle of approach, Douglas manages to slip past Blunt's guard. Douglas delivers a crippling blow to the back of Blunt's knee, hamstringing him. Blunt immediately loses the use of his leg and falls to one knee. Douglas presses his advantage and swiftly dispatches the hapless Blunt with a thrust beneath the breastplate. Lifeless, Blunt crashes to the ground.

Douglas vs. Blunt Choreography

Fig. 1 Douglas (left): advance right foot forward, cut to left hip beneath Blunt's shield. Blunt: stationary, shield parry three.

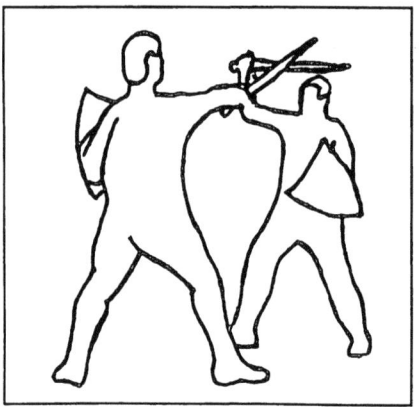

Fig. 2 Douglas (left): advance on the circle, right foot leading, molinello on right side, cut center head. Blunt: retreat to the right on the circle, right foot leading, and sword parry five.

Fig. 3 Douglas (right): advance on the circle right foot leading, cut left chest above Blunt's shield. Blunt: retreat with right foot leading on a circle, shield parry three.

Fig. 4 Douglas (left): advance on the circle with the right foot leading, cut left shoulder. Blunt: advance on the circle to the right, right foot leading, shield parry high three.

Fig. 5 Douglas (right): pass forward onto left foot, circle blade above head to left side, cut behind right knee with "false" edge (exposed view).

Fig. 6 Blunt (right): kneel on right knee, sword and shield held out to each side. Douglas: pass forward onto right foot, draw sword hilt back toward right side, thrust in half-pronation upstage of Blunt's body outline at stomach level beneath breastplate, flat of blade contact on Blunt's body. Blunt: pain reaction follows blade contact. (Illustrated view would be hidden from audience.)

The last few moments of the duel between Douglas and Blunt is witnessed by Hotspur and he praises his heroic ally.

O Douglas, hadst thou fought at Holmdon thus,
I never had triumph'd upon a scot.

Following the quick dispatch of heroic Blunt by Douglas, there is a brief scene of self congratulation with the victorious Douglas and the rebel Hotspur. This intensifies the impression that the Rebels are winning the battle. Shakespeare further reinforces this impression with the subsequent duel between the aging and enfeebled King Henry and the vigorous Douglas.

Douglas vs. King Henry

From the beginning, the fight between King Henry and Douglas is woefully mismatched. The King is quite likely older than Douglas, and the King also lacks robust health. This impression of a physically unhealthy monarch is suggested by Henry himself in the opening line of the play,

So shaken as we are, so wan with care,...

If King Henry's age and general relative infirmity is sufficiently established by the actor portraying Henry, then the King's vulnerability becomes more poignant when the Prince leaves him for a moment in the thick of battle without any soldiers or attendants. This window of vulnerability is then exploited by Douglas, who enters and accosts the King.

Doug.
Another King? they grow like Hydra's heads.
I am the Douglas, fatal to all those
That wear colors on them. What art thou
That counterfeit'st the person of the king?

King.
The King himself, who, Douglas, grieves of heart
So many of his shadows thou hast met
And not the very King. I have two boys
Seek Percy and thyself about the field,
But seeing thou fall'st on me so luckily,
I will assay thee, and defend thyself.

Doug.
I fear thou art another counterfeit,
And yet in faith thou bearest thee like a king.
But mine I am sure thou art, whoe'er thou be,
And thus I win thee.

[They fight; the king being in danger, enter the Prince of Wales.]

Douglas descends upon King Henry with a running thrust to the King's left flank. King Henry parries the thrust with his shield and simultaneously deflects the force of the running thrust by displacing his body to the right. Following the King's parry, Douglas continues running past King Henry, and immediately turns to face the King once again.

Douglas repeatedly strikes his own shield with his word as he closes the distance between them. Douglas then quickly passes diagonally to the right and cuts to King Henry's right knee, which the King parries with his sword. Douglas continues to press the attack with a series of cuts to the flank, head and knee, driving the King backwards and around in a circle. In a desperate bid to gain space to breathe, the King jumps in toward Douglas and drives his shield against Douglas with all his strength. The King's attempt to upset Douglas' balance proves to be futile, for Douglas protects himself with his shield and firmly stands his ground. Douglas then pushes the King backwards almost effortlessly. The old man staggers back winded and gasping for breath.

Douglas again begins to smash his own sword against his own shield, which induces the King to deliver a wild thrust at Douglas' exposed knee. In that instant, Douglas passes backwards and simultaneously cuts the King's right wrist. King Henry drops his sword and staggers back. Douglas triumphantly pounds at the King's shield with his sword, literally attempting to smash his way through the King's defenses. These powerful blows drive the King to his knees and a final slash from Douglas' shield sweeps the King's shield from his grasp, leaving the King defenseless.

Douglas vs. King Henry Choreography

Fig. 7 Douglas (right): run into fighting distance, halt with right foot leading, thrust to the left hip beneath King Henry's shield. King Henry: lunge to the right onto right foot, shield parry three.

Fig. 8 Douglas (left): run past King Henry, pivot 180 degrees, close distance while banging sword on shield five times. When in distance, pass to the left onto right foot, cut to right side of right knee. King Henry: stationary, counter cut sword parry two.

Fig. 9 Douglas (right): pass to the left onto left foot, cut right chest. King Henry: pass to the left onto right foot, sword parry three.

Fig. 10 Douglas (right): pass to the left onto right foot, molinello on left side, cut center head. King Henry: pass to the left onto left foot, shield parry five.

Fig. 11 Douglas (right): pass to the left onto left foot, diagonal cut to right knee. King Henry: pass to the left onto right foot, sword parry two.

Fig. 12 King Henry (left): maintain blade contact, pass forward onto left foot, extend shield forward at arm's length toward Douglas' center chest. Douglas: stationary, protect center chest with his shield (They are now locked in a corps a corps).

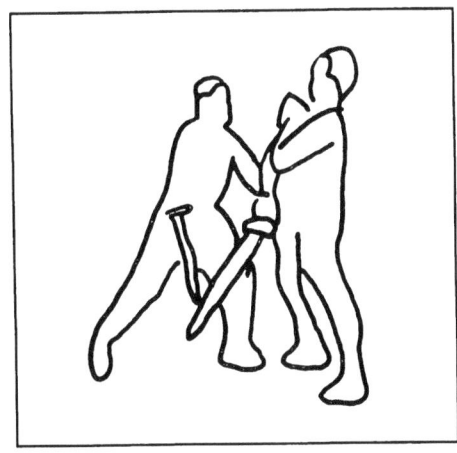

Fig. 13 Douglas (right): pass forward onto right foot. King Henry: react backwards with double pass, break contact. Douglas: bang sword against his shield five times.

Fig. 14 King Henry (left): on Douglas' fifth shield strike, passes forward onto left and right foot, (in distance) thrust in supination to right knee. Douglas: pass back avoidance onto right foot, right side molinello, contact right wrist with flat of blade and pull sword back to low right side for follow through.

Fig. 15 King Henry (left): drop sword, pass back. Douglas: pass forward onto right foot, cut left shoulder. King Henry: shield parry high three.

Fig. 16 Douglas (left): stationary, cut right shoulder. King Henry: shield beat parry high four with inside edge.

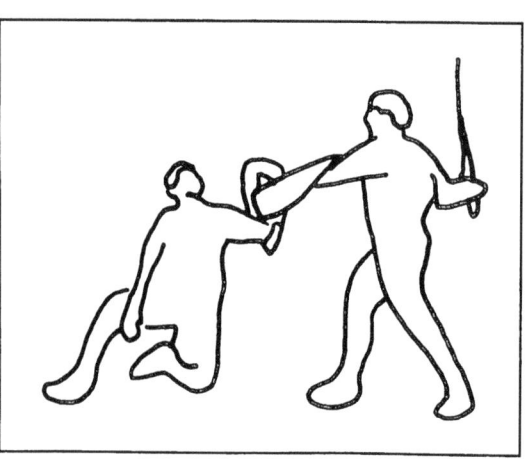

Fig. 17 King Henry (left): immediately following the parry with shield, kneel on left knee. Douglas: stationary, strike left edge of shield against left inside edge of King Henry's shield. King Henry: release shield following impact.

Douglas raises his sword to deliver the death-stroke when he is halted by the Prince of Wales.

Douglas vs. Prince Henry

PRINCE.
Hold up thy head, vile Scot, or thou art like
Never to hold it up again! The spirits of
Valiant Shirley, Stafford, Blunt are in my arms,
It is the Prince of Wales that threatens thee,
Who never promiseth but he means to pay.

[They fight: Douglas flieth]

Here is a match more worthy of the "vile Scot"! Douglas turns from the vulnerable monarch and faces Prince Hal. He sees a warrior whose armor is covered with blood, some of which is the prince's own. For it has been established earlier in the scene that Hal has been wounded.

In lines 1 and 2 of this scene, the King advises Prince Hal to leave the battle.

KING.
I prithee, Harry,
Withdraw thyself, thou bleedest too much.

However, from the Prince's actions, it is clear that the wound has not hampered him overmuch.

The prince is armed with a hand-and-a-half bastard sword, and a heavy metal war gauntlet which covers his left arm up to the elbow. For theatrical effect, the gauntlet is studded with spikes which protrude from the knuckles.

Douglas once again initiates the attack and cuts at Hal's right knee, which the Prince parries with his sword. Douglas follows this attack by swinging his shield at Hal's exposed left flank, and Hal avoids the shield attack by leaping backwards.

Douglas has momentarily exposed his left flank by sweeping his shield across Hal's left flank, and Hal leaps in with a cut to Douglas' left flank. Douglas parries the cut with his shield, without a moment to spare. Finding the Prince to be both cunning and very quick in his responses, Douglas steps back out of distance and begins to cautiously circle the Prince, in order to find an opening in his defenses.

This time Hal begins the offensive and delivers a powerful head cut, which causes Douglas to raise his shield in order to parry the blow. The Prince immediately steps in toward Douglas and strikes him on his chest with the Gauntlet, below Douglas' upraised shield. Douglas staggers back from the strength of the blow upon his chest.

The Prince follows his successful attack with a number of lightening quick cuts to varies targets, which places Douglas on the defensive. In an effort to halt Hal's furious advance, Douglas thrusts out toward Hal's right side with his sword. Hal parries Douglas' thrust and binds Douglas' sword with his own, causing Douglas to lose his grip and be disarmed, the sword flying from his grasp upstage. Without a sword, Douglas knows he hasn't a prayer of surviving Hal's next attack! Douglas turns and races off of the stage, armed only with a shield.

Douglas vs. Prince Henry Choreography

Fig. 18 Douglas (left): pass forward onto left foot, molinello on right side, cuts right knee. Prince Henry: pass back onto right foot, counter cut parry two.

Fig 19. Douglas (left): stationary, sweep shield in a horizontal arc from left to right. Prince Henry: pass back avoidance onto left foot, keep sword below waist.

Fig. 20 Prince Henry (right): pass forward onto left foot, circle sword above head, cut to right chest. Douglas: stationary, shield beat parry four.

HENRY IV, PART 1 39

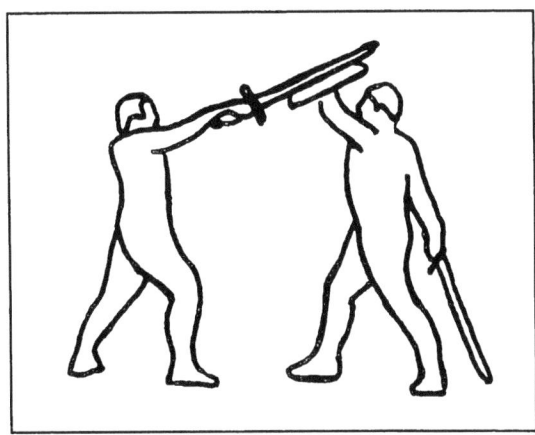

Fig. 21 Douglas (right): pass back out of distance, circle counter-clockwise 180 degrees. Prince Henry: circle counter-clockwise 180 degrees, pass forward onto right foot, cut center head. Douglas: pass back onto left foot, shield parry five.

Fig. 22 Prince Henry (left): pass forward onto left foot, strike center chest with left gauntlet. Douglas: pass back twice, ending up with right foot leading.

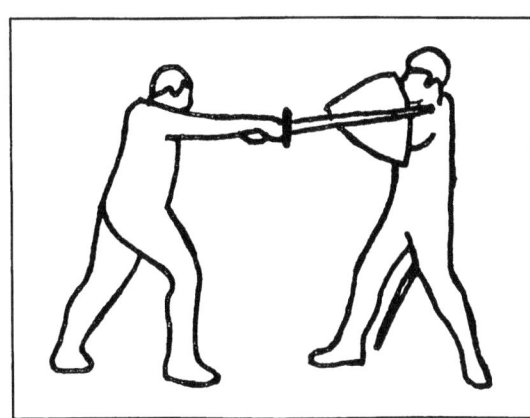

Fig. 23 Prince Henry (left): pass forward onto right foot, right side molinello, cut left shoulder. Douglas: shield parry high three.

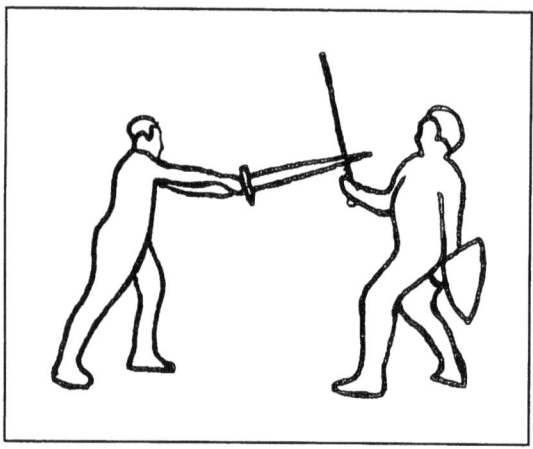

Fig. 24 Prince Henry (left): passes forward onto left foot, cut right shoulder. Douglas: pass back onto right foot, counter cut sword parry high three.

Fig. 25 Prince Henry (left): pass forward onto right foot, cut left knee. Douglas: pass back onto left foot sword parry one.

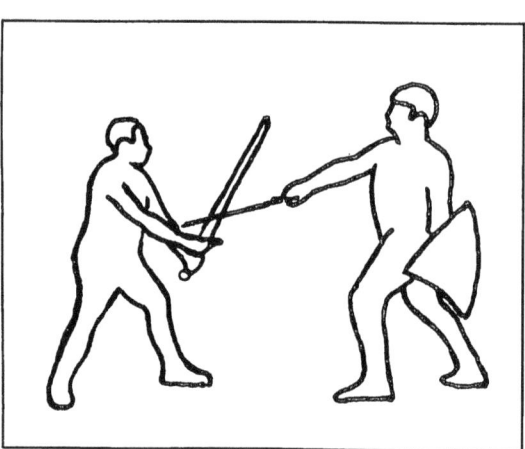

Fig. 26 Douglas (right): pass forward onto left foot, thrust in supination to right hip below breastplate. Prince Henry: passes back onto right foot, counter cut parry three.

 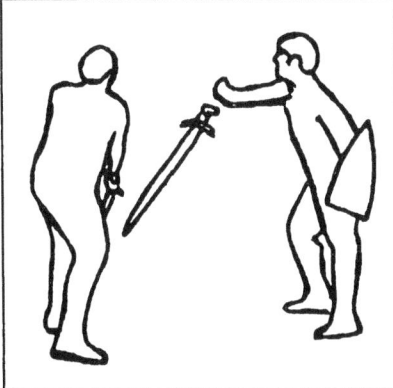

Figs. 27 & 28 Prince Henry (left): stationary, bind sword to low inside. Douglas: control sword release so it slides upon the floor to a designated upstage corner.

The Prince turns to the King to assess the extent of his injuries. Here there is a momentary hiatus in the battle, as father and son begin to reconcile. But the tide of the battle is yet uncertain, and there is little time for personal matters. The King exits to aid in Sir Nicholas Gawsey's rescue and to afford the Prince time alone on stage to, "stay and breathe a while." The King deliberately presents his sword to Hal prior to exiting.

Hotspur vs. Prince Hal

When the King and Prince Hal pause to briefly share a moment of reconciliation, they remove their helmets. Hotspur then enters to see the face of his rival. He recognizes the Prince and removes his own helmet, as he announces his name. The fight that follows their challenges is fought bare headed in order to afford the actors more opportunities to heighten the drama of this climactic duel.

HOTSPUR.
If I mistake not, thou art Harry Monmouth.

PRINCE.
Thou speak'st as if I would deny my name.

HOTSPUR.
My name is Harry Percy.

PRINCE.
Why then I see
A very valiant rebel of the name.
I am the Prince of Wales, and think not, Percy,
To share with me in glory any more.
Two stars keep not their motion in one sphere,
Nor can one England brook a double reign
Of Harry Percy and the Prince of Wales.

HOTSPUR.
Nor shall it, Harry, for the hour is come
To end the one of us, and would to God
They name in arms were now as great as mine!

PRINCE.
I'll make it greater ere I part from thee,
And all the budding honors on thy crest
I'll crop to make a garland for my head.

HOTSPUR.
I can no longer brook thy vanities.

[They fight.]

In this celebrated duel between Hotspur and Prince Hal, the culmination and resolution of the conflicts engendered by duality is artfully explored in *King Henry IV, Part 1*. Opposites meet and the victor speaks for order over chaos, reason over passion, duty over glory!

Hotspur is the fiery emblem of heroic youth. His unbridled vigor and passion leading him to apparent greatness. His reputation is enhanced by heroic feats in battle. Even Prince Hal acknowledges the unsullied reputation of his foe that is known to all,

...this same child of honor and renown,
This gallant Hotspur, this all-praised knight,

However the very qualities of courage, valor and bravado, which have hoisted Hotspur into the precarious world of power and conquest, also point to serious flaws in his character. He lacks mental balance and is very easily swayed by his passions. His name bespeaks impatience and an incautious recklessness. His father says of Hotspur that he is "a wasp-stung and impatient fool." In battle, these flaws can prove to be fatal.

Opposite Hotspur on this violent field of destiny stands Harry, the Prince of Wales. He has shown the audience that his profligate ways are over. He has recognized and denounced his rampant passions. His sense of duty to his kingdom and to his father has taken precedent in his heart and mind. He has become the symbol of divine reason and order. His choices will not be rash. He has set his course towards redemption. He is determined to wash his sins clean in the blood of his father's enemies. What Hotspur interprets as "vanities" are merely statements of fact.

It is fitting then that Hotspur launches the first wild attack upon his foe. With a triumphant shout, Hotspur races directly at Hal and slams his shield against Hal's extended sword, driving the Prince backwards, who unsuccessfully attempts to stand his ground. Hal staggers back and Hotspur rains more savage blows towards Hal's unprotected head, which Hal parries with his sword.

On the third head cut, which Hotspur directs at Hal with all of his strength, Hal slips aside to avoid the blow and spins around to Hotspur's unprotected right side. Hotspur's head blow continues harmlessly to the ground.

In that instant, Hal cuts to Hotspur's unprotected right flank and Hotspur is forced to desperately avoid the flank cut with an awkward leap to the left. Hal presses his advantage with a series of cuts to Hotspur's legs. Which Hotspur parries with his sword.

Shamed by this attack and a bit enraged by Hal's skill, Hotspur whips his shield across Hal's face. Prince Hal ducks beneath the shield and immediately slashes up to slightly graze Hotspur's exposed shield arm.

Shocked by the unexpected wound, Hotspur gives ground a few paces and Hal holds his position to cautiously await Hotspur's next gambit.

Meanwhile, Falstaff has entered to witness this last exchange and the wounding of Hotspur. This prompts Falstaff's lines of encouragement and braggadocio on Hal's behalf.

Douglas then enters and there ensues a comic chase scene between Falstaff and Douglas. They encircle the continuing fight between Hotspur and Hal.

Hotspur circles Hal looking for an opening in Hal's defenses; finding none, Hotspur again resorts to brute force. Hotspur cuts at Hal's legs, head and flank furiously in the hope of overpowering the Prince by sheer might. Hal retreats as he defends himself from Hotspur's series of attacks. He is driven all the way across the stage. We can see that he does not have the strength to match Hotspur directly.

Just as Hal runs out of room for any further retreats, He strikes out with a counter-thrust at Hotspur's knee and quickly escapes to the side. Hotspur parries the knee thrust with his sword and continues to pursue Prince Henry.

The Prince begins a succession of evasive maneuvers, artfully avoiding Hotspur's wild slashing blade. Hal is attempting to fatigue Hotspur and to draw him into exposing a vulnerable target.

During this episode of slashes and avoidances between our principal characters, Falstaff has contrived to fall down and play dead, in an attempt to avoid Douglas' retribution.

At this point the questions arise: Why does Douglas leave the stage, instead of helping Hotspur defeat Prince Hal? Is there a moment where Douglas offers to aid Hotspur and Hotspur proudly indicates that he requires no help, as this is a private quarrel? Why then wouldn't Douglas remain merely to observe the final result, or to be there just in case the outcome of Hotspur's duel with the Prince goes awry? Does a group of the king's soldiers suddenly arrive, forcing Douglas to defend himself as he battles his way off the stage? Do Hotspur and Hal themselves momentarily battle their way off the stage, so that Douglas also exits from the stage to follow them, not returning when the principal combatants return? Or does Douglas witness the defeat of Hotspur and flee the stage to save himself?

In Act V, Scene v, Prince Hal relates the subsequent fate of the warrior Douglas.

The Noble Scot, my lord Douglas, when he saw
The fortune of the day quite turn'd from him
The noble Percy slain, and all his men
Upon the foot of fear, fled with the rest,
And falling from a hill, he was so bruis'd
That the pursuers took him.
At my tent The Douglas is; and I beseech
   your Grace
I may dispose of him.

One choice would be to have Douglas leave the stage prior to the death of Percy. Douglas could either be pursued by the king's forces, or he could encounter a passing foe, such as John of Lancaster, and exit fighting. This would leave the stage free for the audience to focus upon the final moments of the Hal and Hotspur fight. The final choice, of course, would be the director's. And so, to return to Hal and Hotspur.

Hotspur's pursuit of Hal becomes more incautious, as Hotspur is becoming frustrated with his elusive foe. After a particularly wild slash and skillful avoidance by Hal, the Prince returns a powerful thrust at Hotspur's chest, which Hotspur beats aside with his Shield. Stepping in between Hotspur's sword and shield, Prince Henry drives his gauntleted left fist upwards, striking Hotspur on the face. Hotspur staggers backwards from the force of the blow and he drops his shield to the ground.

Hal pursues Hotspur and cuts at his head. Hotspur parries the head cut. Hal then quickly drops to one knee, below Hotspur's lifted sword, and with a powerful thrust, mortally wounds Hotspur across the stomach.

Percy drops his sword and begins to sink to his knees. Hal discards his sword and shield and catches his adversary. Prince Henry gently lowers him to the ground—valiant enemies in battle and honorable brothers in death.

Hotspur vs. Prince Henry Choreography

Fig. 29 Hotspur (left): pass forward into distance, extend shield at arm's length, sword held overhead, contact Prince Henry's sword. Prince Henry: stationary, right foot forward, grasping foible of sword with left gauntlet, extends sword horizontally forward.

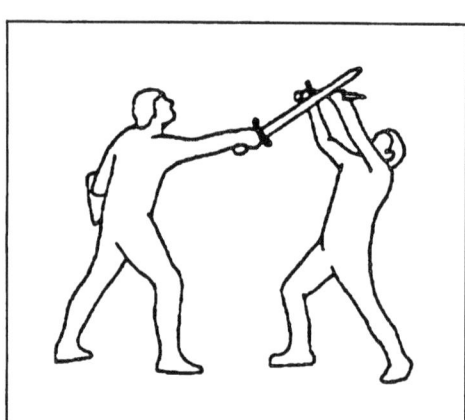

Fig. 30 Hotspur (left): pass forward onto left foot. Prince Henry: pass back four steps, breaking contact. Hotspur: pass forward three steps, right foot forward, cut center head. Prince Henry: parry five with sword held by foible and hilt.

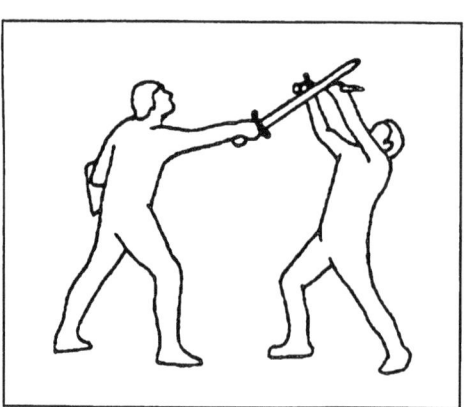

Fig. 31 Hotspur (left): stationary, again cut center head. Prince Henry: stationary, parry five with sword held by foible and hilt.

Fig. 32 Hotspur (left): passes back onto right foot with right side molinello and then pass forward onto right foot, cut center head. Prince Henry: diagonal pass avoidance to the right onto left foot.

Fig. 33 Prince Henry (left): pivot on left foot, pass diagonally to the left onto right foot, cuts diagonally downward to right rear shoulder. Hotspur: avoid by pivoting on right foot and sweep left foot counter clockwise 180 degrees.

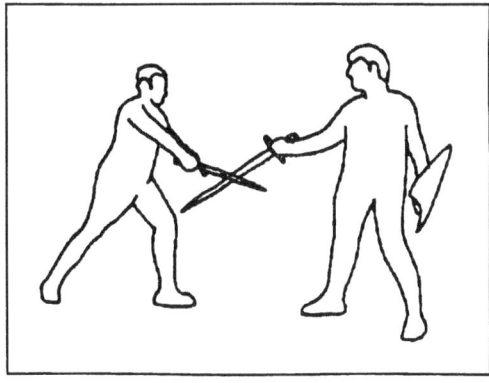

Fig. 34 Prince Henry (left): stationary, shift weight to leading left foot, turn torso to face Hotspur, cut to inside of left knee. Hotspur: stationary, pivot on the balls of his feet to face Prince Henry, left foot leading, counter cut sword parry seven.

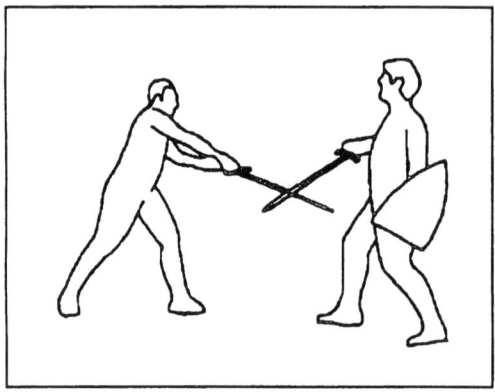

Fig. 35 Prince Henry (left): stationary, sweep blade overhead, cut to outside of right knee. Hotspur: stationary, sword parry two.

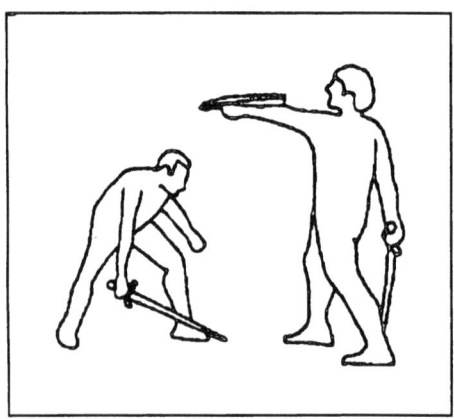

Fig. 36 Hotspur (right): stationary, sweep shield horizontally left to right. Prince Henry: duck beneath shield.

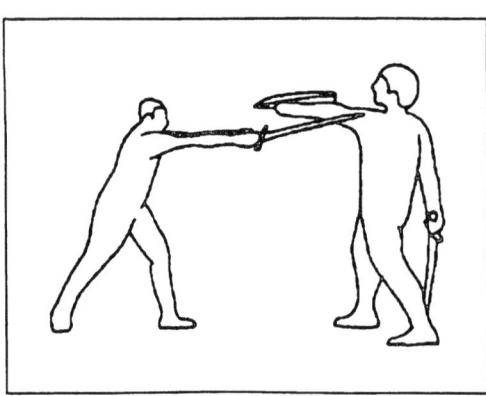

Fig. 37 Prince Henry (left): stationary, cut diagonally upward and place flat of blade against Hotspur's left upper arm. Prince Henry: stationary, pull blade away from contact and follow through diagonally downward to low outside line. Hotspur: immediately after Hal's follow through, react by passing back three steps.

Fig. 38 Hotspur (right): out of distance, circle 90 degrees, pass forward two steps, with right foot leading cut left knee. Prince Henry: stationary, left foot leading, beat parry one.

Fig. 39 Hotspur (right): pass forward onto left foot, circle blade on right side, cut center head. Prince Henry: pass back onto left foot, two handed parry high four.

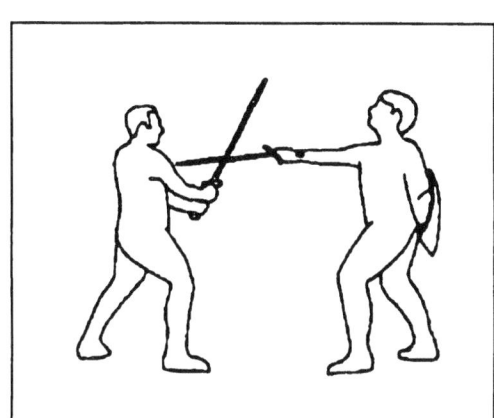

Fig. 40 Hotspur (right): stationary, cut left chest. Prince Henry: stationary, two handed parry four.

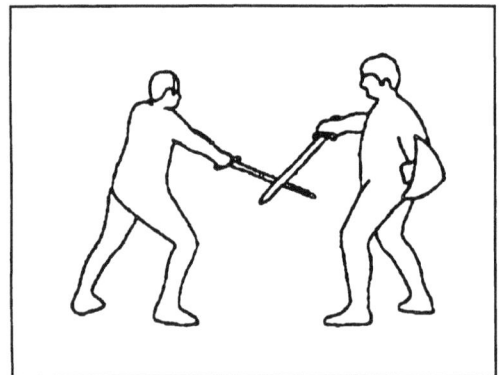

Fig. 41 Prince Henry (left): stationary, shift weight forward onto leading right foot, thrust in supination with one hand to right knee. Hotspur: stationary, counter cut sword parry two.

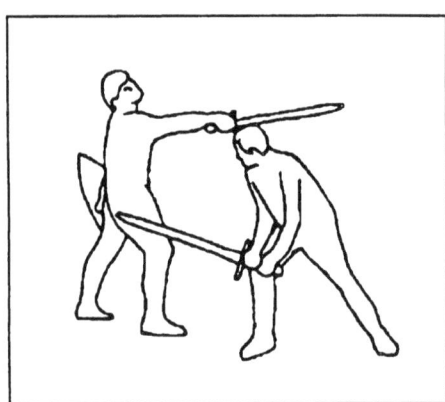

Fig. 42 Prince Henry (right): following the thrust, move out of distance and counter-clockwise 90 degrees around Hotspur. Hotspur: pivot, with the right foot leading, to face Prince Henry. Hotspur: pass forward twice onto left and right foot, overhead molinello, slash diagonally downward, from right side, to left shoulder. Prince Henry: diagonal pass avoidance to the left onto the right foot.

Fig. 43 Prince Henry (left): pass diagonally forward onto left foot, pivot to face Hotspur. Hotspur: pass forward toward Hal onto left foot, slash horizontally from the inside line, to stomach. Prince Henry: backward leap avoidance out of distance, land with right foot leading.

HENRY IV, PART 1   49

Fig. 44 Hotspur (right): pass forward onto right foot with overhead molinello, diagonal slash from high inside to left shoulder. Prince Henry: diagonal pass avoidance to the right onto the left foot.

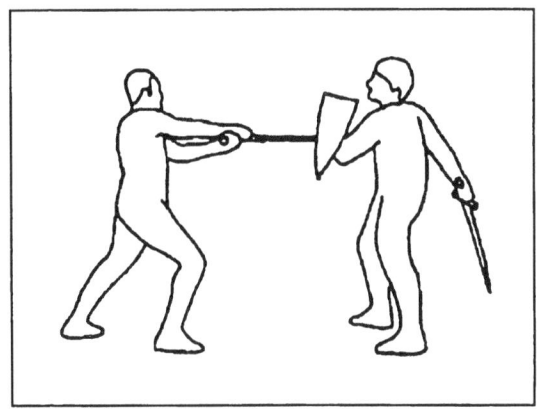

Fig. 45 Prince Henry (left): pivot on left foot, pass forward toward Hotspur onto right foot, thrust in pronation to right chest. Hotspur: stationary, parry four with inside edge of shield.

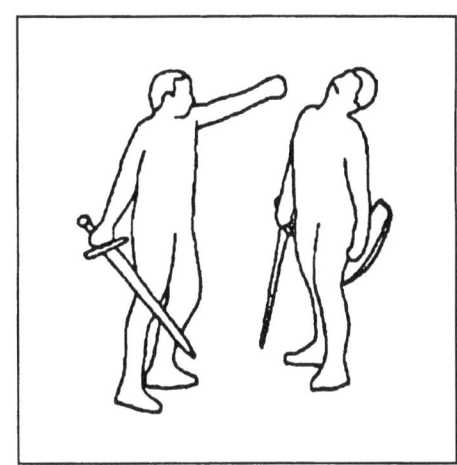

Fig. 46 Prince Henry (left): pass forward onto left foot, strike upward with back of left gauntlet to right-outside of Hotspur's face. Hotspur: react by snapping head back and step backwards onto right foot, drop shield.

Fig. 47 Prince Henry (left): pass forward onto right foot, right side molinello, cut center head. Hotspur: stationary, sword parry five.

Fig. 48 Prince Henry (left): kneel onto left knee, half-pronated thrust upward from low outside to left side of Hotspur's stomach level, flat of blade contact to right side. Hotspur: close elbow onto sword—hiding blade contact from audience—drop sword to the outside. Prince Henry: following disarm, discard sword to the outside, catch Hotspur around the waist with the right arm, slowly lower Hotspur to the floor onto Hotspur's right side.

HENRY IV, PART 2

Here's a goodly tumult!

Falstaff vs. Pistol

A more lazy, indulgent, perjuring, pilfering, lecherous, amoral, debauched, endearing, witty, thoroughly delightful clown has never been seen in dramatic literature. This is, of course, Falstaff.

In Act II, Scene iv, the audience is in for a riotous display when Shakespeare pits the vain Falstaff in a battle with that emotional firecracker, Pistol. Pistol (as his name suggests) is outrageously argumentative under normal circumstances. In this scene, his explosive temper is exacerbated by his being drunk.

To round off the foolish affair, we have the excitable Hostess Quickly, the slatternly Doll Tearsheet, the dissolute Bardolph and Falstaff's Page. The action takes place at the Boar's Head Tavern in Eastcheap.

The fight between Falstaff and Pistol occurs rather late in the scene. The drunken Pistol enters and he is exceptionally rowdy and loud. He has annoyed the assembled group and Falstaff has ordered Bardolph to kick Pistol out.

BARD.
Come, get you down stairs.

PIST.
What? Shall we have incision? shall we imbrue?[*Snatching up his sword.*]
Then death rock me asleep, abridge my doleful days!
Why then let grievous, ghastly, gaping wounds
Untwind the Sisters Three! Come, Atropos, I say!

HOST.
Here's goodly stuff toward!

FAL.
Give me my rapier, boy.

DOLL.
I pray thee, Jack, I pray thee do not draw.

FAL.
Get you down stairs.

[Drawing, and driving Pistol out.]

HOST.
Here's a goodly tumult! I'll forswear keeping house afore I'll be in these tirits and frights.
So! murder, I warrant now. Alas, alas, put up your naked weapons, put up your naked weapons.

[Exeunt Pistol and Bardolph.]

DOLL.
I pray thee, Jack, be quiet, the rascal's gone. Ah, you whoreson little valiant villain, you!

HOST.
Are you not hurt i' the groin? Methought 'a made a shrewd thrust at your belly.

[Enter Bardolph.]

FAL.
Have you turn'd him out a' doors?

BARD.
Yea, sir. The rascal's drunk; you have hurt him, sir, i' th' shoulder.

Although Falstaff says, "Give me my rapier, boy," Falstaff fights with a broadsword. Falstaff is notorious for misapplication of fencing terms. In *Henry IV, Part 1*, Falstaff fights with the sword and buckler, but he indiscriminately describes his fighting style as that of either the rapier or the sword and buckler. It can safely be assumed that his weapons haven't changed for this play. [*Henry IV, Part 2*, is virtually a continuation of *Part 1*.] Pistol also carries a broadsword. Neither fighter uses a buckler in this scene.

Seated at a table, with a tankard of ale in one hand and the sword given to him by his page in the other, Falstaff roars, "Get you down stairs," and pitches the ale into Pistol's face. Falstaff then throws the tankard to the floor and drawing his sword from its sheath, shoves his great bulk onto his feet. Hostess Quickly, Doll Tearsheet, the Page and Bardolph move back against the walls to escape injury.

Temporarily blinded, Pistol, who was standing on the other side of the table from Falstaff, waves his sword about wildly trying to hit anything at all. With a triumphant laugh, Falstaff begins to chase Pistol around the table.

They circle the table twice as Falstaff tries to cut Pistol in the backside. The drunken Pistol just barely manages to stay out of harm's way. Meanwhile, Hostess Quickly is adding her voice to the madness.

HOST.
Here's a goodly tumult! I'll forswear keeping house afore I'll be in these tirits and frights. So! murder, I warrant now.

After two ridiculous revolutions around the table Falstaff is exhausted and breathing heavily. He takes another clay tankard of ale from off the table and begins to quench his thirst. Bleery-eyed, Pistol spies an opportunity.

Pistol thrusts at Falstaff's groin from across the table. Tearsheet and Quickly scream in fright. Falstaff spits out a mouthful of ale and by sheer luck parries the thrust by pinning Pistol's sword to the table with his own sword.

For a moment the action stops, as Falstaff looks down aghast that Pistol had dared to choose such a dastardly (and tender) target! Falstaff lifts his head and fixes Pistol with a baleful gaze. Pistol responds with a sheepish grin.

Enraged, Falstaff smashes the clay tankard over Pistol's shoulder. Dripping with ale, Pistol howls, Doll Tearsheet screams, and Hostess Quickly shouts, "Alas, alas, put up your naked weapons, put up your naked weapons."

Falstaff lifts his sword and cuts at Pistol's head. Pistol ducks under the table, leaving his sword upon it. Falstaff's blade slams harmlessly into the table and Pistol scrambles out from underneath. Bardolph steps in and hoists Pistol up by his hair and drags him off stage. (For the hair pulling technique please see, Martinez, J.D., *Combat Mime, A Non-Violent Approach to Stage Violence*. Chicago: Nelson Hall Publishers, Inc., 1983.)

Falstaff picks up Pistol's sword and throws it off stage. Doll Tearsheet rushes to the furious Falstaff, hugs him around his massive waistline with both arms and pleads, "I pray thee, Jack, be quiet, the rascal's gone."

Falstaff vs. Pistol Choreogaphy

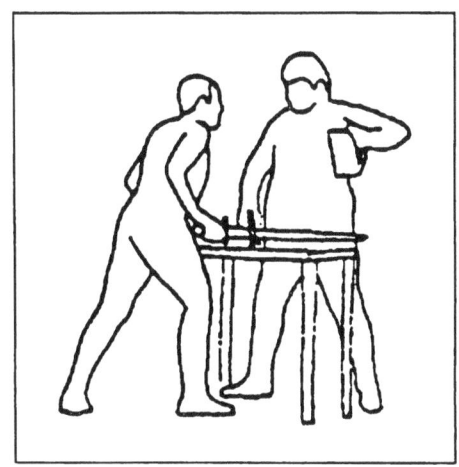

Fig. 49 Pistol (left): stationary, thrust in pronation horizontally, two inches above table, to center groin. Falstaff: take a mouthful of liquid, head to one side to secretly observe the thrust, trap Pistol's blade onto table with a low parry five and spit liquid out of mouth onto Pistol.

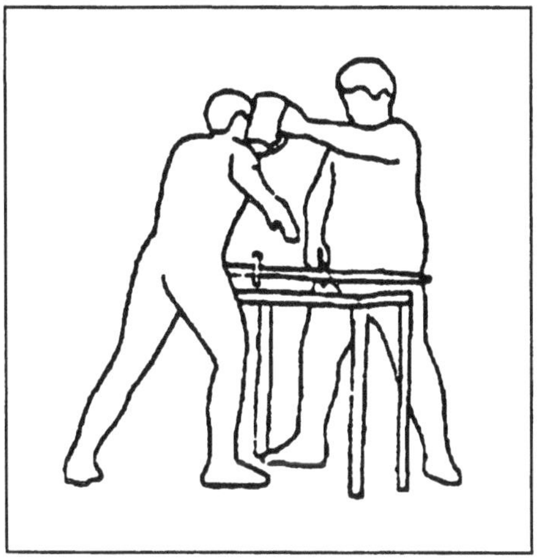

Fig. 50 Falstaff (right): stationary, maintain blade contact, raise trick "break-away" tankard above left shoulder, strike vertically downward onto right shoulder. Pistol: release sword onto table.

Fig. 51 Falstaff (right): stationary, raise blade up to high outside, cut vertically downwards to the inside of Pistol's body outline, strike edge of sword onto table top. Pistol: duck below table.

HENRY VI, PART 1

Thou art an Amazon,
And fightest with the sword of Deborah.

Shakespeare has not created the heroic, saintly, Joan of Arc (Joan De Pucelle) with whom most of us are familiar. Consistent with his manipulation of history to serve his dramatic purposes and his characteristic English patriotism, Joan is portrayed as a devious witch bent upon the destruction of the English.

In Shakespeare's view, Joan De Pucelle's powers actually come from the devil. We learn this later in the play (Act V, Scene iii), when Joan and the French forces are losing to the English. In desperation, Joan calls upon those who have given her her skills, strength and supernatural insights. In a ritual of classic conjuration, Joan spills her own blood and calls not the angels, but rather the devil's helpers. Nor is this the first time that she has called upon them, for in the same scene Joan laments,

JOAN.
Cannot my body nor blood-sacrifice
Entreat you to your wonted furtherance?

Charles vs. Joan De Pucelle

In Act I, Scene ii, however, we can only accept on faith that Joan De Pucelle has been visited by divine spirits who have invested her with supernatural powers. In attempting to convince Charles that he should give her the leadership of his army in order to raise the siege of Orleance, Joan claims that her powers come from heaven.

JOAN.
Heaven and our Lady gracious hath it pleas'd
To shine on my contemptible estate.

Charles (heir to the king of France) may be foppish and an ineffectual leader, but he is no fool. Despite her protestations of divinity he does not take this strange girl's bold rhetoric to mean that she is fated to lead his army. Instead, he thinks that he will amuse himself by putting her to a test of combat and thus expose her as a fraud.

He is in for a rude awakening. Joan may be hiding from whence her powers spring, but there is no doubt that she possesses them.

CHAR.
Thou hast astonish'd me with thy high terms.
Only this proof I'll of thy valor make,
In single combat thou shalt buckle with me;
And if thou vanquishest, thy words are true,
Otherwise I renounce all confidence.

PUC.
I am prepar'd; here is my keen-edg'd sword,
Deck'd with [five] flower-de-luces on each
 side,

The which at Touraine, in Saint Katherine's
  churchyard,
Out of a great deal of old iron I chose forth.

CHAR.
Then come a' God's name, I fear no woman.

PUC.
And while I live, I'll ne'er fly from a man.

[Here they fight, and Joan de Pucelle Overcomes.]

CHAR.
Stay, stay thy hands! Thou art an Amazon,
And fightest with the sword of Deborah.

PUC.
Christ's Mother helps me, else I were too
  weak.

Joan fights with her enchanted singlehand broadsword. Charles uses a singlehand broadsword as well. Neither Joan nor Charles are wearing armor. Charles does wear a pair of gloves, while Joan grips her sword bare-handed.

Charles smiles in self confidence as he nonchalantly circles around Joan. Joan, calm and alert, pivots in place to face Charles with her blade extended in front of her. Abruptly, Charles jabs with the point of his sword at Joan's leg. Joan parries the thrust. Charles laughs and continues his circling manuever around her.

Without any warning Joan passes forward and swings her sword in a mighty cut to Charles' head. The smile leaves Charles' face as he jumps backwards and parries Joan's powerful head cut.

Joan continues her advance towards Charles by driving him backwards with a cut to his chest and a slash at his knees. Charles retreats parrying her chest cut and barely leaps backwards in time to avoid her slash at his knees.

Joan relentlessly pursues Charles with a thrust at his chest and another cut at his head and a diagonal slash at his shoulder. Charles is now completely on the defensive as he scarcely has time to protect himself from Joan's thrust to his chest. He then clumsily parries her head cut and throws himself to the side to avoid her slash at his shoulder.

Increasing the tempo of her attacks and forcing Charles to retreat, Joan thrusts twice in succession at Charles' stomach and slashes horizontally at his head. Charles stumbles backwards as he desperately beats Joan's thrusts aside and narrowly ducks in time to avoid her head slash.

Rising from his crouched position, Charles advances on Joan and cuts at her head. Joan parries his head cut and without breaking contact with his blade, she quickly steps in close to Charles and grasps his sword arm at the wrist with her left hand. Maintaining control of his sword arm, Joan draws her own sword backwards and drives the pummel of her sword into Charles' shoulder.

She releases Charles' sword arm as the force of the blow to his shoulder causes him to reel backwards and fall to the floor. Charles loses his grip on his sword as he falls backwards and the blade skids across the stage.

Joan strides forward to straddle the prostrate Charles. He is filled with conflicting emotions as he pleads with this extraordinary woman.

CHAR.
Stay, stay thy hands!

Charles vs. Joan De Pucelle Choreography

Fig. 52 Charles (left): encircle Joan 360 degrees clockwise. Joan: pivot to face him. Charles: stationary, right foot leading, thrust in half pronation to right thigh. Joan: right foot forward, counter cut parry two.

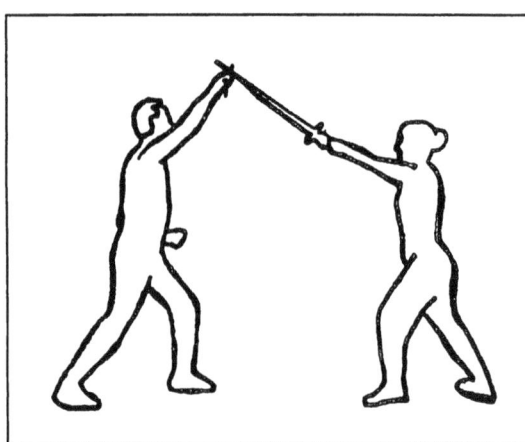

Fig. 53 Charles (left): circle Joan clockwise 90 degrees. Joan: pass forward onto left foot with right side molinello, cut center head. Charles: pass back onto right foot, parry five.

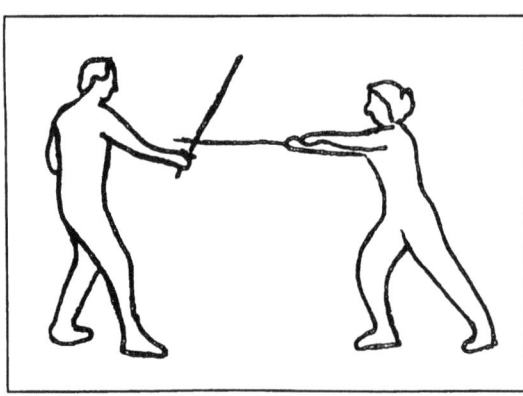

Fig. 54 Joan (right): pass forward onto right foot, cut right chest. Charles: retreat, right foot forward, parry three.

HENRY VI, PART 1

Fig. 55 Joan (right): pass forward onto left foot, slash in pronation horizontally from inside to outside at ankle level (insure proper fighting distance!). Charles: backward leap avoidance, land with the right foot leading.

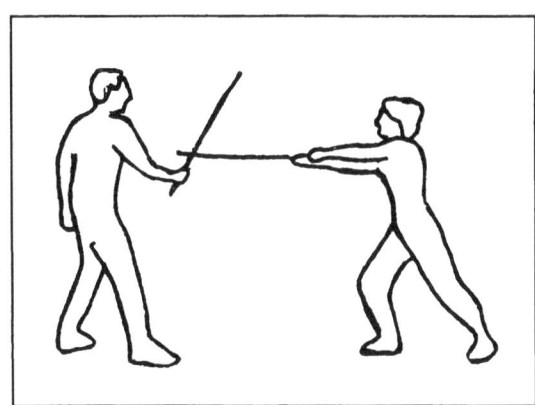

Fig. 56 Joan (right): pass forward onto right foot, cut in supination to left chest. Charles: stationary, parry four.

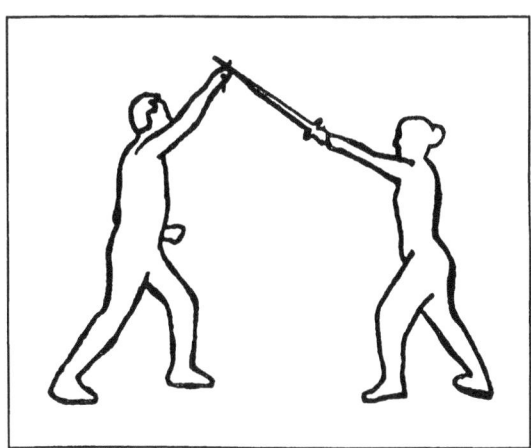

Fig. 57 Joan (right): pass forward onto left foot with a left side molinello, cut center head. Charles: pass back onto right foot, parry five.

Fig. 58 Joan (right): pass onto right foot, diagonal cut from high inside to right shoulder. Charles: avoidance to the left.

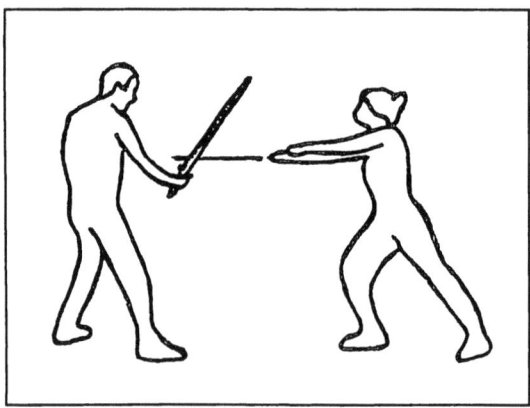

Fig. 59 Joan (right): pass onto left and right foot, thrusts in half-pronation at left hip. Charles: pass back onto left foot, parry four.

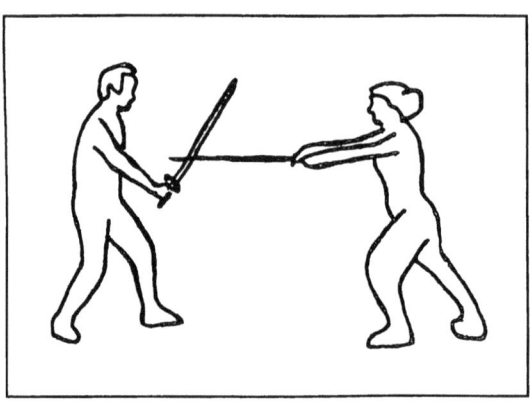

Fig. 60 Joan (right): pass forward onto left foot, thrust in supination to right hip. Charles: pass back onto right foot, parry three.

HENRY VI, PART 1

Fig. 61 Joan (right): pass forward onto right foot, slash in supination from high outside to low inside above Charles' head. Charles: pass back onto left foot, duck beneath head slash.

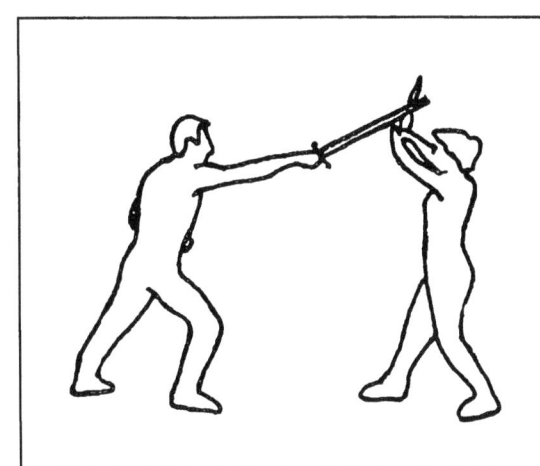

Fig. 62 Charles (left): rise from crouch, advance, right foot forward, right side molinello, cut center head. Joan: stationary, parry five.

Fig. 63 Joan (right): maintain blade contact in parry five, pass forward onto left foot, grasp Charles' right wrist with left hand, move sword above and over to his right side, draw pummel of sword back over right shoulder.

Fig. 64 Joan (left): stationary, extend pummel forward, strike Charles' left shoulder with forearm for a simulated pummel blow to left chest. (Combatants are reversed in illustration to expose technique.) Charles: react with a backward fall. Following fall, control disarm so that blade slides to safe area.

Fig. 65 Joan (right): close distance, stand with right foot between Charles' splayed legs, left foot to the outside of Charles right leg, hand on hip in contempt.

Joan's next encounter is with a much more ferocious adversary, but he fares no better than the Dauphin.

Talbot vs. Joan De Pucelle

The English Army, under the command of Lord Talbot, has besieged the French town of Orleance. The French Army, under the command of Joan De Pucelle, has come to raise the siege and are now attacking the English.

This thrilling duel takes place during the chaos and rout of the English forces. Talbot, the most renowned of England's warriors, cannot keep his men from fleeing in retreat. He aches for a chance to face Joan.

TAL.
Where is my strength, my valor, and my force?
Our English troops retire, I cannot stay them;
A woman clad in armor chaseth them.

[Enter Pucelle.]

Here, here she comes. I'll have a bout with thee;
Devil or devil's dam, I'll conjure thee.

Blood will I draw on thee—thou art a
    witch—
And straightway give thy soul to him thou
    serv'st.

Puc.
Come, come, 'tis only I that must disgrace
    thee.

[Here they fight.]

Tal.
Heavens, can you suffer hell so to prevail?
My breast I'll burst with straining of my
    courage,
And from my shoulders crack my arms asunder,
But I will chastise this high-minded strumpet.

[They fight again.]

Puc.
Talbot, farewell, thy hour is not yet come.
I must go victual Orleance forthwith.

[A short alarum: then enter the town with
    soldiers.]

O'ertake me if thou canst, I scorn thy
    strength.
Go, go, cheer up thy hungry-starved men;
Help Salisbury to make his testament.
This day is ours, as many more shall be.

[Exit.]

    Talbot and Joan wear open-faced helmets, metal gauntlets and full body armor. Joan's singlehand broadsword counters Talbot's bastard sword. It is obvious that Talbot is larger and stronger than Joan, but the skills of warfare have been mysteriously invested into the french "witch." She uses her supernatural skills to balance the strengths of her adversary.
    During the opening dialogue, Talbot and Pucelle circle each other warily. With Pucelle's taunt of, "Come, come, 'tis only I that must disgrace thee," Talbot can no longer contain his desire to destroy this woman who dares to stand up to him.

    He rushes upon her and slashes mightily at her leading leg. In defiance, Joan stands her ground and parries the cut. She then sweeps Talbot's blade up over her head.
    Talbot renews his attack by passing forward and cutting at Joan's head. She passes back and parries the head cut and again sweeps Talbot's blade aside.
    Undaunted, Talbot presses his attack by passing forward and thrusting at Joan's leading leg. Joan quickly pivots her leg out of the path of the thrust, parries Talbot's thrust with her sword and envelopes Talbot's blade into a huge circular arc, forcing his blade aside once again.
    She follows this dynamic display of skill with a horizontal slash at Talbot's head. Talbot ducks the head slash and scrambles backwards. Joan continues to advance menacingly towards Talbot.
    Talbot's look of confusion and disbelief on his face at this woman's ability to fight is almost comical. He shakes off his momentary doubts and with a war cry he rushes forward to thrust at Joan's leg. With great economy she parries the thrust.
    Talbot passes forward and cuts at Joan's chest. Joan simply passes back and parries the chest cut. Then, with a savage suddenness, Joan De Pucelle passes forward and rakes the sharp edges of the gauntleted fingers of her left hand across Talbot's naked face.
    Bright red bloody wounds appear on Talbot's face. He reels backwards, out of reach of Joan's sword. Painfully reacting to his face wounds, Talbot circles Joan De Pucelle. She laughs with pleasure.

Tal.
Heavens, can you suffer hell so to prevail?
My breast I'll burst with straining of my
    courage,
And from my shoulders crack my arms asunder,
But I will chastise this high-minded strumpet.

With grim determination, Talbot launches another attack by running in upon Joan. Building momentum with a large molinello, he slashes at Joan's head. She ducks the head slash.

Immediately swinging his sword in a wide arc, Talbot slashes diagonally at Joan's shoulder. She leans deeply to the side and avoids the slash.

Talbot again raises his sword and performs another diagonal slash at Joan's opposite shoulder. And again, calmly, almost contemptuously, Joan leans aside and avoids the shoulder slash.

In terrible frustration, Talbot strides forward and slashes at Joan's stomach. She avoids the slash by jumping backwards. There is a taunting, wry expression on her face.

Closing the fighting distance by passing forward, Talbot tries another Molinello and head cut. Without retreating, Joan parries the head cut. Quickly passing forward, she cuts at Talbot's chest and leg.

Talbot gives ground and parries Pucelle's sharp cuts to his chest and leg. Then, reaching forward, Talbot thrusts at Joan's chest. The force of the thrust seems capable of piercing right through her body armor. Joan lightly passes back and parries the thrust to her chest.

Taking advantage of Talbot's overextended position, Joan slides her edge along Talbot's sword and takes control of his blade. She sweeps his blade into an ever widening circle which (given his unbalanced position) causes the sword to be torn from his grasp.

Talbot's blade flies in a glistening spiral through the air and falls to the stage floor. Joan draws her weapon back and slashes at Talbot's stomach. Talbot, wrenching his body backwards, leaps out of the way of Joan's razor-like slash.

Unarmed, Talbot stoically awaits his fate. However, Pucelle makes no move to murder her vulnerable opponent.

The sounds of the offstage battle increase and Joan knows she is needed elsewhere. Besides, it will enhance her reputation and strike fear into the hearts of her enemies to have Talbot relate the tale of his defeat at her hands. She laughs, and as she exits she scornfully tosses her parting words at the humiliated Talbot.

PUC.
Talbot, farewell, thy hour is not yet come.
I must go victual Orleance forthwith.

[A short alarum: then enter the town with soldiers.]

O'ertake me if thou canst, I scorn thy strength.
Go, go, cheer up thy hungry-starved men;
Help Salisbury to make his testament.
This day is ours, as many more shall be.

[Exit.]

Talbot vs. Joan De Pucelle Choreography

Fig. 66 Out of fighting distance, Talbot and Joan circle each other 180 degrees. Talbot (left): close distance with a double pass, with right foot forward, diagonal cut to inside of right knee. Joan: stationary, counter cut parry seven.

HENRY VI, PART 1

Fig. 67 Joan (right): stationary, bind sword to his high right side.

Fig. 68 Talbot (left): pass forward onto left foot with a right side molinello, cut center head. Joan: pass back onto right foot, parry five.

Fig. 69 Joan (right): stationary, bind sword to his low right side.

Fig. 70 Talbot (left): pass forward onto right foot, diagonal cut to left knee. Joan: pivot back onto left foot, parry one.

Fig. 71 Joan (right): stationary, envelop blade in a large clockwise circle to Talbot's low right side.

Fig. 72 Joan (right): stationary, slash from high inside to high outside above Talbot's head. Talbot: duck beneath head slash and simultaneously pass back two steps.

Fig. 73 Talbot (left): pass forward two paces with a left and right side molinello, cut left knee. Joan: stationary, beat parry one.

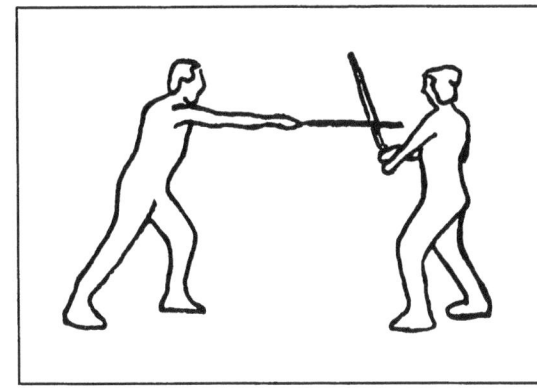

Fig. 74 Talbot (left): pass forward onto left foot with overhead molinello, cut to right chest. Joan: pass back onto right foot, counter cut parry three.

Fig. 75 Joan (right): maintain blade contact, pass forward onto right foot, bend left wrist, cover Talbot's right cheek from audience's view.

Fig. 76 Joan (right): draw left hand sharply downwards (no facial contact) to low inside. Talbot: respond to face scratch with a double pass back.

Fig. 77 Talbot (left): out of distance, circle 180 degrees counter-clockwise around Joan. Joan: pivot to face Talbot. Talbot: double pass forward into distance with an overhead molinello. With right foot forward, slash from high inside to his high outside above Joan's head. Joan: stationary, duck head slash.

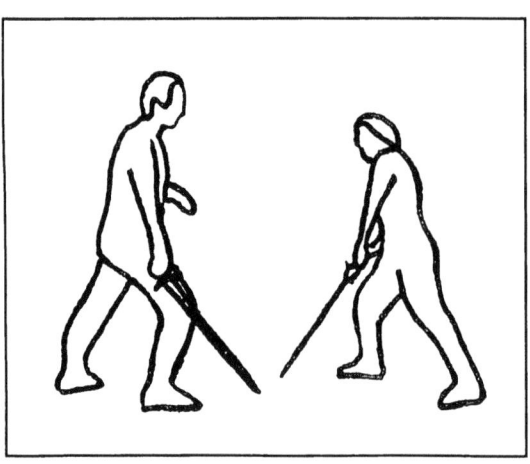

Fig. 78 Talbot (left): stationary, diagonal slash to left shoulder. Joan: lunge avoidance onto left foot out to left side.

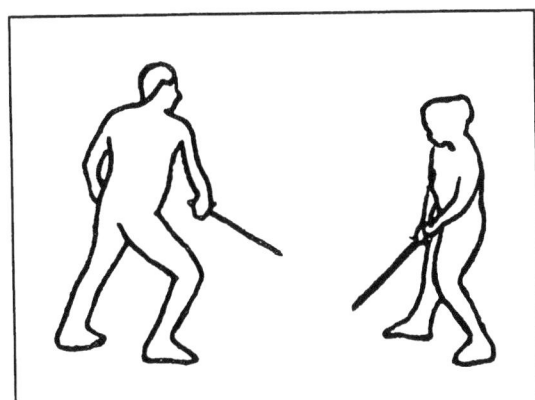

Fig. 79 Talbot (left): stationary, diagonal slash from high inside to right shoulder. Joan: stationary, avoid by shifting torso over right foot.

Fig. 80 Talbot (left): pass forward onto left foot, slash horizontally in supination from inside to outside at Joan's stomach level. Joan: backward leap avoidance, land with right foot forward.

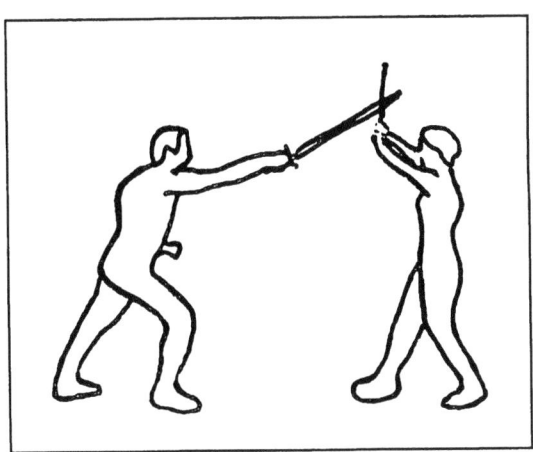

Fig. 81 Talbot (left): pass forward onto right foot with right side molinello, cut center head. Joan: stationary, parry five.

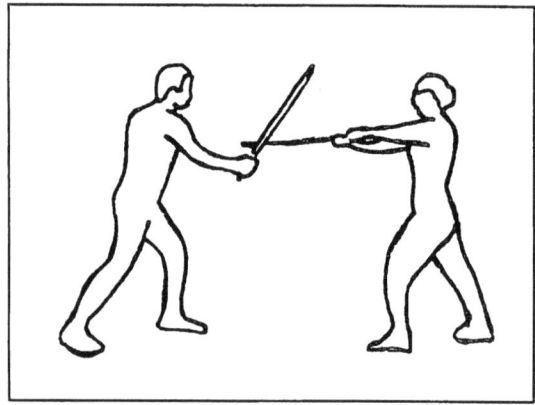

Fig. 82 Joan (right): pass forward onto left foot, cut left chest. Talbot: pass back onto right foot, parry four.

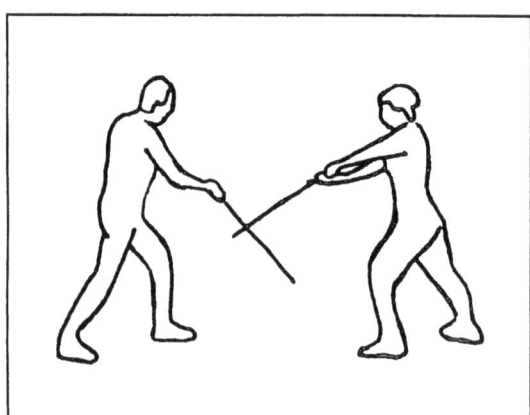

Fig. 83 Joan (right): stationary, cut left knee. Talbot: stationary, counter cut parry seven.

Fig. 84 Talbot (left): pass forward onto right foot, overextend in a thrust to right chest. Joan: pass back onto left foot, parry four.

Fig. 85 Joan (right): envelop Talbot's sword in a large circle to his high right side. Talbot: control release of his sword at conclusion of envelopment.

Fig. 86 Joan (right): stationary, slash in pronation from inside to outside at level of Talbot's stomach. Talbot: backward leap avoidance.

HENRY VI, PART 2

With thy brave bearing should I be in love,
But that thou art so fast mine enemy.

Horner vs. Peter

Henry VI, Part 2 continues the story of the War of the Roses. This is a play fueled by the passions of rival factions. In this scene we see yet another set of factions—the masters and their apprentices. In a balanced world these groups should work harmoniously together, but this world is "out of joint."

Shakespeare's rendition of a formal "Trial By Combat"—that curious medieval institution for determining the truth through armed conflict—between an armorer and his apprentice (based perhaps on the Davy vs. John Catour Combat of 1446) degenerates into a raucous farce. The irony inherent in this usually solemn event viewed by the king, his queen and ministers would not be lost on Shakespeare's audience.

A picture of polar opposites in the persons of Horner and Peter could not be crafted in a more obvious fashion. Horner is grotesquely confident and reveling among his loud drunken peers. Peter is meek and terrified, but his angry compatriots are trying to raise his flagging spirits.

Enter at one door [Horner] the armorer and his Neighbors,
drinking to him so much that he is drunk; and he enters
with a Drum before him and his staff with a sand-bag
fastened to it; and at the other door [Peter] his man,
with a Drum and sand-bag, and Prentices drinking to him.

This is a very noisy affair. Horner and his neighbors are in high spirits and prematurely toasting Horner's victory. Horner quaffs a sickening variety of alcoholic drinks with his friends. In contrast, Peter will not drink with his fellow apprentices because he fears for his life and considers himself a dead man.

PETER.
I thank you all. Drink, and pray for me, I pray you, for I think I have taken my last draught in this world.

Both men are armed with quarterstaffs, which have a sandbag affixed to one end. At first glance, these appear to be very curious weapons indeed, but the choice is appropriately theatrical and underscores the combatants' lowly social status. In any case, these weapons prove to be quite lethal.

Neither Horner nor Peter is wearing any armor. Perhaps Horner sports a pair of gloves to protect his hands, but Peter is gloveless. It may be that both men are stripped to the waist, or wear leather body suits as depicted in a fourteenth century German manuscript (see Bibliography).

With the blare of trumpets and the shouting of onlookers, the battle begins and ends rather quickly.

[Alarum] They fight, and Peter [hits him on the head and] strikes him down.

Overconfident, Horner rushes upon the frightened Peter. Horner delivers a crushing cut to Peter's head and groin. Peter backs away from the attack and manages to parry both cuts.

Belligerently pressing his attack, Horner swipes at Peter's head. Peter ducks out of the way and they circle each other.

Horner is a little dizzy from the circling maneuver and wildly slashes at Peter. Peter nimbly avoids the slash, steps behind Horner and strikes him on the back. Horner reacts with a howl of pain and rage. Horner's faction raises a cacophony of outrage and the apprentices yell in triumph.

Horner again rushes upon Peter and rains a volley of cuts to Peter's chest and legs. Peter, breathing heavily, parries Horner's attacks. On the last leg cut and parry, Peter sweeps Horner's staff aside and strikes Horner in the stomach.

The breath is knocked out of Horner and he doubles over. Taking advantage of Horner's momentary vulnerability, Peter strikes Horner on the back of his head with the heavy sandbagged end of the quarterstaff, knocking Horner to the ground. The head blow will prove to be fatal.

HOR.
Hold, Peter, hold! I confess, I confess treason.
 [He dies.]

YORK.
Take away his weapon. Fellow, thank God, and the good wine in thy master's way.

Horner vs. Peter Choreography

Fig. 87 Horner (right): pass forward four paces, the right foot forward, strike fore end to center head. Peter: stationary, parry head with middle of staff.

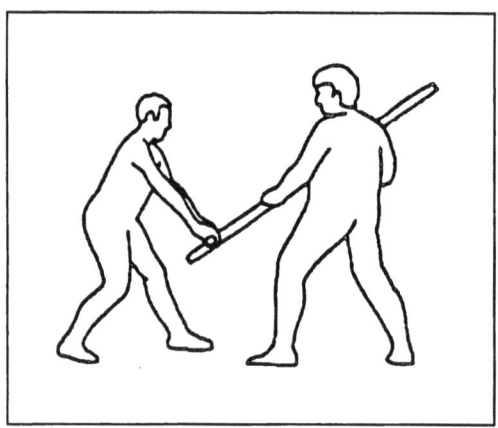

Fig. 88 Horner (right): pass forward onto left foot, strike upward with butt end to center crotch. Peter: pass back onto right foot, parry crotch with middle of staff.

Fig. 89 Horner (right): pass forward onto right foot, fore end slash from high outside to high inside above Peter's head. Peter: duck head slash.

Fig. 90 Peter and Horner move in a circle counter clockwise 360 degrees. Horner (right): stationary, right foot forward, fore end diagonal slash from high outside to left shoulder. Peter: with a diagonal pass avoidance to the left onto right foot.

HENRY VI, PART 2

Fig. 91 Peter (left): diagonal pass toward Horner onto left foot, fore end thrust and strike to backside of upper right arm and react with pass right and left.

Fig. 92 Horner (right): pivot to face Peter, pass forward onto left and right foot, fore end thrust to left chest. Peter: stationary, parry right chest with middle of staff.

Fig. 93 Horner (right): stationary, fore end strike to right knee. Peter: stationary, butt end parry right knee.

Fig. 94 Peter (left): stationary, bind Horner's staff to his high right side.

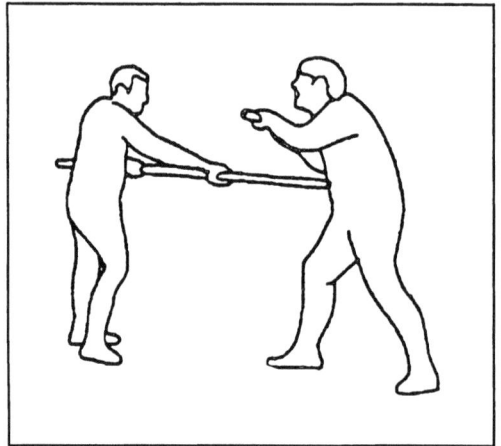

Fig. 95 Peter (left): stationary, fore end thrust to center stomach (no forward energy on contact!). Peter: following contact, react by bending over at waist.

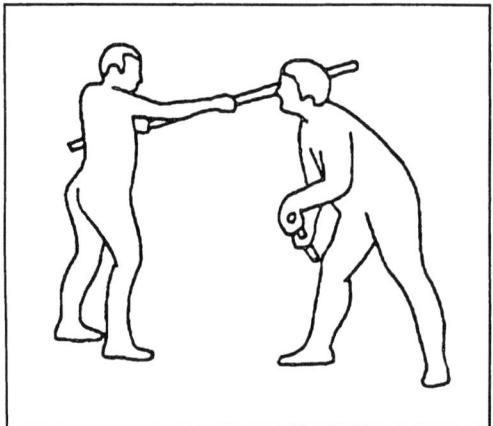

Figs. 96 & 97 Peter (left): stationary, fore end strike to above Horner's left shoulder at level of Horner's head (creating the illusion of a blow to the head). Horner: shout in pain at moment of supposed impact, control release of quarterstaff to right outside, sink to floor.

Cade vs. Iden

Judging from the way in which he presents his various rebels, Shakespeare must have been a kind-hearted person. The rebel, Cade is one of Shakespeare's comic villains whose braggadocio and supreme self-confidence somehow make him sympathetic. Coupled with a broad regional accent and a hilarious turn of phrase, this opportunistic ne'er-do-well was sure to please the groundlings.

We find Cade down on his luck hiding in the garden of Alexander Iden, a Kentish gentleman. Cade's rebellion (an effort to place himself upon the throne of England!) has been crushed. He hasn't eaten for five days. By chance Iden enters with his servants and discovers the interloper.

In typical fashion, Cade saucily challenges Iden and his five servants to do battle. Whatever else he may be, Cade is no coward. Iden is unaware of Cade's true identity as the celebrated insurgent sought by the King.

Cade and Iden are both armed with the double-edged bastard sword. Cade is wearing Sir Humphrey Stafford's armor that he acquired in Act IV, Scene iii. Iden is not wearing any armor.

CADE
Steel, if thou turn the edge, or cut not out the burly-bon'd clown in chines of beef ere thou sleep in thy sheath, I beseech [God] on my knees thou mayst be turn'd to hobnails.

Here they fight [and Cade falls down].

Defiantly, Cade attacks Iden with a cut to the chest. Iden parries the cut and riposts with a thrust to the stomach.

Cade parries the thrust and slashes at Iden's head. Iden ducks the slash and pivots around Cade.

Iden cuts at Cade's head and chest and thrusts at his stomach. Cade parries the attack and retorts with a cut at Iden's head. Then immediately stepping in to close the distance, Cade strikes Iden in the stomach with his fist. Iden reacts backwards.

Cade leaps forward and hurls several vicious cuts at Iden's chest. Iden retreats, narrowly protecting himself.

Iden halts Cades advance by sweeping Cade's sword aside in an arc and slashing at Cade's face. Cade ducks beneath Iden's hurtling blade.

In a dastardly gesture, Cade grabs up some dirt and flings it into Iden's eyes. Momentarily blinded, Iden gives ground and circles away from Cade.

Cade stumbles in exhaustion. The deprivation of the last few days is catching up with him and he is not able to pursue Iden as swiftly as he should. By the time Cade pitches his next attack, Iden has been able to recover much of his sight.

Cade cuts at Iden's head and slashes at his stomach. Iden parries the head cut and hurling himself backwards, avoids the stomach slash.

Cade, with his last bit of energy, swings his blade at Iden's head. Iden drops to one knee, avoiding the head slash.

From the kneeling position, Iden thrusts upwards—driving the point of his sword beneath Cade's breastplate and deep into Cade's stomach.

With a cry of pain, "O, I am slain!" Cade crumples to the ground. The thrust is fatal, but Cade hangs on for 15 more lines. His lifeless body is unceremoniously dragged from the stage to end the scene. Thus Cade, however sympathetic, shares a fate common to Shakespeare's rebels.

Cade vs. Iden Choreography

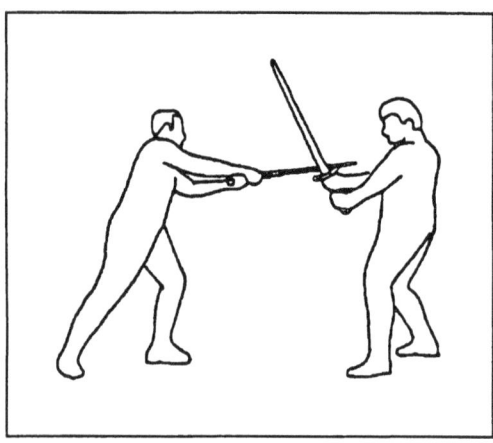

Fig. 98 Cade (left): pass forward onto left foot, cut in pronation to right chest. Iden: pass back onto right foot, parry three.

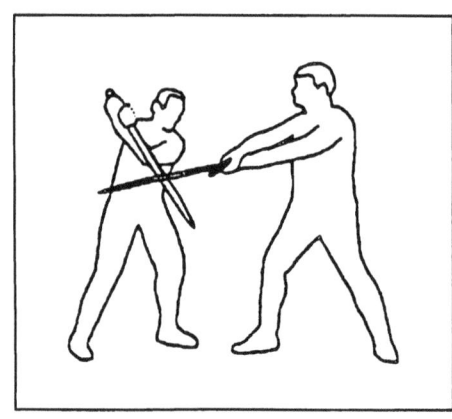

Fig. 99 Iden (right): pass forward onto right foot, thrust half-pronated to center stomach. Cade: stationary, counter cut parry two.

Fig. 100 Cade (left): slashes from high outside to high inside, above Iden's head. Iden: duck head slash.

HENRY VI, PART 2

Fig. 101 Iden (left): circle counter clockwise 180 degrees around Cade. Cade: pivot to face Iden. Iden: stationary, right side molinello, cut center head. Cade: stationary, parry five.

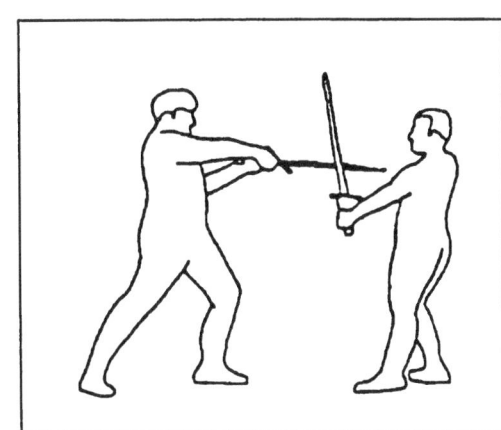

Fig. 102 Iden (left): pass forward onto left foot, cut to right chest. Cade: pass back onto right foot, parry three.

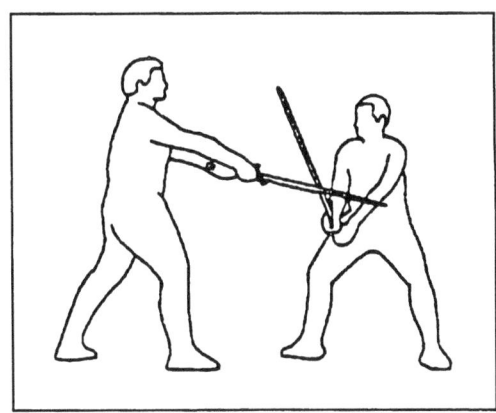

Fig. 103 Iden (left): pass forward onto right foot, thrust half-pronated to left hip. Cade: pass back onto left foot, beat parry four.

Fig. 104 Cade (right): stationary, cut to center head. Iden: stationary, parry five.

Fig. 105 Cade (right): pass forward onto left foot, left hand stage stomach punch. Iden: react back then pass back onto right and left foot.

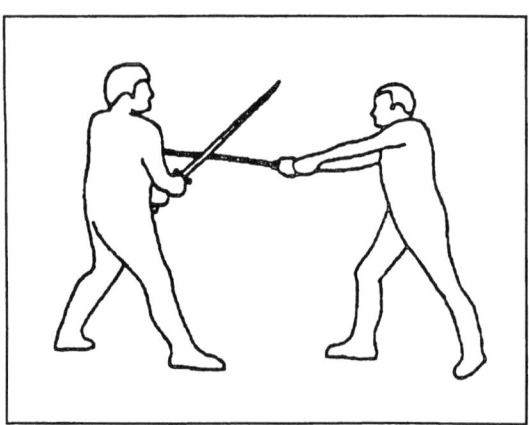

Fig. 106 Cade (right): pass forward onto right foot, cut to Iden's left chest. Iden: stationary, parry four.

HENRY VI, PART 2   79

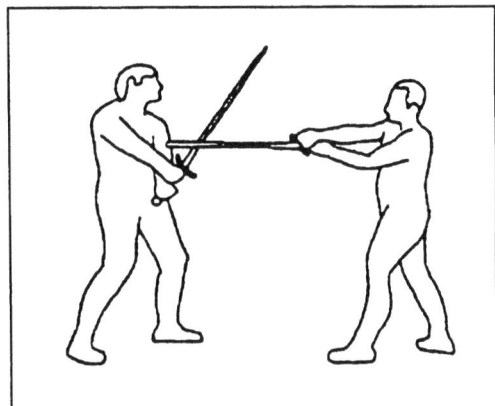

Fig. 107 Cade (right): pass forward onto left foot, cut to right chest. Iden: pass back onto right foot, parry three.

Fig. 108 Iden (left): stationary, bind sword down to Iden's low right side.

Fig. 109 Iden (left): stationary, slash from high inside to high outside above Cade's head. Cade: duck head slash.

80   THE SWORDS OF SHAKESPEARE

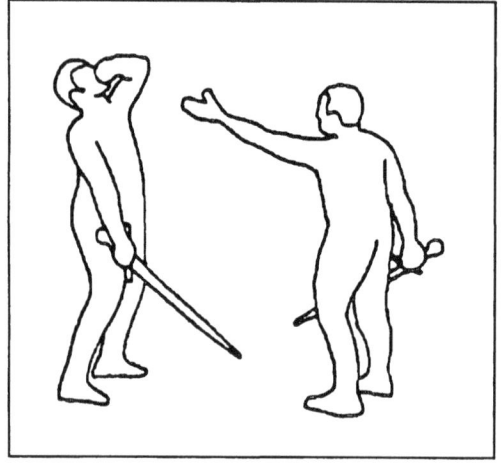

Fig. 110 Cade (right): pick up debris from stage floor, draw hand back as cue, throw debris toward Iden after Iden covers eyes with forearm (work on timing to create proper illusion).

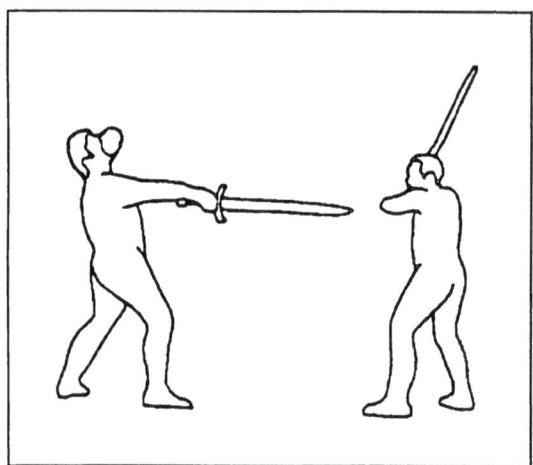

Fig. 111 Iden (left): cover face with forearm, sword extended toward Cade, circle counter clockwise 90 degrees around Cade.

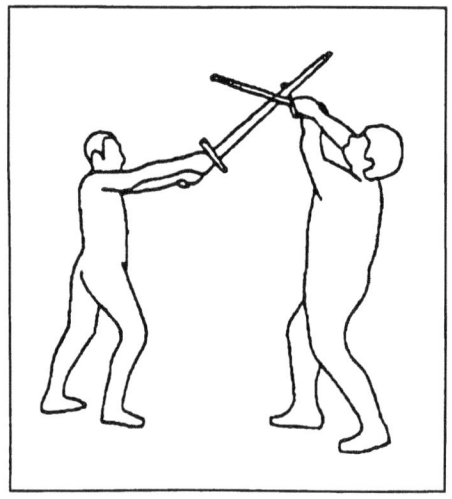

Fig. 112 Cade (left): double pass forward, cut to center head. Iden: stationary, parry five.

HENRY VI, PART 2 81

Fig. 113 Cade (left): stationary, right foot forward, slash from inside to outside at Iden's stomach level (observe fighting distance). Iden: backward leap avoidance; land with right foot forward.

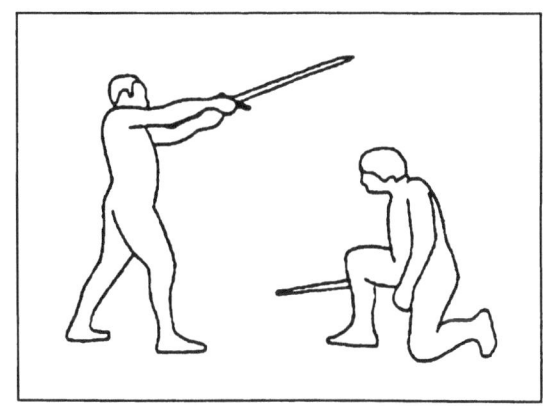

Fig. 114 Cade (left): double pass forward, overhead molinello, slash in pronation from high inside to high outside, above Iden's head. Iden: duck head slash, drop to left knee.

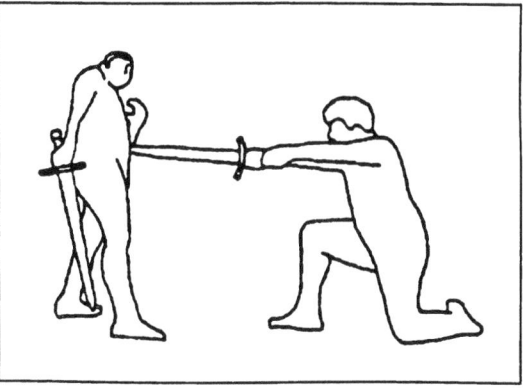

Fig. 115 Iden (right): from kneeling position, thrust in half-pronation, place flat of blade against Cade's left side at waist level. Cade: following contact, close left elbow onto Iden's blade (hide sword from audience).

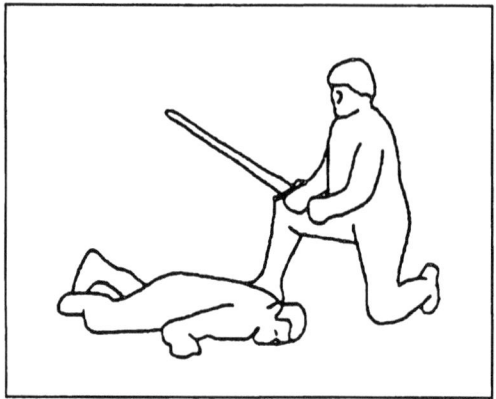

Fig. 116 Iden (right): withdraw sword. Cade: drop sword well out to right side, fall to ground.

Clifford vs. York

A recurrent symbol for the senseless tragedy of war in Shakespeare's plays is the death of fathers and sons. War disrupts the natural and orderly procession from birth, to the joys of youth to the gentle rewards of old age.

Lord Clifford is well past his prime. Although proud and brave, this elderly statesman does not belong on the tumultuous field of battle. He is no match for the virile Duke of York.

Young Clifford laments the death of his father in Act V, Scene ii, lines 45–49,

Wast thou ordain'd dear father,
To lose thy youth in peace, and to achieve
The silver livery of advised age,
And in thy reverence, and thy chair-days, thus
To die in ruffian battle?

In their opening dialogue, prior to the tragic duel, we see that York is not eager to cross swords with his aged adversary. The cold vicissitudes of war and politics force him to perform his onerous duty.

CLIF.
What seest thou in me, York? Why dost thou pause?

YORK.
With thy brave bearing should I be in love, but that thou art so fast mine enemy.

CLIF.
Nor should thy prowess want praise and esteem,
But that 'tis shown ignobly and in treason.

YORK.
So let it help me now against thy sword,
As I in justice and true right express it.

CLIF.
My soul and body on the action both!

YORK.
A dreadful lay! Address thee instantly.

[They fight, and Clifford falls.]

Clifford and York are clothed in battle armor. They wear open-faced helmets and are protected by breast and backplates, cuisse, espauliere, jamb, and gauntlets. They each carry shields and single hand broadswords.

Albeit reluctantly, York begins his deadly task by advancing toward old Clifford and raining a host of powerful cuts at Clifford's head and chest. Clifford reels from the powerful blows, but manages with both his shield and sword to valiantly parry them all.

York finishes his initial attack with a thrust at Clifford's vulnerable groin. Clifford beats the groin thrust aside with his sword. York sweeps his shield across Clifford's face. Clifford avoids York's shield by stepping backward.

Old Clifford heroically strides forward and thrusts at York's chest, as though to pierce his opponent right through his armor.

York easily deflects the thrust with his shield.

So as not to allow his opponent an advantage, Clifford follows his thrust with a cut to York's head.

With his upraised shield, York protects his head. Swiftly striking below Clifford's breastplate with his sword, York slashes Clifford's stomach, opening a deep wound. A pitiful moan escapes the old warrior's lips. Dropping his sword and shield, Clifford slumps in agony to the ground.

CLIF.
La fin couronne les [oeuvres].

[Dies.]

York gently kneels and places the fallen sword across the old man's body.

YORK.
Thus war hath given thee peace, for thou art still.
Peace with his soul, heaven, if it be thy will.

[Exit.]

Clifford vs. York Choreography

Fig. 117 York (right): advance forward with the right foot leading, cut at center head. Clifford: right foot forward stance, retreat, sword parry five.

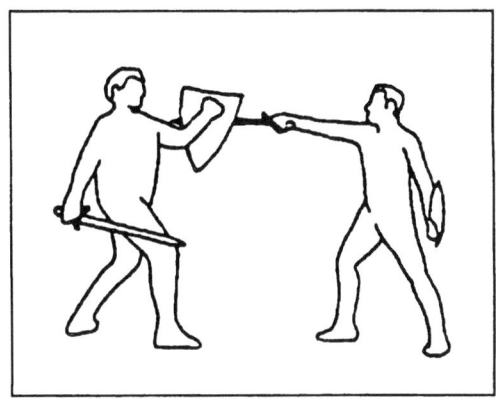

Fig. 118 York (right): advance, cut in supination to left chest above Clifford's lowered shield. Clifford: retreat with shield parry two.

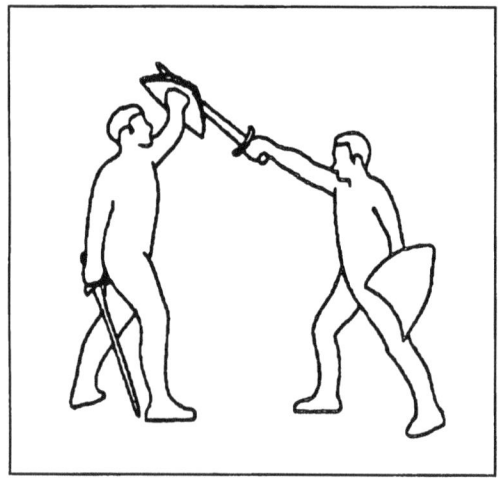

Fig. 119 York (right): advance, cut center head. Clifford: retreat, shield parry five.

Fig. 120 York (right): advance, cut to right chest. Clifford: retreat, sword parry three.

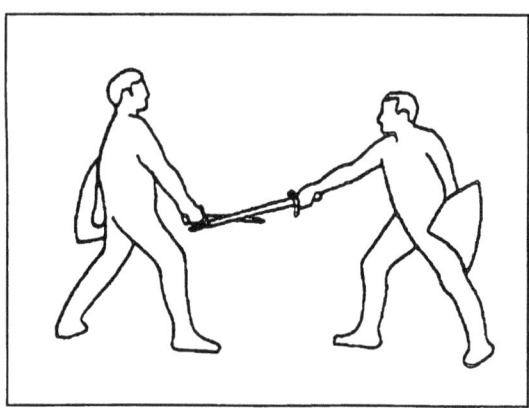

Fig. 121 York (right): advance, thrust in half-pronation to center groin (observe fighting distance!). Clifford: retreat, sword parry low five.

HENRY VI, PART 2

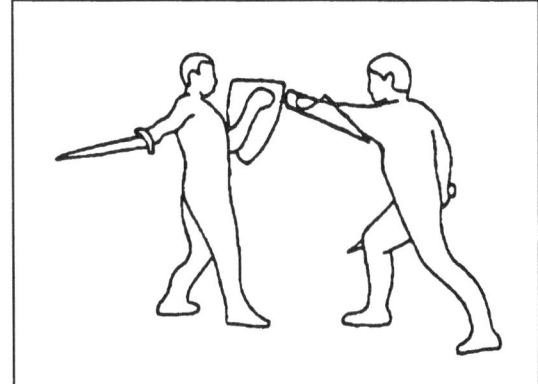

Fig. 122 Clifford (left): stationary, sweep shield from inside to outside lines at level of York's face (fighting distance!). York: retreat avoidance.

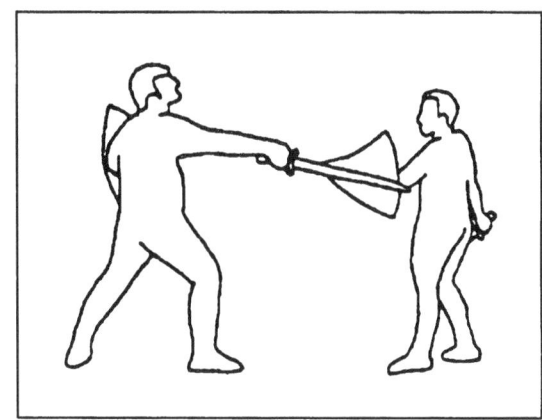

Fig. 123 Clifford (left): pass forward onto left right foot, thrust in half-pronation to left chest. York: pass back onto right foot, shield parry three.

Fig. 124 Clifford (left): advance, right foot leading, molinello on right side, cut center head. York: pass back onto left foot, shield parry five.

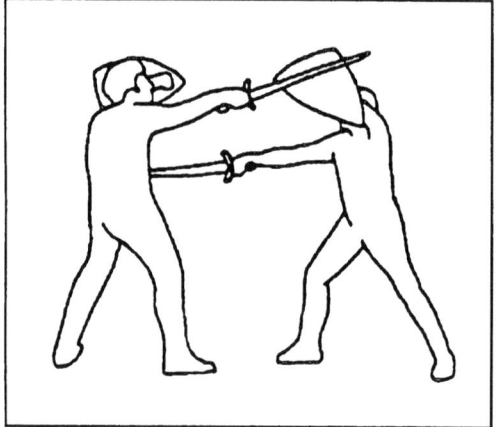

Fig. 125 York (right): stationary, maintain blade contact with shield parry five, cut in supination from the outside. With flat of blade contact Clifford's stomach below breastplate, pull sword away and break body contact, follow through to low inside. Clifford: stationary on blade contact. After York's follow through, drop shield and sword to outside left and right and fall to floor.

Richard vs. Somerset

If for no other reason, we should celebrate the penning of *Henry VI, Part 2*, because in it Shakespeare first begins to shape that deformed, Machiavellian villain, Richard Gloucester (later Richard the Third).

Shakespeare's remarkably vibrant characterization of Richard is further developed in *Henry VI, Part 3* and in *Richard III*. (For a discussion of Richard's physical deformity and how it may alter the way in which he fights, see the introduction to his duel with Clifford in *Henry VI, Part 3* and with Richmond in *Richard III*.) Our initial view of Richard's sinister inner life is revealed in Act III, Scene ii, lines 191–195.

I can add colors to the chamelion
Change shapes with Proteus for advantages,
And set the murtherous Machevil to school.
Can I do this, and cannot get a crown?
Tut, were it farther off, I'll pluck it down.

Enter Richard and Somerset to fight. [Somerset is killed under the sign of the Castle Inn.]

RICH.
So lie thou there;
For underneath an alehouse' paltry sign,
The Castle in Saint Albons, Somerset
Hath made the wizard famous in his death.
Sword, hold thy temper; heart, be wrathful still:
Priests pray for enemies, but princes kill.
[Exit.]

Richard carries a bastard sword (no pun intended), while Somerset fights with a singlehand broadsword and shield.

Eager to begin the fray, Richard and Somerset simultaneously rush at each other. Richard is the first to try a devious ploy by feinting with a thrust in-between Somerset's sword and shield. Somerset leaps to the bait and responds to the feint by attempting to knock Richard's thrust aside with the edge of his shield.

With impeccable timing, Richard drops his sword beneath Somerset's shield and pressing forward, thrusts at Somerset's exposed knee. Caught off guard, Somerset scrambles backwards and barely sweeps the thrust aside with his sword.

Taking advantage of his sword's momentum, Somerset strides forward, whipping his sword in a huge arc, and aims a crushing blow at Richard's head. Richard gives ground and easily parries the head blow.

Unwilling to give his wily opponent any time to riposte, Somerset steps forward and once again cuts at Richard's head. Richard is forced to retreat and, with less confidence, parries this second head blow. Then to deflect and break Somerset's advantage, Richard throws Somerset's blade off to the side and shifts his ground. Somerset and Richard cautiously eye each other as they circle about looking for an opening in each other's guard.

Displaying characteristic tactics, Richard cuts upwards with the razor-sharp edge of his sword at Somerset's crotch. Somerset stands his ground and blocks the cut.

Not to be deterred, Somerset pushes forward and cuts at Richard's flank. Richard, no one's fool, once again gives ground to his opponent and parries the flank cut. Powerfully sliding his blade forward—steel rasping on steel—Richard thrusts below Somerset's shield. Somerset throws himself backwards and deflects Richard's thrust with his shield.

In an attempt to repel his aggressive adversary, Somerset slashes across Richard's stomach and plunges forward to return a thrust at Richard's heart. Richard lightly avoids the stomach slash and parries the thrust.

Richard, with a greater command of strategy than his haphazard opponent, suddenly steps forward and grasps Somerset's sword wrist, and leaving no time for a response, he steps forward again and drives the sharpened point of his broadsword downwards, embedding it deeply into Somerset's back beneath his cuirass. With a most pitiable moan Somerset is transfixed. Richard twists the blade, grinding it past bone and sinew, while gleefully watching the anguished face of his enemy. Arching in unendurable pain, Somerset resembles a frantic specimen hoisted upon a steel pin. As Richard viciously yanks his bloody sword from pliable flesh, Somerset slumps soundlessly, lifelessly, to the ground.

In stark contrast to the tender manner in which Young Clifford lifted and carried his dead father off stage, Richard contemptuously leaves Somerset's ravaged body in the dirt to rot "underneath an alehouse' paltry sign."

Richard vs. Somerset Choreography

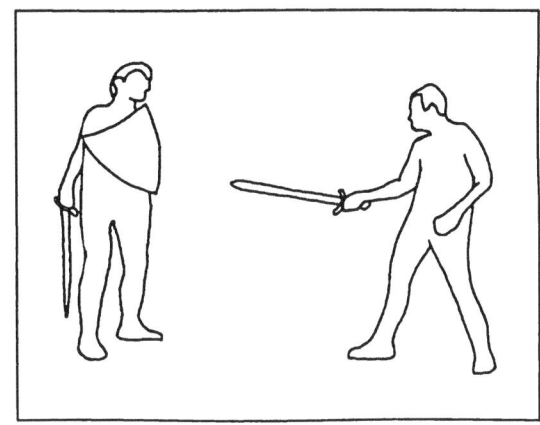

Fig. 126 Richard (right): move forward to fighting distance, right foot forward, *feint* thrust to center chest. Somerset: stationary, shield parry four (note—no weapon contact).

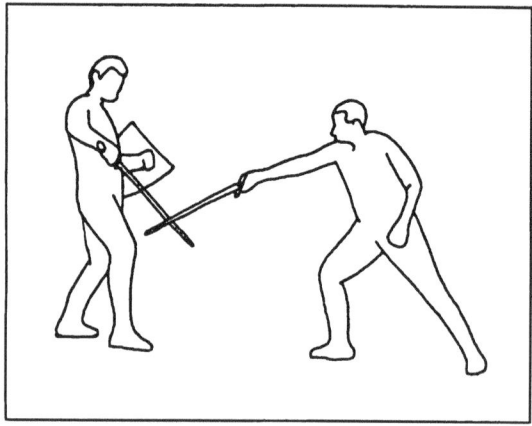

Fig. 127 Richard (right): advance, cut right knee. Somerset: retreat, sword beat parry two.

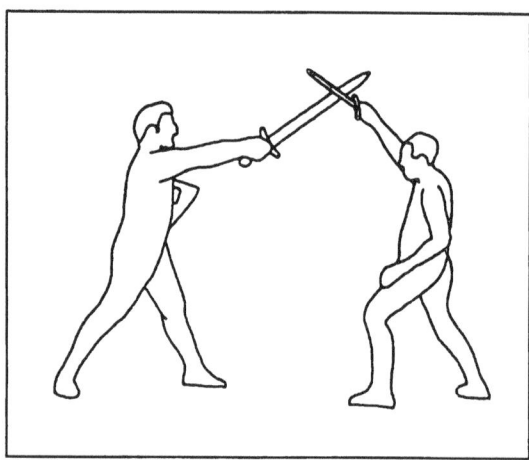

Fig. 128 Somerset (left): pass forward onto left foot, cut head. Richard: pass back onto right foot, parry five.

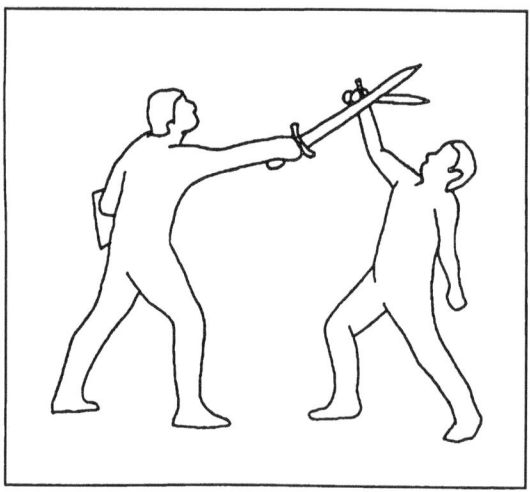

Fig. 129 Somerset (left): pass forward onto right foot, right side molinello, cut head. Richard: pass back onto left foot, parry five.

HENRY VI, PART 2

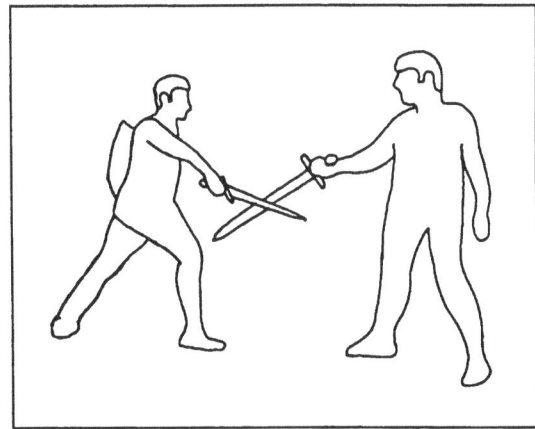

Fig. 130 Richard (right): stationary, bind Somerset's sword to his low right side.

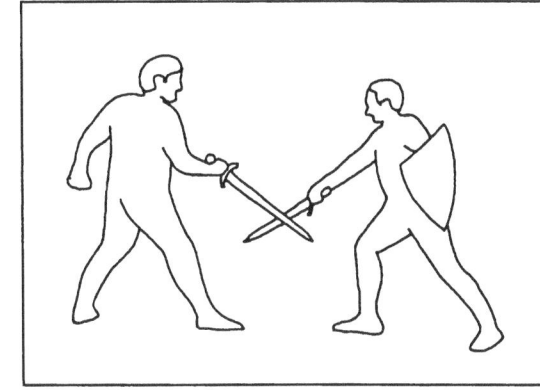

Fig. 131 Somerset and Richard circle each other counter-clockwise 90 degrees. Richard (left): close into fighting distance, right foot forward, cut crotch. Somerset: stationary, parry low five.

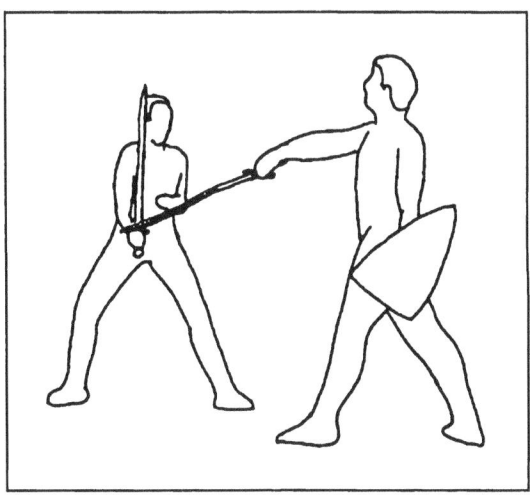

Fig. 132 Somerset (right): pass forward onto left foot, cut right hip. Richard: pass back onto right foot, parry three.

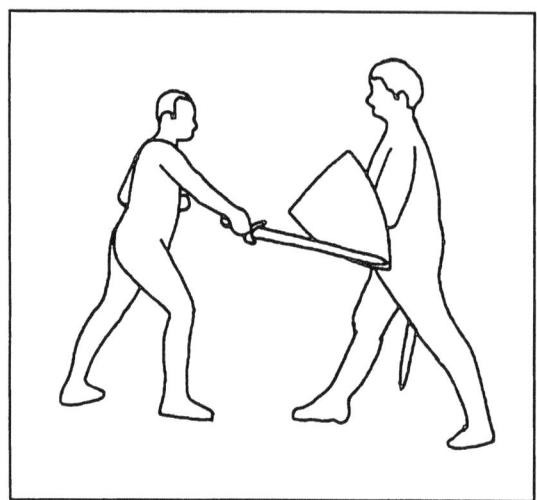

Fig. 133 Richard (left): pass forward onto right foot, glissade and thrust left hip below shield. Somerset: pass back onto left foot, shield parry low three.

Fig. 134 Somerset (right): stationary, sword slash in supination from outside to inside at Richard's stomach level (note—fighting distance!). Richard: leap backward avoidance.

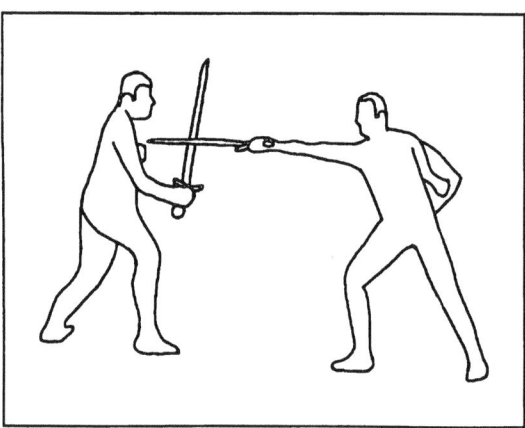

Fig. 135 Somerset (right): close fighting distance, right foot forward, thrust center chest. Richard: stationary, parry three.

HENRY VI, PART 2   91

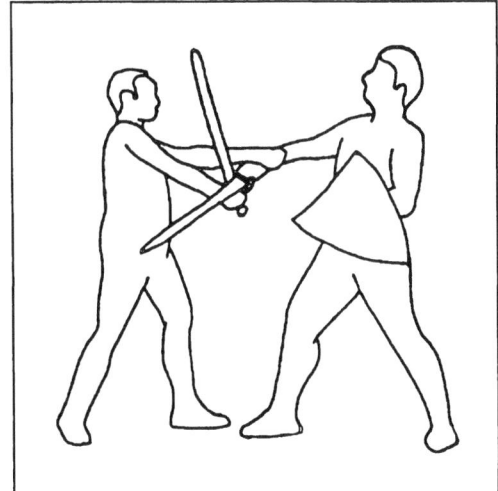

Fig. 136 Richard (left): maintain sword contact, pass forward onto left foot, grasp right wrist with left hand. Somerset: stationary.

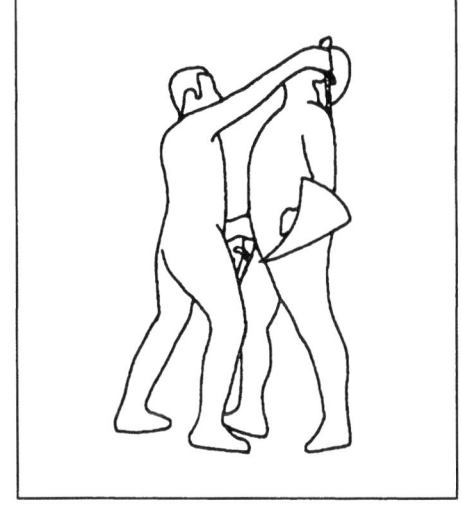

Fig. 137 Richard (left): pull Somerset's sword to his right side, pass forward onto right foot, thrust downward to Somerset's left upper back, place flat of blade against Somerset's left upper back. Somerset: react to wound in back on contact. Richard: mime twisting sword. Somerset: react to sword twist.

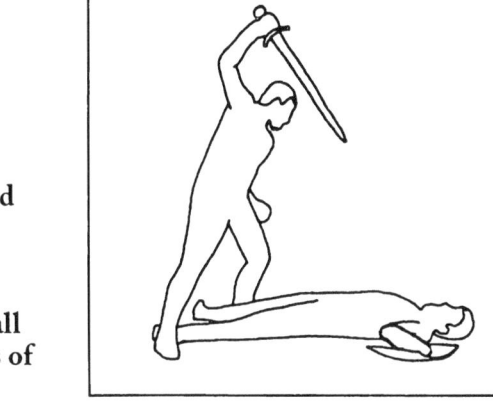

Fig. 138 Richard (left): lift sword away from body contact, follow through by yanking up and away from Somerset. Somerset: after Richard's follow through, backfall to floor (note—control positions of sword and shield on backfall).

HENRY VI, PART 3

...here's the heart that triumphs in their death,

Richard vs. Clifford

The complex personality of one of dramatic literature's most repugnant characters is gradually taking grotesque shape throughout this play. With fascination and horror, it becomes aware that a gleefully malignant villain is beginning to develop within the dark subconscious of our great poet. Richard, son of the Duke of York, is transforming, through bloodshed, into the Duke of Gloucester. His transformation will be complete when next encountered as the treacherous Richard the Third!

Yet one cannot entirely blame Richard for his twisted ambitions and insane compulsions for murder and revenge; after all, the world which his poor misshapen body inhabits is one of war, cruelty and sinister intrigue. Power is prized above all other qualities and woe to the helpless victim who falls into the hands of his opponent. Richard has no mercy in a merciless age.

Henry VI, Part 3 is a play rife with battles, vitriolic arguments, and excessive murders. The play presents a foul picture of England torn apart by the War of the Roses. Victims are psychologically and physically tortured before they are executed. The hatred runs so deep between these adversaries vying for England's throne, that there is a scene in which Clifford's *dead* body is propped up so that Richard and his faction can insult Clifford's spirit before they cut his head off and hoist it on a pole.

Make no mistake, although Clifford and the House of Lancaster are the losers in the fray, there is little sympathy for their fate. Clifford has been as bloodthirsty as Richard in this play. Clifford has brutally murdered Richard's father and his younger brother, Rutland.

There is a passion for killing that is shared by these two manic opponents. The smell of blood is in the air and these wolves are at each other's throat.

Excursions. Enter Richard [at one door] and Clifford [at the other].

RICH.
Now, Clifford, I have singled thee alone:
Suppose this arm is for the Duke of York,
And this for Rutland, both bound to revenge,
Wert thou environ'd with a brazen wall.

CLIF.
Now, Richard, I am with thee here alone:
This is the hand that stabb'd thy father York,
And this the hand that slew thy brother Rutland,
And here's the heart that triumphs in their death,

And cheers these hands that slew thy sire and
    Brother
To execute the like upon thyself-
And so have at thee!

[Alarums.] They Fight. Warwick comes;
    Clifford flies.

RICH.
Nay, Warwick, single out some other chase,
For I myself will hunt this wolf to death Exeunt.

    Richard and Clifford are in full battle armor with open-faced helmets. Clifford's only weapon is a hand-and-a-half broadsword, which he uses for both offense and defense. Richard carries a single-handed broadsword and a shield. Both have been embroiled in the carnage of war and their armor is bloody, scratched and dented.
    There is little doubt that both adversaries are skillful warriors and have had the best tutors in the arts of warfare that England could provide. Richard's physical deformities do not hamper his ability to fight, but the type and quality of his handicaps will affect the way in which he fights.
    In Act III, Scene ii, lines 153–162, Richard is quite explicit about his deformities.

Why, love forswore me in my mother's
    womb;
And for I should not deal in her soft laws,
She did corrupt frail nature with some bribe,
To shrink mine arm up like a wither'd shrub,
To make an envious mountain on my back,
Where sits deformity to mock my body;
To shape my legs of an unequal size,
To disproportion me in every part,
Like to a chaos, or an unlick'd bear-whelp
That carries no impression like the dam.

    A right-handed actor would choose to have his left arm appear "wither'd." It would not be difficult to attach a shield to the deformed arm if the actor is careful not to excessively exaggerate the deformity. The legs of "unequal" sizes pose a problem in balance and mobility. Very often actors have chosen to have the costumer create a boot with an enlarged sole, which creates the illusion of a shorter leg quite nicely, without unduly sacrificing mobility. The "mountain," or hump, on Richard's back need not be an issue at all, unless the actor insists on hunching over to enhance the effect. A good costumer can create the illusion of the hump quite easily without the actor's flexibility in the spine being hampered. The important thing to remember is that the dramatic action requires Richard to be athletic in his movements throughout the play.
    Clifford eagerly begins the contest by running toward Richard, swinging his sword in a circle above his head and cutting at Richard's exposed right flank. Richard takes a step backwards to soften some of the force of Clifford's attack, and parries the flank cut with his sword.
    Clifford cannot contain his violent passions and driving onward, he cuts at Richard's opposite shoulder. Richard passes back and parries the shoulder cut with his shield.
    Clifford is not giving Richard any opportunity to return an attack. Clifford immediately thrusts at Richard's leg below his shield. Richard stands his ground and parries the vicious thrust with his sword.
    Taking advantage of Richard's lowered defenses, Clifford sweeps his blade high and cuts at Richard's head. Richard parries the head cut with a powerful counter parry with his sword. Directly out of the head parry, Richard lifts Clifford's sword high above his head with his own sword, and striding forward, he smashes Clifford full in the chest with his shield. Clifford staggers backwards from the savage force of the blow.
    Rushing in upon the imbalanced Clifford, Richard strikes at his head,

thrusts at his chest and delivers a crushing diagonal cut at Clifford's shoulder. Clifford manages to thwart Richard's ferocious attacks.

After repelling the final diagonal shoulder cut, Clifford binds Richards sword down and to the side and slashes horizontally at Richard's head. Richard ducks and the opponent's circle each other warily.

This time it is Richard's impatience for revenge that spurs his running attack at Clifford's leg. Clifford opposes Richard's cut with his sword and once again binds Richard's blade, sweeping Richard's sword above his head and to the side. Then leaping forward, Clifford delivers a punishing blow to Richard's face. Richard reacts backwards.

At this moment, Warwick enters. Seeing he is outnumbered, Clifford hastily exits. Warwick begins to pursue Clifford, but Richard cuts Warwick off and threatens him with his sword.

RICH.
Nay, Warwick, single out some other chase,
For I myself will hunt this wolf to death.

Richard is enraged and he exits to seek his hated foe.

Clifford and Richard are not afforded a second opportunity to appease their blood-lust upon each other. Clifford, however, does not survive the battle.

Richard vs. Clifford Choreography

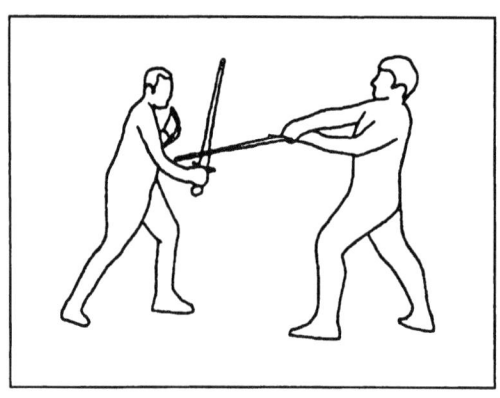

Fig. 139 Clifford (right): run into distance, pass onto left foot, overhead molinello, cut right hip. Richard: pass back onto right foot, sword parry three.

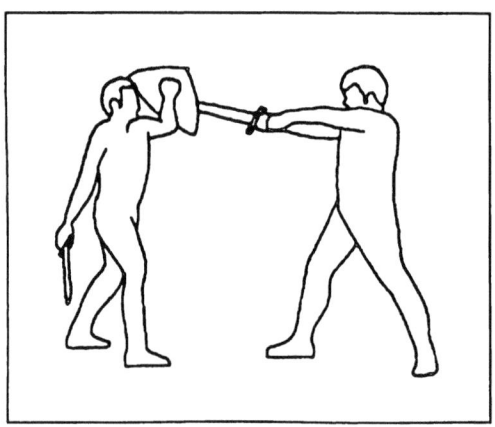

Fig. 140 Clifford (right): pass forward onto right foot, cut left shoulder. Richard: pass back onto left foot, shield parry high three.

HENRY VI, PART 3

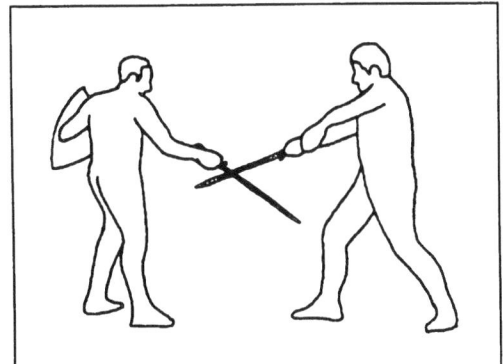

Fig. 141 Clifford (right): stationary, thrust left knee. Richard: stationary, sword parry seven.

Fig. 142 Clifford (right): stationary, cut head. Richard: stationary, sword parry five.

Fig. 143 Richard (left): maintain blade contact, pass forward onto left foot, shield strike to center chest (note—control force of contact). Clifford: react backward two steps.

Fig. 144 Richard (left): close distance, right foot forward, right side molinello, cut head. Clifford: stationary, parry five.

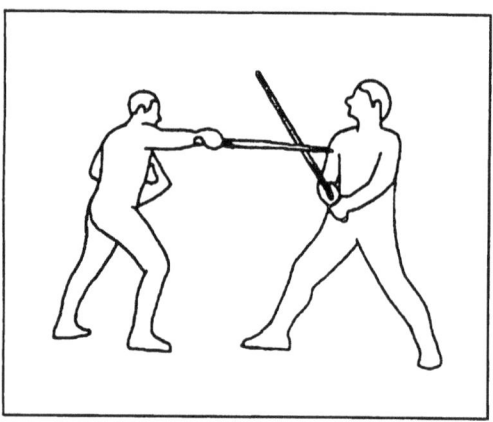

Fig. 145 Richard (left): double pass forward onto left and right foot, thrust at left chest. Clifford: double pass back onto right and left foot, parry four.

Fig. 146 Richard (left): pass forward onto left foot, cut right shoulder. Clifford: pass back onto right foot, parry high three.

HENRY VI, PART 3

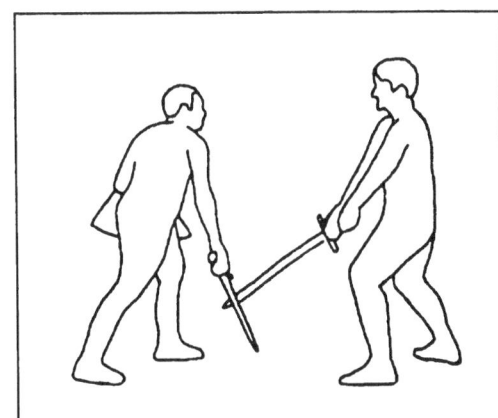

Fig. 147 Clifford (right): stationary, bind sword down to Richard's low outside. Richard: stationary.

Fig. 148 Clifford (right): stationary, slash high outside to high inside above Richard's head. Richard: duck head slash (note—lower blade with body to avoid contact with Somerset's blade).

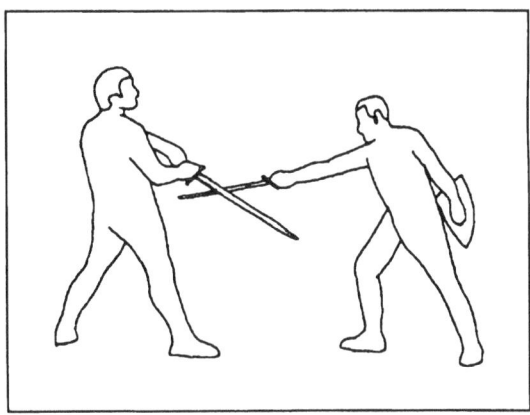

Fig. 149 Richard and Clifford circle each other counter-clockwise 180 degrees. Richard (right): double pass forward onto left and right foot, right side molinello, cut to left knee. Clifford: double pass back onto right and left foot, counter cut parry seven.

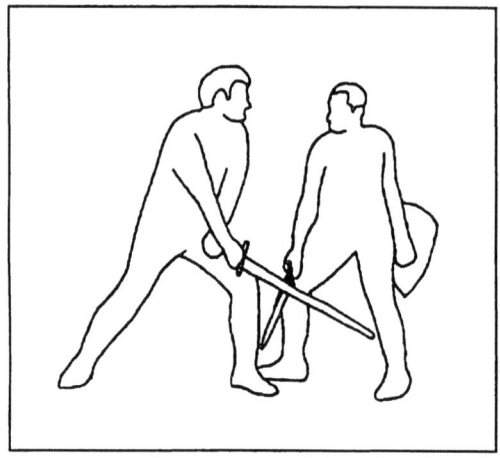

Fig. 150 Clifford (left): pass forward onto left foot, bind sword above Richard's head to his low inside. Richard: stationary.

Fig. 151 Clifford (left): stationary, left backhand punch to outside of Richard's face. Richard: react to face strike by snapping head back and pass back two steps. Warwick enter, Clifford exit.

RICHARD III

Richard vs. Richmond

I have set my life upon a cast,
And I will stand the hazard of the die.

The essential creative decision to be made by the director, the actor portraying Richard and the fight choreographer, is the type and extent of Richard's deformity. (In *Henry VI, Part 3*, Act III, Scene ii, lines 153–162, Richard describes his deformities.) The chosen deformity will affect the fight choreographer's decisions concerning which weapon or weapons will be used and the technique incorporated to dramatize this famous duel.

There are indications in the script that Richard is indeed a formidable warrior despite his deformity. In Act V, Scene iv, Catesby rushes on stage amid loud "alarums" and "excursions" and bellows to Norfolk,

Rescue, my Lord of Norfolk, rescue, rescue!
The king enacts more wonders than a man
Daring an opposite to every danger.
His horse is slain, and all on foot he fights,
Seeking for Richmond in the throat of death.
Rescue, fair lord, of else the day is lost.

Richard himself elaborates on his exploits in this tumultuous battle scene, erasing any doubt of his power and expertise in the art of personal warfare, when he rejects Catesby's offer for rescue in Act V, Scene iv.

Slave, I have set my life upon a cast,
And I will stand the hazard of the die.
I think there will be six Richmonds in the field:
Five I have slain to-day instead of him.
A horse, a horse! my kingdom for a horse!

The assumption here will therefore be that Richard has full use of his legs and his sword arm (many actors have portrayed Richard with a limp and were still able to perform a thrilling stage fight with Richmond). Richard fights with a hand-and-a-half sword, which he uses for both offense and defense.

Richmond, a member of the aristocracy and trained in the use of arms as a matter of social custom, will enter with the traditional hand-and-a-half sword of the fifteenth century and a shield.

The infamous duel between Richard and Richmond takes place on the field of battle in Act V, Scene v. The stage directions are typically scant:

Alarum: Enter [King] Richard and Richmond; they fight; Richard is slain.

The inference, however, is clear that this duel is set off from the battle proper, which presumably continues to rage around the principal combatants somewhere off stage. Many fight choreographers will emphasize the surrounding battle by having soldiers fight across the stage occasionally to punctuate the central dual between Richard and Richmond. This requires adequate stage space, excellent timing and gifted performers, but may add drama to the central action.

Nevertheless, the duel between Richard and Richmond is generally conceived as a somewhat formal climax to the essential conflict between the forces of good and evil in the play. In the dialogue presented above, it is disclosed that Richard has been ferociously seeking Richmond throughout the battle. Richmond, it may be surmised, has likewise been searching for Richard.

When they meet face to face a pause in the action heightens the dramatic tension. Richmond, seeing that Richard is armed only with a sword, casts his own shield aside upstage in a chivalrous gesture.

Richard laughs scornfully at Richmond's magnanimity and immediately launches a ferocious attack, driving Richmond backwards. Richard cunningly trips Richmond, who loses his footing and falls to the ground.

Richard lifts his sword above his head with both hands to land a crushing blow on the prostrate Richmond, but Richmond avoids the blow by rolling to the side and Richard's powerful cut misses Richmond by inches. Richmond then quickly rises to his feet, and the opponents circle each other.

A few exploratory cuts and parries are delivered as the combatants test each other's strength, speed and resolve. Richmond then attempts to lure Richard into dropping his guard by performing a false thrust to Richard's legs and immediately slashing at Richard's head. Richard ducks the blow, and Richmond's sword flashes above Richard's head. Whereupon Richard closes the distance and strikes Richmond in the torso with his heavily padded shoulder, knocking him backward. Richard relentlessly renews his attack, taking advantage of Richmond's momentary imbalance. Richmond avoids harm by a deft and desperate parry with one hand upon his sword and an evasive technique.

Richmond then retorts with several powerful cuts as he advances upon Richard and with a binding action, Richmond successfully disarms Richard and immediately deals him a mortal wound. Richard staggers back, realizing that he has been fatally wounded.

With an appalling scream, Richard throws himself upon Richmond and clutches him about the throat, strangling him with both hands. Richmond strikes Richard repeatedly upon the back with the pommel of his sword, but because of Richard's desperate tenacity the pommel blows fail to break Richard's strangle hold. Richmond then draws back the tip of his sword and stabs Richard in the stomach. Richard then releases his hold upon Richmond's throat and staggers back, refusing to fall.

Richard stumbles forward slowly, attempting to again reach Richmond with his bare hands, but loses momentum and stops before he reaches him. Richmond lowers his sword and watches as Richard slowly drops to one knee, then to both knees. Richard removes the crown from his head and clutches it possessively and finally sinks to the floor dead. Richmond steps forward and drags the crown from Richard's lifeless fingers to complete the duel.

Richard vs. Richmond Choreography

Fig. 152 Richard (right): run into fighting distance, right side molinello, head cut. Richmond: counter cut parry five.

Fig. 153 Richard (right): pass forward onto left foot, thrust right chest. Richmond: pass back onto right foot, parry three.

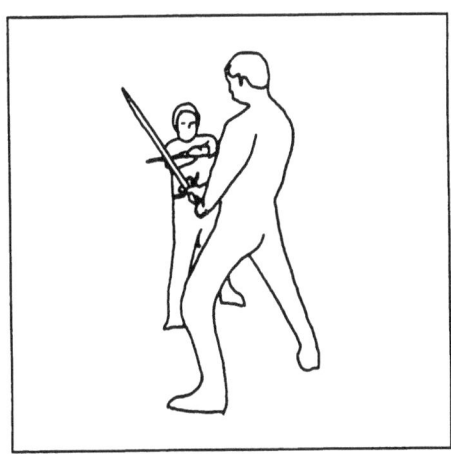

Fig. 154 Richard (left): pass forward onto right foot, cut left chest. Richmond: pass back onto left foot, parry four.

102 THE SWORDS OF SHAKESPEARE

Fig. 155 Richard (right): pass forward onto left foot, cut head. Richmond: pass back onto right foot, parry five.

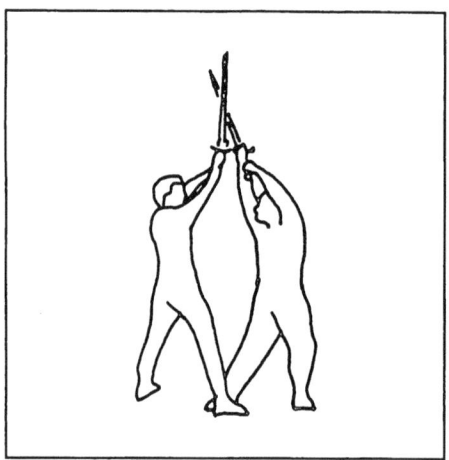
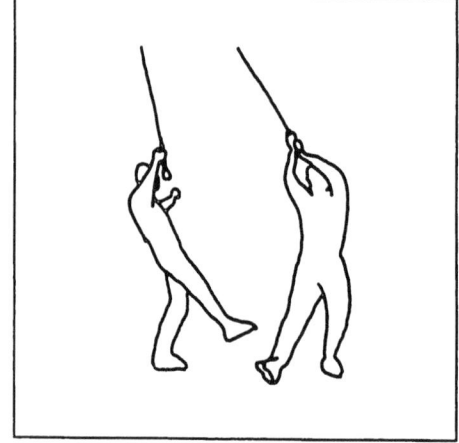

Figs. 156 & 157 Richmond (left): sweep right foot forward, hook Richmond's left foot, raise right foot for trip (note—take cue from Richmond for trip). Richmond (left): fall backward, retain sword in right hand.

Figs. 158 & 159 Richard (left): weight on forward right foot, diagonal slash to floor beyond Richmond's left side. Richmond (right): roll to right side avoidance.

RICHARD III

Fig. 160 Richmond (right): rise, circle 180 degrees counter-clockwise around Richard. Richard (left): pivot to face Richmond. Richmond: pass forward onto left foot, cut right knee. Richard: pass back onto right foot, one handed parry two.

Fig. 161 Richard and Richmond circle each other counter-clockwise 90 degrees. Richmond (right): pass forward onto left foot, cut head. Richard: pass back onto left and right foot, parry five.

Fig. 162 Richard (right): stationary, stomach slash left to right. Richmond: backward jump avoidance.

104 THE SWORDS OF SHAKESPEARE

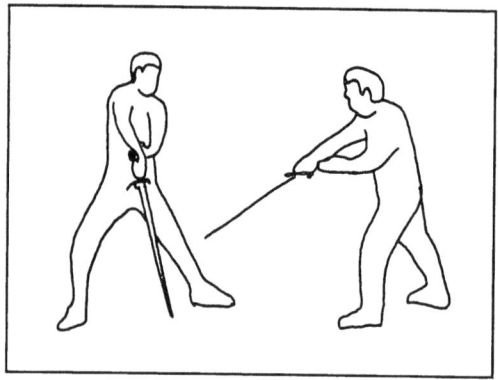

Fig. 163 Richmond (left): pass forward onto left foot, feint right knee thrust. Richard: pass back onto right foot, parry two.

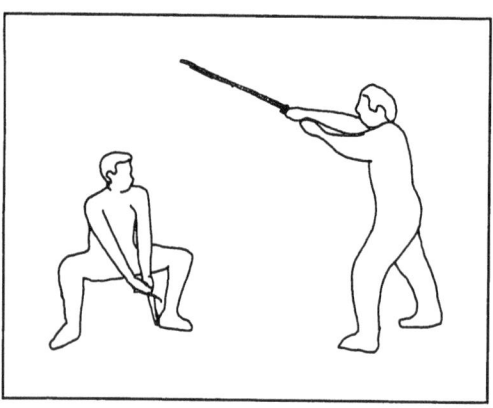

Fig. 164 Richmond (right): stationary, head slash right to left. Richard: duck avoidance.

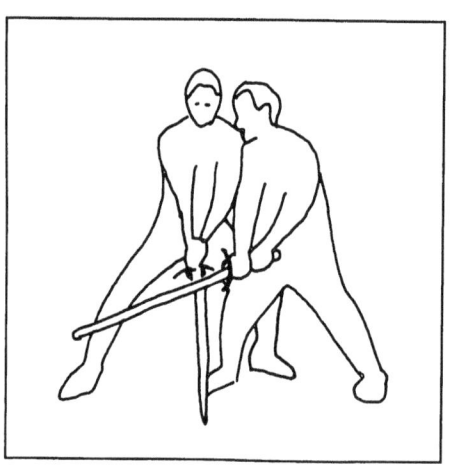

Fig. 165 Richard (right): pass forward onto right foot, strike Richmond on his left shoulder with right shoulder. Richmond: react backwards out of fighting distance.

RICHARD III

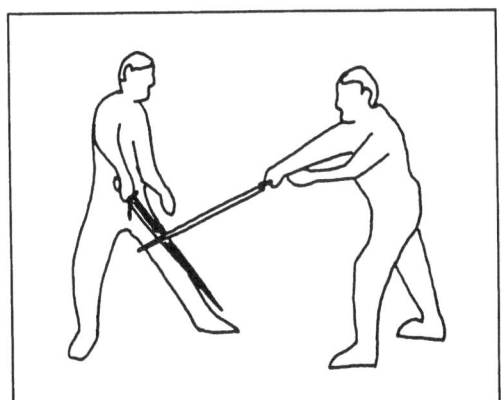

Fig. 166 Richard (right): close to fighting distance, cut right knee. Richmond: stationary, (right hand grip only) parry two.

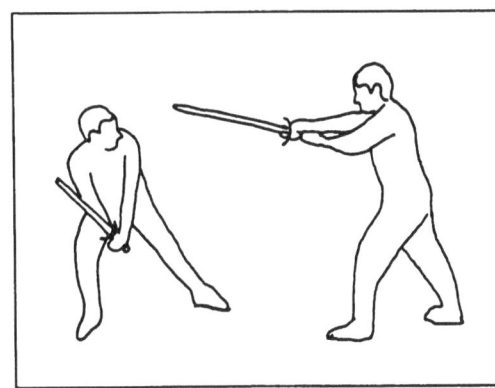

Fig. 167 Richard (right): stationary, slash above head from high outside to low inside. Richmond: step onto right foot to the right side, lean torso over right knee to avoid slash.

Fig. 168 Richmond (right): out of fighting distance, circle clockwise 90 degrees around Richmond. Richard: pivot to face Richmond. Richard: pass forward onto left and right foot, cut left chest. Richmond: stationary, parry four.

106　THE SWORDS OF SHAKESPEARE

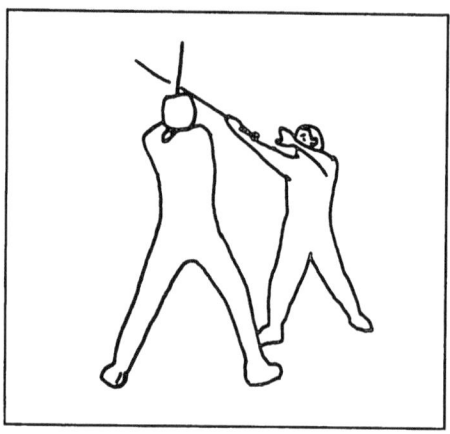

Fig. 169 Richmond (left): stationary, envelopment and bind to Richard's right side. Richmond: stationary, control disarm to safe stage position.

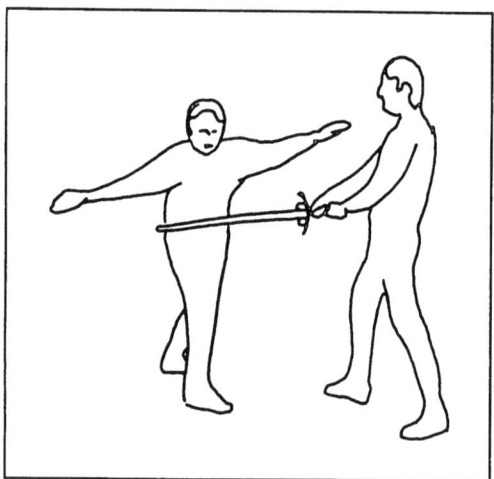

Fig. 170 Richmond (right): stationary, slash from right to left at level of stomach (note—fighting distance). Richard: react to stomach wound, stumble backwards two steps.

Fig. 171 Richard (left): close fighting distance, two hand choke from front, right foot forward.

RICHARD III

Fig. 172 Richmond (right): stationary, grasp right forearm with left hand, pummel blow (use right forearm for contact) to Richard's left upper trapezius or deltoid (note—pummel extends beyond shoulder). Richard: react to pummel blow, but maintain two hand choke hold.

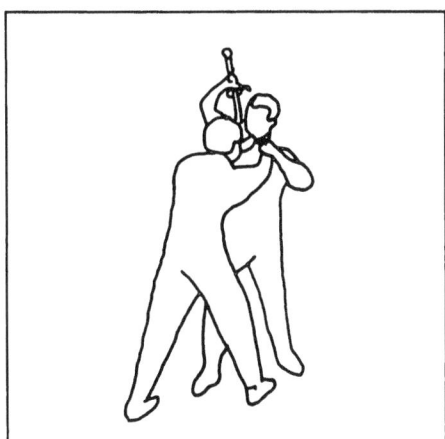

Figs. 173 & 174 Richmond (right): stationary, repeat pummel blow. Richard: react to second pummel blow, but maintain two hand choke hold.

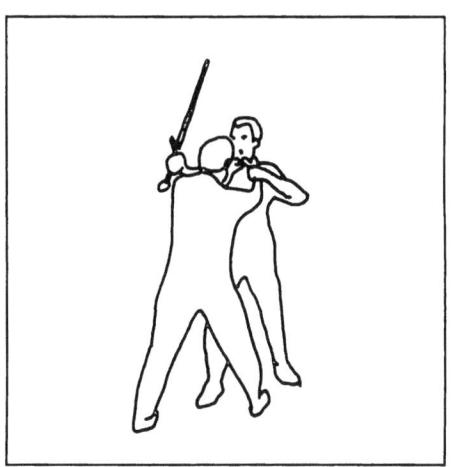

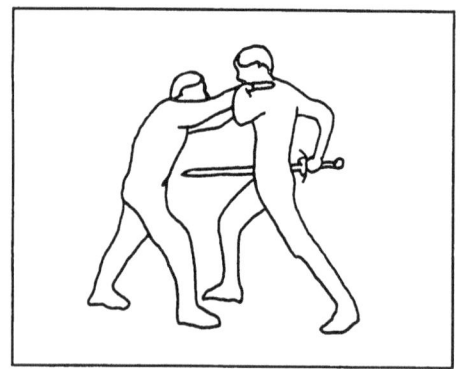

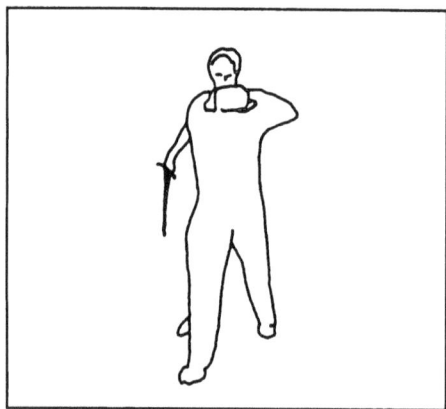

Figs. 175, 176 & 177 Richmond (right): stationary, maintain left hand grip on Richard's right wrist, draw sword back to low outside, thrust to left flank and place flat of blade onto flank (hide contact from audience). Richard: stationary, react to thrust on contact, release choke hold. Richmond (back): break contact and draw sword back to low outside. Richard: pass back three steps, pass forward two steps with hands reaching out toward Richmond's throat, drop to both knees, remove crown and clutch it possessively, fall forward to stage floor. Richmond (right): close distance, remove crown from Richard's lifeless fingers and raise it triumphantly over head.

ROMEO AND JULIET

The very butcher of a silk button,
a duellist, a duellist;

Is it exaggeration to say that *Romeo and Juliet* is the world's most famous play? It is certainly safe to state that *Romeo and Juliet* is the quintessential example of how Shakespeare weaves the art of swordplay into the very fabric of his dramatic action.

The fate of the principal characters is intimately linked with the outcome of several duels. In fact, Shakespeare begins this passionate play with a tumultuous mass battle scene between the household servants of the feuding Capulet and Montague families. This battle graphically displays the ludicrous and dangerous feud which will be resolved so tragically in the death of the lovers.

Beyond the marvelous opportunities for staging thrilling dueling scenes, *Romeo and Juliet* is a particular favorite of stage fight choreographers for what Shakespeare reveals about sixteenth century swordplay. This is because Shakespeare appears to express the attitudes of the sixteenth century English Masters of Defence who were attempting to preserve their monopoly as purveyors of the combat arts in London and provincial England.

The English Masters of Defence were under siege from an onslaught of Spanish and Italian Masters of Arms who had set up fashionable schools in Elizabethan England. The Elizabethan courtiers were enamored with the new "fashionable" styles of swordplay and were equally charmed by the elegant and often frivolous rules of etiquette surrounding the duel promoted by these new Masters of Arms from the continent. As a result, the rage for dueling and swordfighting on the streets of the capital began to rise. The English Masters of Defence taught a more common-sense approach to swordplay and were bitterly opposed to the new fashions and the new weaponry introduced by these foreign interlopers. They were also opposed to the impact upon their pocketbooks as students abandoned their schools for foreign instruction!

Shakespeare uses Mercutio as the vehicle to condemn the new fashion in manners and the new-fangled art of swordplay which were being accepted so readily by the fashion conscious Elizabethan nobility and sons of the merchant class. Tybalt, on the other hand, symbolizes the new fashion in manners and swordplay promoted by the Italian and Spanish Masters of Defence. Shakespeare ridicules Tybalt and what he represents in Act II, Scene iv, lines 19–35. Mercutio is describing Tybalt to Benvolio.

MER.
... O, he's the
courageous captain of compliments. He fights
as you sing prick-song, keeps time, distance, and
proportion; he rests his minim rests, one, two, and the
third in your bosom: the very butcher of a silk button,
a duellist, a duellist; a gentleman of the very first
house, of the first and second cause. Ah, the immortal
passado, the *punto reverso*, the *hay!*

BEN.
The what?

MER.
The pox of such antic, lisping, affecting
[phantasimes], these new tuners of accent! "By, Jesu,
a very good blade! a very tall man! a very good
whore!" Why, is this not a lamentable thing, grand-
sire, that we should be thus afflicted with these strange
flies, these fashion-mongers, these [pardon] me's, who
stand so much on the new form, that they cannot sit at
ease on the old bench? O, their bones, their bones !

Although Shakespeare is obviously contemptuous of the "fashion-mongers," as personified by the hot-headed dandy, Tybalt, it should not be inferred from this that he was therefore in complete agreement with the English Masters of Defence. This play expresses Shakespeare's disgust with the rampant urban violence of the late sixteenth century and with dueling in particular.

Today there is the dangerous misuse of firearms, which are all too readily available and daily cause terrible tragedies on city streets. In Shakespeare's time, the flagrant misuse of hand-held weapons and the indiscriminate penchant for dueling was a serious problem in London and in other cities throughout the continent.

In *Romeo and Juliet,* Shakespeare takes a verbal stab at the violent tendencies of his English contemporaries. In Act III, Scene i, lines 5–30, Mercutio accuses Benvolio of the current violent malaise (although it would actually appear that Mercutio is, in truth, describing himself).

MER.
Thou art like one of these fellows that, when
he enters the confines of a tavern, claps me his sword
upon the table, and says, "God send me no need of
thee!" and by the operation of the second cup draws
him on the drawer, when indeed there is no need.

BEN.
Am I like such a fellow?

MER.
Nay, and there were two such, we should
have none shortly, for one would kill the other. Thou?
why, thou wilt quarrel with a man that hath a hair
more or a hair less in his beard than thou hast. Thou
wilt quarrel with a man for cracking nuts, having no
other reason but because thou hast hazel eyes.
What eye but such an eye would spy out such a
quarrel? Thy head is as full of quarrels as an egg is
full of meat, and yet thy head hath been beaten as
addle as an egg for quarrelling. Thou hast quarrell'd
with a man for coughing in the street, because he
hath waken'd thy dog that hath lain asleep in the sun.
Didst thou not fall out with a tailor for wearing his new
doublet before Easter? with another for tying his new
shoes with old riband? and yet thou wilt tutor me from quarreling?

Benvolio vs. Tybalt

Shakespeare's obvious disenchantment with his countrymen's excessive use of violence for settling quarrels is a powerful undercurrent throughout this play. As it shall be seen, he is intent on clearly showing his audience that violence never solves an argument. Aggression only breeds itself and inevitably leads to tragedy.

He places the responsibility for this climate of senseless violence squarely upon the blades of the nobility. Shakespeare wastes no time in demonstrating his thesis by opening his play with a serio-comic scene of violence between the servants of the feuding families. This ludicrous exchange between the clumsy and cowardly servants escalates into something much more serious when Benvolio and Tybalt enter the fray. Very cleverly, the audience is led from the attitude that swordfighting is just a form of adolescent fun, into the realization that this kind of "fun" all too readily escalates into dangerous violence.

Assuming that Benvolio faithfully narrates the violent conflicts of which he is a part, there emerges a valuable indication of Shakespeare's intent when staging this mass battle. In Act 1, Scene i, lines 106–115, Benvolio describes the opening battle and the sequence in which the battle takes place.

BEN.
Here were the servants of your adversary,
And yours, close fighting ere I did approach.
I drew to part them. In the instant came
The fiery Tybalt, with his sword prepar'd,
Which, as he breath'd defiance to my ears,
He swung about his head and cut the winds,
Who, nothing hurt withal, hiss'd him in scorn.
While we were interchanging thrusts and blows,
Came more and more, and fought on part and part,
Till the Prince came, who parted either part.

It can be inferred from Benvolio's description that he doesn't enter onstage until the fighting between the servants is already in full swing. He draws his sword to part the combatants, but it appears that Tybalt enters before Benvolio is able to stop the fighting. Therefore, the servants continue to fight during the verbal exchange between Tybalt and Benvolio.

Benvolio also supports the impression that the "Fiery Tybalt" is acting quite wildly by indiscriminately slashing his sword through the air "about his head." This would definitely be frightening to Benvolio, as Tybalt has a reputation for being "fiery" and an accomplished swordsman. There is no indication in the script that Benvolio is a skilled swordsman. (Mercutio's dubious description of Benvolio being a hot-headed duelist notwithstanding.) Therefore, we have a mismatched pair in relation to the levels of skill in swordsmanship possessed by these characters. The dominance of Tybalt over Benvolio during their fight would help to foreshadow the danger of the subsequent duels between Tybalt/Mercutio and Tybalt/Romeo.

The fight between Benvolio and Tybalt should also include both "thrusts and blows." The Italian or Spanish system of swordfighting with the rapier, as practiced by Tybalt, stressed the use of the thrust over the cut. In contrast to Tybalt, Benvolio could be a proponent of the sixteenth century English system which focused on the supremacy of the cut over the thrust.

While the principal characters are fighting it would appear that more combatants enter the stage to swell the number of fighters. Benvolio clearly states that others "Came more and more, and fought on part and part." These other combatants who swell the scene and fight "part on part," are probably members of the feuding households. However, there are citizens who are not attached to either the Capulet or Montague families as the dialogue of some of the entering combatants is derogatory toward both factions.

These late entering citizens fight with "clubs or partizans" (partizan being a wooden pole with a metal blade attached to one end and was the weapon of choice of sixteenth century guards), breaking in between the fighting servants and creating new combinations of combatants. To heighten the drama, however, Benvolio and Tybalt continue to fight each other throughout the fray until they are stopped by the Prince. In fact, in order to dramatize the feud between the Montagues and Capulets, it should be Tybalt and Benvolio who are the last of the combatants to be subdued by the Prince's rancor.

Because the stage is filled with other combatants and many other characters not directly involved in the mass battle, such as the elder Capulets and Montagues, the fight between Tybalt and Benvolio would be best confined to a small downstage area. Confining Tybalt and Benvolio to a limited space may not be the most dramatically effective way to stage this fight, but it will be the *safest* method. The general melee, therefore, forms a backdrop for the principal characters.

Shakespeare is quite explicit in indicating that the servants fight with sword and buckler. Samsons, "remember thy washing blow" is a colloquial phrase referring to a common practice of smashing your sword against your own shield to create a noise that would disconcert your opponent. (The term "swashbuckler" is surmised to be an ancient term to describe the proponents of the sword and buckler.) By the end of the sixteenth century, the sword and buckler were considered the weapons of the lower classes. The aristocracy had completely accepted the rapier as the weapon of fashion. Fighting with the sword and buckler was considered less refined. Fighting with these weapons is a noisy affair and the technique would lend itself more easily to comic maneuvers. The juxtaposition of the clownish servants with the more deadly Tybalt/Benvolio duel is a masterly stroke and serves to dramatize the irony inherent in the feud between the Capulets and Montagues.

Enter Benvolio

GRE.
Say "better," here comes one of my master' kinsmen.

SAM.
Yes, better, sir.

ABR.
You lie.

SAM.
Draw, if you be men. Gregory, remember thy washing blow.

BEN.
Part, fools!
Put up your swords, you know not what you do.
[*Beats down their swords.*]

Enter Tybalt

TYB.
What, art thou drawn among these heartless hinds?
Turn thee, Benvolio, look upon thy death.

BEN.
I do but keep the peace. Put up thy sword,
Or manage it to part these men with me.

TYB.
What, drawn and talk of peace? I hate the word
As I hate hell, all Montagues, and thee.
Have at thee, coward! [*They fight*].

Enter three or four citizens with clubs or partisans.

[Citizens.] Clubs, bills, and partisans! Strike! Beat them down!
Down with the Capulets! Down with the Montagues!

Enter old Capulet in his gown, and his wife [Lady Capulet].

CAP.
What noise is this? Give me my long sword ho!

LA. CAP.
A crutch, a crutch! why call you for a sword?

CAP.
My sword, I say! Old Montague is come,
And flourishes his blade in spite of me.

Enter old Montague and his wife [Lady Montague].

MON.
Thou villain Capulet!—Hold me not, let me go.

LA. MON.
Thou shalt not stir one foot to seek a foe.

Enter Prince Escalus with his Train.

PRINCE.
Rebellious subjects, enemies to peace,
Profaners of this neighbor-stained steel—
That quench the fire of your pernicious rage
With purple fountains issuing from your veins—
On pain of torture, from those bloody hands
Throw your mistempered weapons to the ground,
And hear the sentence of your moved prince.

Benvolio fights with an English broadsword and dagger of the late sixteenth century. These weapons were light enough to counter the rapid movements of the rapier and poinard, which are brandished by Tybalt.

Tybalt slices the air with his rapier in wide circular molinellos as he delivers his tirade to Benvolio. Immediately out of the sweeping downward arc of his final molinello, Tybalt leaps forward and attempts to scar Benvolio's face with a diagonal slash.

Benvolio leaps to the side and avoids the slash and quickly attempts to move around to Tybalt's more vulnerable poniard hand. Tybalt pivots quickly, steps forward and thrusts at Benvolio's leading knee with his rapier. Benvolio passes back and parries the knee thrust with his sword. Benvolio then beats Tybalt's rapier aside with his dagger and cuts at Tybalt's chest with his sword. Tybalt jumps backwards and allows Benvolio's sword to whistle harmlessly by.

Immediately taking advantage of Benvolio's vulnerability, Tybalt lunges forward and thrusts with his rapier at Benvolio's stomach. Benvolio stands his ground and just manages to parry Tybalt's powerful thrust by crossing his sword and dagger together in a classic cross parry.

With his rapier pinned by Benvolio's blades, Tybalt steps forward and thrusts at Benvolio's exposed shoulder with his poniard. Not releasing the cross parry which controls Tybalt's rapier, Benvolio leans violently to the side and avoids Tybalt's poniard thrust. With lightning reflexive speed, Tybalt drives the pummel of his poniard upward into Benvolio's jaw, driving Benvolio backwards in pain.

Benvolio, down on one knee and bleeding at the mouth, awaits Tybalt's next deadly gambit. Tybalt merely pauses to laugh contemptuously at his pitiful adversary. (These pauses are deliberately built into the fight so that the actors can better coordinate the timing of their fight with the rest of the action taking place on stage. Although all of the fighters on stage are choreographed carefully to a particular tempo, it is inevitable that minor variations will occur. The difficulty here is in timing the entire melee so that it corresponds with the dialogue that punctuates the action. In addition, the principal fight between Benvolio and

Tybalt must outlast the mass battle. Thus the choreographed pauses in Benvolio and Tybalt's duel are inserted to act as a window for the actors to ascertain whether they need to slow down or slightly speed up their subsequent actions.)

Just as Benvolio rises from his knee, Tybalt leaps forward with a slash at Benvolio's head. Benvolio ducks beneath Tybalt's rapier and slips past and behind Tybalt. Tybalt turns to face his elusive foe.

With a series of powerful thrusts at Benvolio's legs and chest with his rapier, Tybalt begins to drive the hapless Benvolio backwards. Benvolio is becoming desperate and fearful for his life. He is appearing awkward and only barely succeeding in warding off Tybalt's repeated attacks. Benvolio must do something quickly to halt the relentless Tybalt.

After parrying with his sword Tybalt's last thrust at his leg, Benvolio sweeps Tybalt's rapier up into the air with a binding action and immediately cuts low to Tybalt's exposed knee. Tybalt yanks his leg back out of harm's way. Benvolio then presses his advantage with a cut high to Tybalt's head, which Tybalt cross parries with his Rapier and poniard. Benvolio passes forward immediately and swings his sword in a reverse arc and up to Tybalt's groin. Tybalt passes back and lowers his cross parry to protect himself.

Passing in again, Benvolio cuts downward toward Tybalt's shoulder in an attempt to wound him with his dagger. Tybalt stops the dagger cut by sliding the hilt of his rapier upwards in a high parry.

Now both Tybalt's and Benvolio's blades are locked together in their parry positions. At that instant, Tybalt slams his chest forward against Benvolio's chest and pushes Benvolio backwards a few steps. Grunting with effort, Benvolio manages to stop Tybalt's forward pressure. There is a hiatus in the action as both men strain against each other in a corps a corps.

At this point the Prince has entered and is admonishing everyone to stop fighting. The Prince's guards have begun to quell the battle with their halberds. They are working their way downstage toward Tybalt and Benvolio. Then, as fate would have it, Benvolio trips and falls prostrate to the ground, as his rapier and dagger leave his grasp and skid out of reach.

Mercifully, (and because we need him throughout the rest of the play) the Prince's guards take this moment to intercede. They prevent the fiery Tybalt from exacting his punishment upon the prone Benvolio.

Benvolio vs. Tybalt Choreography

Fig. 178 Tybalt (left): advance, right foot forward, overhead molinello, rapier slash high outside to low inside above Benvolio's head. Benvolio: step to the left and lean torso over left knee to avoid diagonal slash.

Fig. 179 Benvolio (left): circles clockwise 90 degree around Tybalt as he pivots to face Benvolio. Tybalt: double pass forward onto left and right foot, rapier thrust to right knee. Benvolio: pass back onto right foot, sword parry two.

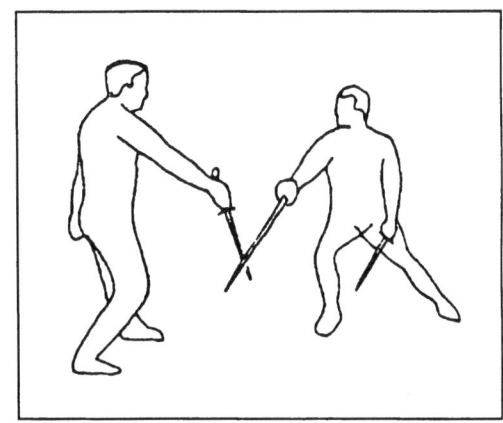

Fig. 180 Benvolio (left): stationary, dagger beat parry low seven.

Fig. 181 Benvolio (left): stationary, sword slash from right to left at chest level. Tybalt: leap back avoidance (note—lift weapons clear of slash on leap).

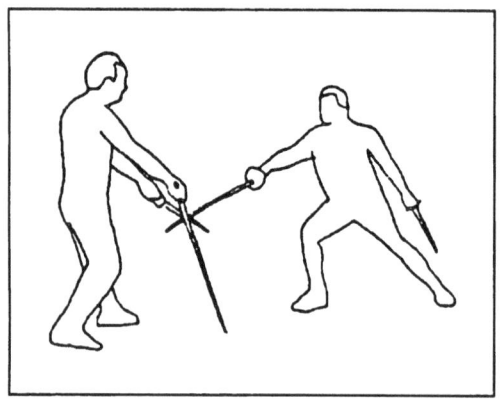

Fig. 182 Tybalt (right): lunge forward, right foot leading, rapier thrust to center stomach. Benvolio: stationary, cross parry low five.

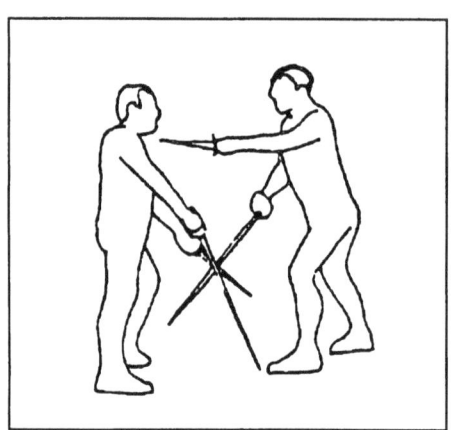

Fig. 183 Tybalt (right): pass forward onto left foot, poniard thrust to right shoulder. Benvolio: maintain cross parry blade contact, avoidance to left side by leaning torso over left leg.

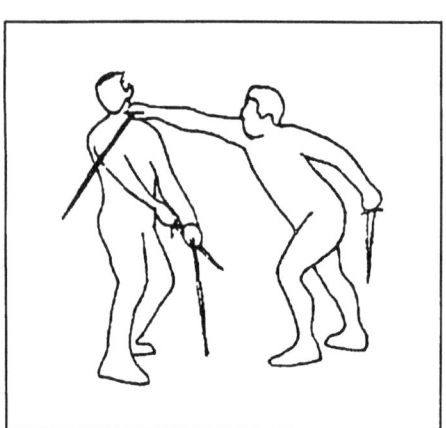

Fig. 184 Tybalt (right): stationary, rapier pummel blow to above left shoulder at level of Benvolio's face (create illusion of pummel blow to face). Benvolio: react to pummel blow, pass back two steps, fall to left knee.

Fig. 185 Benvolio (left): rise, right foot forward. Tybalt: pass forward onto right foot, rapier slash in pronation from high inside to high outside above Benvolio's head. Benvolio: stationary, duck head slash.

Fig. 186 Benvolio (right): circles 180 degrees counter-clockwise around Tybalt as he pivots to face Benvolio. Tybalt: lunge forward onto right foot, rapier thrust right knee. Benvolio: pass back onto right foot, sword parry two.

Fig. 187 Tybalt (left): pass forward onto left foot, rapier thrust left chest. Benvolio: retreat, dagger parry three.

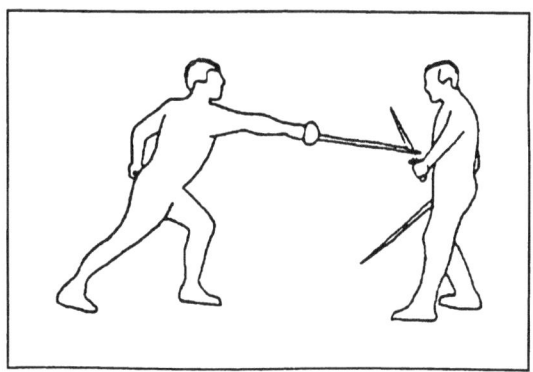

118   THE SWORDS OF SHAKESPEARE

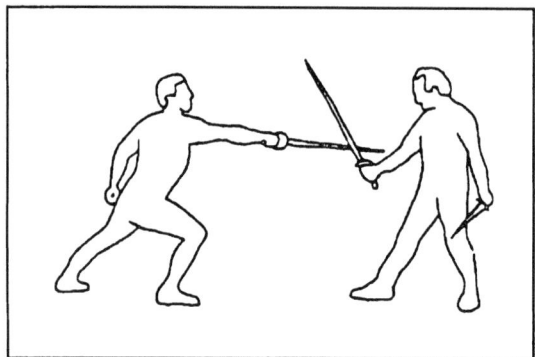

Fig. 188 Tybalt (left): pass forward onto right foot, rapier thrust right chest. Benvolio: pass back onto left foot, sword parry three.

Fig. 189 Tybalt (left): pass and lunge onto left foot, rapier thrust right knee. Benvolio: large retreat, sword parry two.

Fig. 190 Benvolio (right): stationary, with sword, bind Tybalt's rapier up to his high left side.

Fig. 191 Benvolio (right): stationary, sword slash in supination from high outside to low inside across Tybalt's left knee (note—fighting distance). Tybalt: pass back onto left foot avoidance.

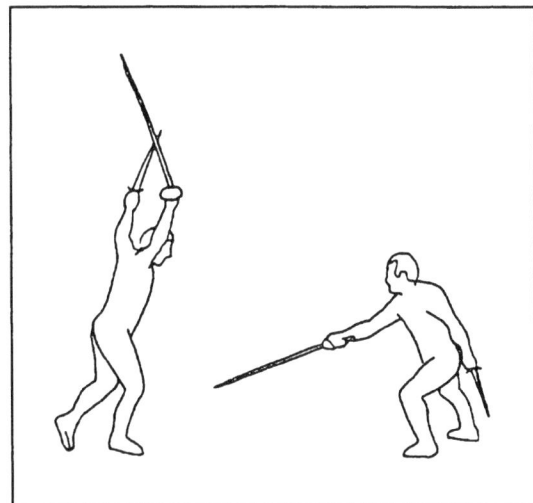

Fig. 192 Benvolio (right): pass forward onto right and left foot, left side molinello, sword cut to head. Tybalt: stationary, cross parry five.

Fig. 193 Benvolio (right): pass forward onto right foot, left side molinello, sword cut to crotch. Tybalt: pass back onto right foot, cross parry low five.

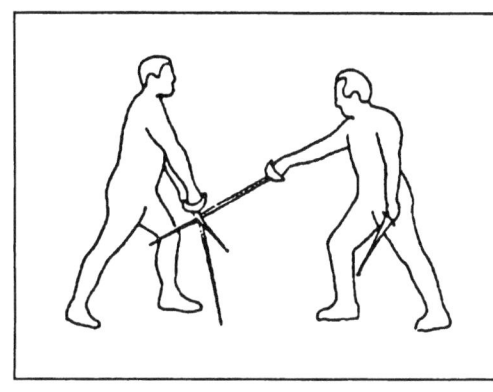

120 THE SWORDS OF SHAKESPEARE

Fig. 194 Benvolio (right): maintain sword contact with rapier and dagger, pass forward onto left foot, dagger thrust to right shoulder. Tybalt: stationary, maintain poniard contact with sword, rapier parry one.

Fig. 195 Benvolio and Tybalt locked in corps a corps. Tybalt (left): double pass forward. Benvolio: double pass back, (create illusion of being forced backwards by Tybalt) trip, backward fall.

Tybalt is blocked from approaching the fallen Benvolio by palace guards.

The duel between Benvolio and Tybalt is fortuitously interrupted. Shakespeare will see to it that good fortune will not visit either the Capulets or Montagues again.

Mercutio vs. Tybalt

Mercutio and Tybalt are the young champions of the noble houses of Montague and Capulet. They are the symbols of arrogant pride that afflicts their masters. Each is supremely confident of his swordfighting abilities and they are eager to test their prowess at any provocation—real or imagined. In Shakespeare's deft control of his plot, their violent encounter is inevitable and inevitably leads to the death of innocence.

This celebrated duel is especially fascinating because it reveals the historic conflict between several methods of swordplay in vogue in Elizabethan England. By 1595, the likely date for the penning of Romeo and Juliet, a heated dispute existed between the English Masters of Defence and the Italian Masters of Arms who had gained popularity among the nobility.

Shakespeare may have had in mind something he overheard one of his contemporary English Masters of Defence say against a sixteenth century Italian Master of Defence, Signor Rocco, when he wrote Mercutio's contemptuous description of Tybalt in Act II, Scene iv, lines 18–26.

[BEN.]
Why, what is Tybalt?

TYB.
O, he's the
courageous captain of compliments. He fights as you sing prick-song, keeps time, distance, and
proportion; he rests his minim rests, one, two, and the
third in your bosom: the very butcher of a silk button,
a duellist, a duellist; a gentleman of the very first
house, of the first and second cause. Ah, the immortal passado, the punto reverso, the hay!

Shakespeare introduces more sixteenth century swordfighting terminology in this play than in any other. He was very conscious of the differing styles of swordplay in vogue and how the young hotheads of his era exploited those differences.

In staging this particular duel, the differences in style between the traditional English methods of swordplay are accentuated from the Spanish or Italian methods. Borrowing from historic manuals of defense, of which Shakespeare was believed to be familiar, very specific techniques for both Mercutio and Tybalt have been chosen.

To illustrate how far a stage fight may be influenced by historic research, the following duel is described using a number of technical terms from several sixteenth and early seventeenth century manuals of defense. Occasionally, the authors' names are referred to (please see Bibliography). As usual, a pictorial representation of this duel follows this conceptual framework and narration.

In recreating this duel, the basic storyline has been taken from the narration of our faithful Benvolio, as he relates his version of the events to the Prince in Act III, Scene i, lines 158–169. However, some dramatic liberties have been taken and an attempt to slavishly follow Benvolio's description has not been made.

BEN.
...Tybalt deaf to peace, but that he tilts
With piercing steel at bold Mercutio's breast,
Who, all as hot, turns deadly point to point,
And, with a martial scorn, with one hand beats
Cold death aside, and with the other sends
it back to Tybalt, whose dexterity
Retorts it. Romeo he cries aloud,
"Hold, friends! friends part!" and swifter than his tongue,
His [agile] arm beats down their fatal points,
And 'twixt them rushes; underneath wose arm
An envious thrust from Tybalt hit the life
Of stout Mercutio, and then Tybalt fled;
But by and by comes back to Romeo,
Who had but newly entertain'd revenge,
And to't they go like lightning, for, ere
I Could draw to part them, was stout Tybalt slain;

Mercutio fights with sixteenth century English broadsword and dagger. Tybalt fights with sixteenth century Italian rapier and poniard.

MER.
Come, Sir, your "Passado."

Mercutio invites an attack from Tybalt by apparently opening himself up with Swetnam's "lasie or careless guard." Both of his weapons are held "overthwart" his body to the left, exposing his centerline and outside lines. Tybalt, confident of his skill, begins Saviolo's low ward (left foot leading in an open stance, both knees bent "as though about to sit in a chair," with the rapier hilt pulled back to the outside of the lower right thigh, point threatening the opponent, and the poniard held fully extended at arms length, just beyond the tip of the rapier point, with the poniard's tip also pointed at the opponent).

Tybalt performs a passado (passing forward on his right foot), launching a stoccata thrust upwards at Mercutio's belly. With a laugh, Mercutio performs a jumping slip to the left and with both his weapons parries Tybalt's thrust, driving Tybalt's sword beyond Mercutio's right hip, then traversing forward and to the left with his left foot, Mercutio delivers a wrist cut to Tybalt's head and immediately passes back with his left foot. This is an historic offensive attack performed while on the retreat.

Tybalt parries the head cut with his rapier and immediately slashes at Mercutio's stomach with his poniard, but Mercutio has already removed himself from the close measure. Tybalt then begins to circle Mercutio, looking for a vulnerable target.

Tybalt is shifting his wards as he circles, testing Mercutio's reactions in time. Mercutio is enjoying the display Tybalt is making of "time, distance and proportion." Mercutio is mocking Tybalt as he circles.

ROM.
Draw, Benvolio, beat down their weapons.

Benvolio draws his sword and is matched by a threatening Petrucio (Tybalt's manservant and second in this impromptu duel). They warily eye each other, but do not fight.

Gentlemen, for shame forbear this outrage! Tybalt,...

Mercutio jumps in toward Tybalt, leading with his left foot, passes forward with his right foot, and using Silver's forehand guard, "puts by" Tybalt's extended rapier with his dagger.

Tybalt immediately races backwards to maintain his distance and not be forced into close fighting, but Mercutio pursues him and delivers a head cut and a reverse cut with the true edge to Tybalt's right chest.

Tybalt passes back and parries the head cut dubble (with both weapons crossed). Tybalt then performs an incartata, sweeping his right foot behind his left and parries the right chest cut with a dubble (parry with rapier and poniard).

Mercutio continues to advance and slams into Tybalt's left shoulder with his own right shoulder, driving Tybalt backwards and off-balance. However, before Mercutio can take advantage of Tybalt's imbalance, Romeo rushes forward and grabs Mercutio from behind, pulling Mercutio backwards away from Tybalt.

ROM.
.......Mercutio, the Prince expressly hath Forbid this bandying in Verona streets.

Romeo leaps in front of Mercutio and is now in between Mercutio and Tybalt. Tybalt recovers. It appears that Tybalt is contemplating taking advantage of Romeo's vulnerability with a dastardly thrust. Mercutio sees this, and elbows Romeo savagely out of the way just in the nick of time.

Tybalt launches a low stoccata at Mercutio's leading knee. Mercutio "removes" the knee by stepping backwards with that foot and parries the thrust by driving Tybalt's rapier downward with both sword and dagger.

Tybalt slashes at Mercutio's face with his poniard. (In stage fighting the actor slashes below the face as the defender supports the illusion of a face slash by accentuating an avoidance of the supposed face slash.) Mercutio desperately avoids the slash by throwing himself into a pass backward, his face leading the motion and with both of his weapons held well back out of the way.

ROM.
...Hold, Tybalt!

Tybalt, quickly stealing ground (à la Saviolo's forerunner to the Balaestra), launches an imbrocata to Mercutio's center chest. (This thrust is actually aimed at the actor's right shoulder and should only be attempted *if* the combatant playing Tybalt is an excellent stage fighter.)
Mercutio slips to the left and parries the center chest thrust with his parallel sword and dagger.
Tybalt traverses to his own left side with his leading right foot and delivers a punta riversa to Mercutio's right hip.
Mercutio, passes back on his right side, parries Tybalt's right chest thrust with his sword in tierce, and passing back again, in order to "indirect his poynt" (à la G. Silver), binds Tybalt's rapier from Mercutio's outside line to low inside line.
In the instant following Mercutio's bind of Tybalt's sword, and as Mercutio's sword is overthwart his body to the left, Romeo rushes in and grasps Mercutio's right sword arm at the wrist.

ROM.
...Good Mercutio!

Romeo lifts Tybalt's sword arm up into the air above their heads and in an attempt to wrest Mercutio's sword from his grip, Romeo steps back, still retaining a grip upon Mercutio's right wrist above their heads, exposes Mercutio's right chest to Tybalt.

[Tybalt under Romeo's arm thrusts Mercutio in.]

Tybalt, without malice aforethought, sees a vulnerable target and his instincts as a duelist prevail—he delivers a stramazone upwards (à la the montante of A. Marozzo, 1536, 1550, 1568) into Mercutio's abdomen, puncturing his intestines. (The stramazone is preferred over the obvious stoccata, because it is safer for the combatants, given the problem of a tight and possibly confused target in between Romeo and Mercutio. It is possible to create the illusion of a thrust using the technique of a stramazone.)
For a moment there is absolute stillness, a tableau—Mercutio and Tybalt are staring at each other, both realizing what has happened. Romeo is focused on Mercutio, not comprehending the moment. Tybalt's sword is suspended in Mercutio's body. The moment is soon over and Tybalt withdraws his sword.
Mercutio moans and collapses into Romeo's arms, watching Tybalt depart over Romeo's back. He futilely and feebly slashes at Tybalt's retreating form with his sword.

Away Tybalt [with his followers]

MER.
I am hurt.
A plague a'both houses! I am sped.
Is he gone and hath nothing?

Mercutio vs. Tybalt Choreography

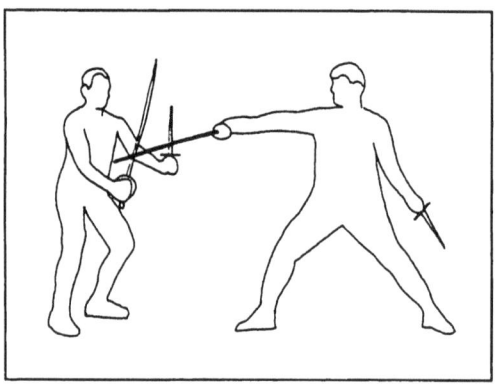

Fig. 196 Tybalt (right): pass forward onto right foot, rapier thrust upward from low outside to right hip. Mercutio: jump to left side, land with right foot forward, sword and dagger parallel parry three.

Fig. 197 Mercutio (left): pass forward to left side onto left foot, sword cut to head (note—head cut is quick and controlled from wrist), pass back onto left foot. Tybalt: stationary, rapier parry five.

Fig. 198 Tybalt (right): stationary, poniard slash in supination from inside to outside at level of Mercutio's stomach (note—Mercutio is already out of fighting distance).

Fig. 199 Mercutio (right) and Tybalt circle each other counter-clockwise 180 degrees. Mercutio: jump into distance, left foot forward, pass forward onto right foot, beat Tybalt's rapier to his right side with dagger. Tybalt: stationary.

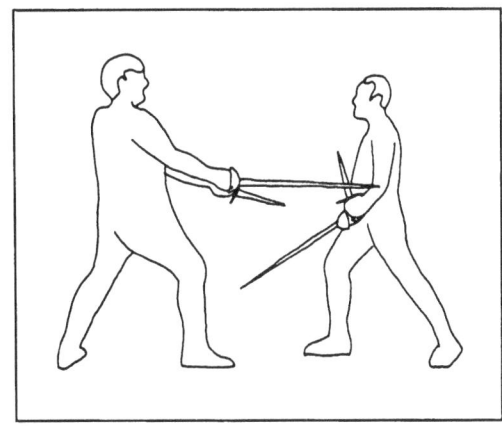

Fig. 200 Mercutio (right): pass forward onto left foot, sword cut to head. Tybalt: pass back onto right foot, cross parry five with rapier and poniard.

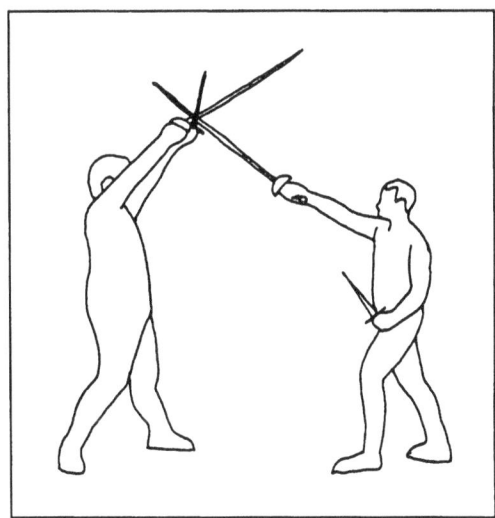

Fig. 201 Mercutio (left): pass forward onto right foot, sword cut in pronation to right hip. Tybalt: pivot right foot behind left foot (demi-volte), cross parry two with rapier and poniard.

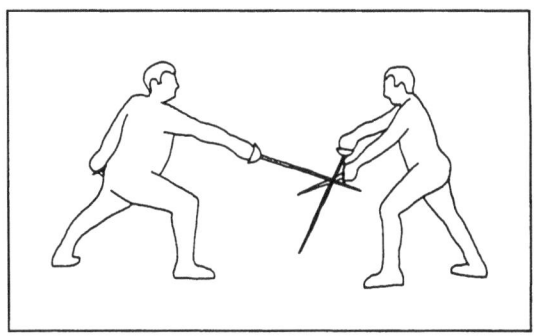

Fig. 202 Mercutio (left): pass forward onto left foot, strike Tybalt's left shoulder with right shoulder. Tybalt: react backwards four steps. Romeo: close distance, right foot forward, hug Mercutio from behind and entrap his upper arms. Mercutio: stationary, left elbow blow to Romeo's left chest.

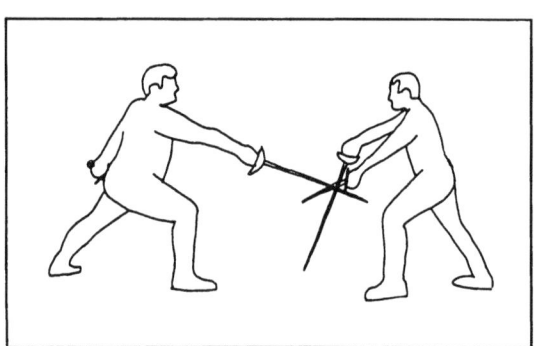

Fig. 203 Tybalt (left): close distance, lunge onto right foot, rapier thrust to right knee. Mercutio: pass back onto right foot, cross parry two.

Fig. 204 Tybalt (left): stationary in lunge position, poniard slash in supination from left to right below Mercutio's face (note—fighting distance!). Mercutio: pass back onto left foot avoidance.

Fig. 205 Tybalt (left): double pass forward onto left and right foot, rapier thrust in supination at right shoulder. Mercutio: advance to the left side, right foot leading, sword and dagger parallel parry three.

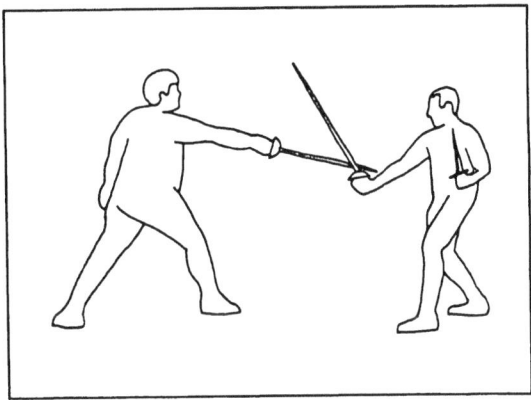

Fig. 206 Tybalt (left): advance clockwise right foot leading, rapier thrust in supination to right hip. Mercutio: pass back onto right foot, sword parry three.

Fig. 207 Mercutio (right): pass back onto left foot and simultaneously sword bind Tybalt's rapier to low right side.

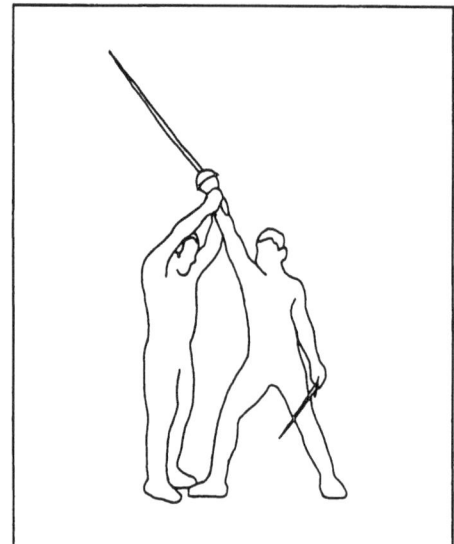

Fig. 208 Romeo (left): close distance left foot forward, grab Mercutio's right wrist with both hands (left hand pronated & right hand supinated on wrist), lift sword arm above Mercutio's head to expose his right flank.

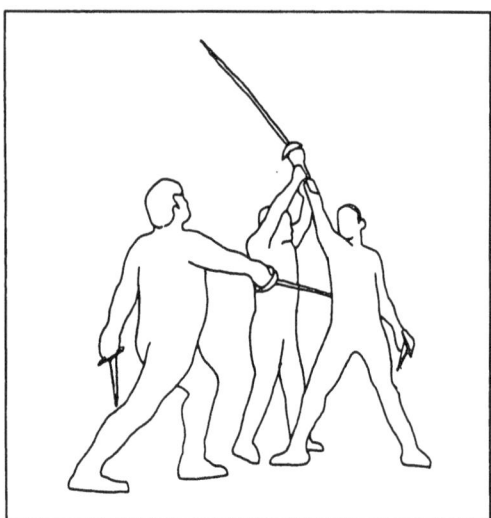

Fig. 209 Tybalt (left): lunge onto left foot, rapier thrust (thrust performed with cutting technique) to Mercutio's right flank (hide contact from audience). Romeo and Mercutio: stationary.

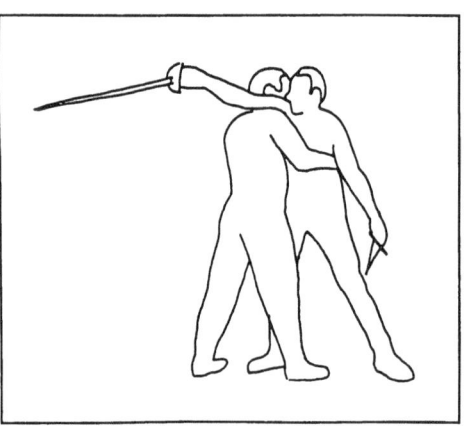

Fig. 210 Tybalt: break body contact and withdraw rapier to low outside. Mercutio (right): collapse over Romeo's right shoulder. As Tybalt exits, feebly sword slash at his retreating form.

Romeo vs. Tybalt

There is scarcely time to mourn the death of the noble Mercutio and for the audience to ruminate upon the consequences of this murder, before the action once again "gallops apace." With Tybalt's entrance, all hope of reconciliation between the houses of Montague and Capulet vanish utterly.

Romeo's intent is to avenge the death of his dear friend Mercutio. Romeo blames himself for Mercutio's death. Romeo believes that his love for Juliet weakened his natural inclinations for dueling and the dutiful defense of his honor. Romeo believes that he, not Mercutio, should have fought with Tybalt. To add insult to injury, Mercutio accused Romeo of interference in the swordfight, which directly resulted in Mercutio's mortal wound. Romeo is stricken with a combination of guilt and grief.

Earlier in the same scene, the stage directions read,

[Enter Tybalt, Petruchio, and others.]

However, prior to Tybalt's duel with Romeo, the stage directions read,

[Enter Tybalt]

Is it probable that Petruchio and the "others" did not return to the scene of the crime with Tybalt, because they justifiably feared the Prince's wrath? Everyone certainly knew that this type of duel was punishable by death. Tybalt's retainers would be prime scape-goat candidates for official retribution. In any case, one assumption is that Tybalt returned alone.

Tybalt has now returned. Why? To fulfill his curiosity about the ultimate fate of Mercutio. Is he dead? Should Tybalt flee the country to escape punishment? Is Tybalt relentlessly pursuing the offender of his wounded honor? Whatever the reason for Tybalt's return to the scene of his crime, as Shakespeare would have it, Tybalt and Romeo collide.

Tybalt, according to the laws of honor, must continue his quest for demanding satisfaction from Romeo or lose face. Both Tybalt and Romeo are experiencing mixed emotions that fuels the bravado prior to the fight.

It is Romeo, however, who lacks emotional control. He is in a rage of regret and frustration. He is operating on pure instincts. We are about to witness in Romeo a tragic flaw common to youth—the subservence of reason to emotion. This same youthful weakness can lead to innocent, spontaneous love, or to an untimely death. Once again, blind fate tips the scales.

ROM.
This gentleman, the Prince's near ally,
My very friend, hath got this mortal hurt
In my behalf; my reputation stain'd
With Tybalt's slander—Tybalt, that an hour
Hath been my cousin! O sweet Juliet,
Thy beauty hath made me effeminate,
And in my temper soft'ned valor's steel!

[Enter Benvolio]

BEN.
O Romeo, Romeo, brave Mercutio is dead!
That gallant spirit hath aspir'd the clouds,
Which too untimely here did scorn the earth.

ROM.
This day's black fate on moe days doth depend,
This but begins the woe others must end.

[Enter Tybalt]

BEN.
Here comes the furious Tybalt back again.

ROM.
He [gone] in triumph, and Mercutio slain!
Away to heaven, respective lenity,
And fire[-ey'd] fury be my conduct now!
Now, Tybalt, take the "villain" back again
That late thou gavest me, for Mercutio's soul

Is but a little way above our heads,
Staying for thine to keep him company.
Ether thou or I, or both, must go with him.

TYB.
Thou wretched boy, that didst consort him
  here,
Shalt with him hence.

ROM.
This shall determine that.

They fight; Tybalt falls.

To seek a method to choreograph this fight, one must turn to Benvolio's description of the fight to the Prince in Act III, Scene i, lines 172–4.

BEN.
And to't they go like lightening, for, ere I
Could draw to part them, was stout Tybalt
  slain;
And as he fell, did Romeo turn and fly.

This description from Benvolio surely indicates that the fast and furious bout between these boys was brief. So brief in fact that Benvolio never drew his sword. Is Benvolio telling the truth?

My assumption is that Benvolio is indeed faithfully describing Shakespeare's intent, i.e., the duel should be violent and very short. The fight should leave the impression of a primitive ferocity unconcerned with personal safety—at least on Romeo's part.

In both the Italian and English manuals of defense extant in sixteenth century England, the writers warn of losing control. They caution that a combatant who loses control has a tendency to swing his sword wildly. Because it is more natural for a person to cut rather than to thrust with a sword when out of control, combatants will naturally make more cuts than thrusts. This would certainly be true for Romeo, whose training, like Mercutio's, appears to be in the system of the English Masters of Defence.

Even Tybalt, whose training would stress the supremacy of the point over the edge, might lose some of the finer points of swordplay and also resort to slashing cuts, à la the infamous "stramazone" of Marozzo.

Romeo has initially entered the scene unarmed, but he has picked up Mercutio's fallen sword and uses that in the fight. Tybalt re-enters with his rapier drawn. His poniard is sheathed.

ROMEO.
This shall determine that.

They fight; Tybalt falls.

What would be the first target of a desperate, violent man? For Romeo, I am guessing that the first target would be Tybalt's scornful face.

Romeo shouts and rushes towards Tybalt, delivering a slash at Tybalt's face (in stage combat this slash occurs *above Tybalt's head*) which Tybalt avoids by ducking.

Immediately, Tybalt retorts with a low slash at Romeo's stomach. Romeo leaps back to avoid the stomach slash. No sooner do his feet touch the ground again, but he is jumping in to cut savagely downwards at Tybalt's exposed head.

Tybalt parries Romeo's head cut with his sword. Romeo continues to close in on Tybalt and grasps Tybalt around the throat with his left hand.

Tybalt and Romeo are now locked in a corps a corps. Romeo and Tybalt's swords are held against each other above their heads in the position of the previous head cut and parry, while Romeo's free hand is around Tybalt's throat and Tybalt's free left hand is holding Romeo's left wrist in a desperate attempt to remove Romeo's fingers from his throat. They struggle haphazardly about for a moment or two, locked in this savage embrace.

Tybalt, in full view of the audience, releases Romeo's wrist, draws his poniard from behind his back and slashes at Romeo's stomach. Romeo releases Tybalt's throat and leaps backwards to avoid the slash. Romeo then circles his sword above his head and swiftly cuts downward at the back of Tybalt's knee, severing his hamstring.

Tybalt grunts in pain and drops onto his knee. (In stage combat the actor never "drops" onto a knee, but rather "lowers" him or herself onto the knee.)

Romeo has drawn his razor-edged sword from across Tybalt's hamstring and now cuts at Tybalt's head. Tybalt, kneeling and bleeding profusely, parries the head cut with his sword.

Romeo then disengages beneath Tybalt's upraised sword and thrusts deeply into Tybalt's chest, piercing his heart. This wound is instantly fatal.

Tybalt slowly drops his sword and poniard to the floor. And as Romeo's passion ebbs away, he watches in growing horror as Tybalt sinks to the floor in agony and quickly dies. Romeo is transfixed; as his own sword slips from his nerveless fingers to the ground.

BEN.
Romeo, away, be gone!
The citizens are up, and Tybalt slain.
Stand not amazed, the Prince will doom thee death
If thou art taken. Hence be gone, away!

ROM.
O, I am fortune's fool!

BEN.
Why dost thou stay! *Exit Romeo.*

Romeo vs. Tybalt Choreography

Fig. 211 Romeo (right): [shouting] run into distance, molinello over head, right foot forward, slash in supination from right to left above Tybalt's head. Tybalt: stationary, duck head slash.

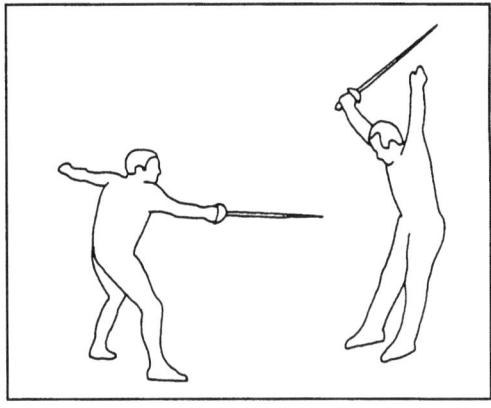

Fig. 212 Tybalt (left): stationary, right foot forward, rapier slash from right to left at level of Romeo's stomach (note—fighting distance!). Romeo: leap backwards avoidance.

Fig. 213 Romeo (right): leap into distance, right foot forward, cut head. Tybalt: stationary, rapier parry five.

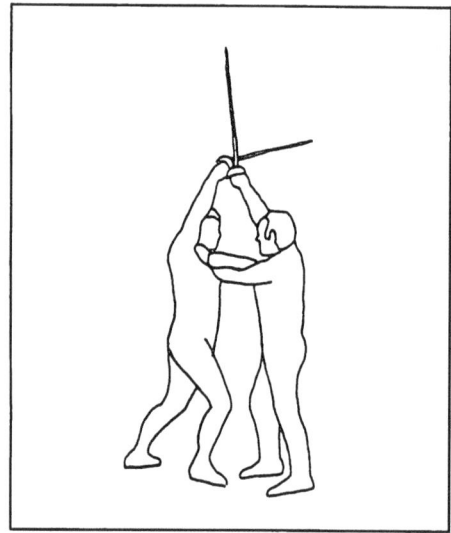

Fig. 214 Romeo (right): maintain sword contact, pass forward onto left foot, one hand choke from front with right hand. Tybalt: stationary, maintain sword contact, grasp Romeo's right wrist with left hand.

Fig. 215 Romeo and Tybalt struggle in a circle 90 degrees clockwise. Tybalt (right): stationary (with back to audience), release Romeo's wrist, draw poniard from sheath behind back, slash from left to right at level of Romeo's stomach (note—fighting distance!). Romeo: release choke hold, leap back avoidance.

ROMEO AND JULIET

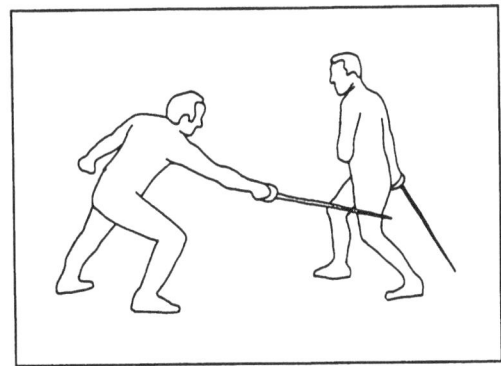

Fig. 216 Romeo (left): lunge to the right side onto the right foot, cut rear left knee (note—control force of contact with edge of sword). Tybalt: stationary, pain reaction (note—illustration is turned to expose technique).

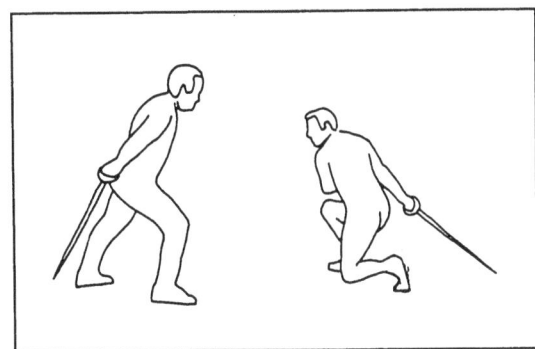

Fig. 217 Romeo (left): lift sword away from body contact and follow through with sword to low outside. Tybalt: kneel onto left knee in pain.

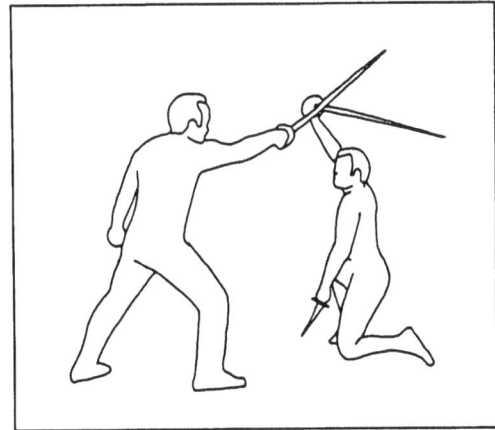

Fig. 218 Romeo (left): stationary, right side molinello, cut head. Tybalt: stationary from left knee, parry five with rapier.

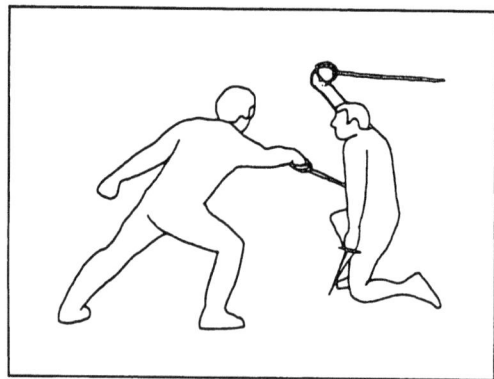

Fig. 219 Romeo (left): stationary, disengage and thrust to the outside of Tybalt's right chest and contact chest with flat side of sword (note—hide wound from audience). Romeo: stationary, lift sword away from body contact, draw sword back to low outside. Tybalt: slowly drop weapons, fall dead, face forward, to the ground (note—control dropped weapons into safe positions).

Romeo vs. Paris

Having witnessed so much senseless violence, followed closely by the end of innocence, must we now endure yet another meaningless death? Although we may tenderly wish it otherwise, Romeo is again the instrument of unwilling destruction.

Romeo enters to commit suicide when he inadvertently meets the grieving Paris in the Capulet sepulchre. Romeo is much changed from the impetuous boy who fell in love with Juliet and passionately avenged his friend Mercutio with the blood of Tybalt. He is older, wiser and resigned to his fate. He does not want to kill Paris nor indeed to cause anymore suffering for anyone. His only need is to die in the arms of his beloved. Romeo is dangerous only to the person who dares to keep him from her. Thus, Paris becomes yet another unfortunate victim of circumstance.

They fight in a very confined space—a burial vault. It is dark and sounds echo off of the stone floors and vaulted ceilings. The mood is ominous and secretive.

Romeo fights with a single hand English broadsword. Paris fights with rapier and lantern. Their swordfighting techniques mirror the differences we have seen in the duel between Mercutio and Tybalt. Romeo fights in the traditional methods of the English Masters of Defence, while Paris uses the Italian/Spanish techniques of a Master like Vincentio Saviolo, circa 1595.

Romeo is in a forehand ward (à la G. Silver): his right foot leading, his sword held midway between the inside and outside lines, the blade sloping upwards, the tip of the sword threatening his opponent and his left hand, covered in a heavy gauntlet, protecting his left chest. Paris is in Saviolo's second guard: his right foot leading, his rapier hilt pulled back next to his right thigh, and a lantern held stiffly forward in his left hand at arm's length (in lieu of a dagger for defense).

ROM.
Wilt thou provoke me? then have at thee, boy!

In an attempt to merely disable Paris, rather than kill him, Romeo quickly passes diagonally forward and, using the false edge of his sword, beats Paris' rapier aside. Paris is now wide open. With extraordinary speed, Romeo cuts to Paris' right knee in order to immobilize him.

Paris passes back and parries the knee cut with a smash from his glowing lantern. He immediately ripostes with a vicious upward thrust to Romeo's belly.

Romeo passes back while parrying the thrust to his belly and springs forward to deliver a blow to Paris' chest.

Paris passes back, parries the chest cut with his rapier and defiantly swings his lantern twice across Romeo's face (above or below the face in stage fighting). Romeo leaps back to avoid the heavy lantern filled with oil and flame (stage lanterns are electric).

Paris renews the attack by feinting high with his rapier, as though to thrust from above Romeo's guard. He then suddenly lowers his rapier and delivers a stealthy stab to Romeo's leading knee.

Romeo slips to the side and parries the thrust. Abruptly pressing in, Romeo grasps Paris' sword wrist with his left hand and strikes Paris in the stomach with the pummel of his sword. Paris reacts to the pummel blow.

Romeo then pushes Paris backwards with the elbow of his sword arm. Paris stumbles backwards. In shame and rage, Paris recklessly rushes forward with his rapier raised above his head, in order to deliver a powerful head cut. Unexpectedly, Romeo drops down onto one knee and delivers a thrust upwards into Paris' exposed underbelly. Most pitifully, Paris slumps to the floor and exclaims,

O, I am slain! [Falls.] If thou be merciful,
Open the tomb, lay me with Juliet. [Dies.]

Romeo vs. Paris Choreography

Fig. 220 Romeo (right): in pronation beat Paris' rapier to his right side with sword, pass forward onto left foot.

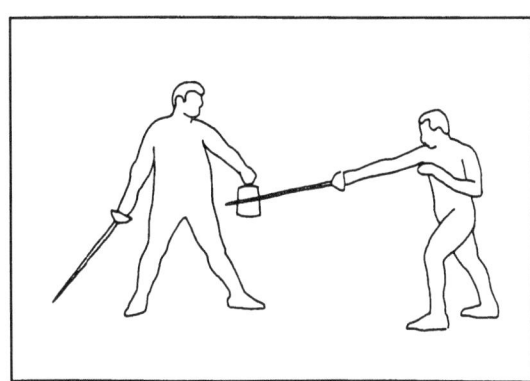

Fig. 221 Romeo (right): stationary, cut right knee. Paris: pass back onto right foot, parry seven with lantern.

Fig. 222 Paris (left): pass forward onto right foot, thrust center stomach. Romeo: pass back onto left foot, counter cut parry two.

Fig. 223 Romeo (right): pass to the left side onto the right foot, cut right chest. Paris: pass back onto right foot, parry high two.

Fig. 224 Paris (left): stationary, sweep lantern twice across Romeo's centerline above or below his face level. Romeo: leap back avoidance, right foot forward.

Fig. 225 Paris (left): stationary, feint by lifting rapier hilt to high outside and threaten Romeo with the point. Romeo: stationary, respond to feint with a high parry one.

Fig. 226 Paris (left): pass to the right side onto the right foot, drop hilt to low outside and thrust in half-pronation to right knee. Romeo: advance to the right, right foot leading, parry one.

Fig. 227 Romeo (right): pass forward toward Paris onto left foot, grasp Paris' right wrist with left hand in pronation (note— when passing forward push Paris' rapier forward with sword in parry position and grasp his wrist by reaching above both hilts).

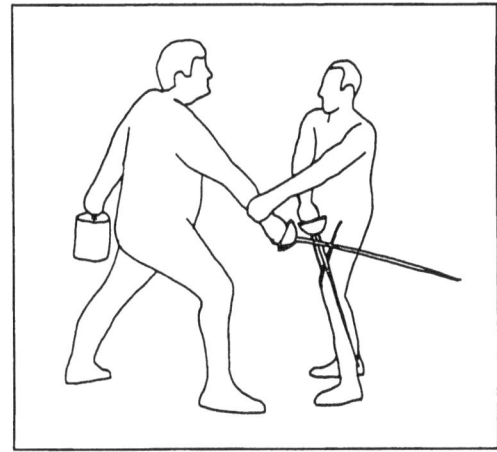

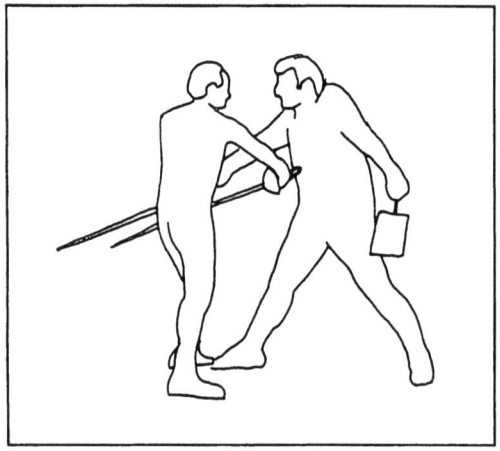

Fig. 228 Romeo (left): stationary, pummel blow to stomach level (note—sword tip is pointing away from Paris and behind Romeo. Pummel does not touch Paris' body—vocal reaction will support illusion.). Paris: stationary, react to pummel blow (view would be hidden from audience).

Fig. 229 Romeo (right): stationary, contact tricep of Paris' right arm with right elbow, lean forward over right knee (create illusion of pushing Paris backwards with elbow). Paris: react backwards two steps.

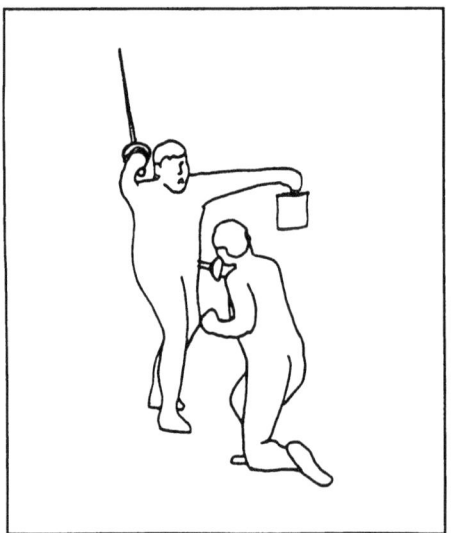

Fig. 230 Paris (left): with sword held overhead, double pass forward onto left and right foot. Romeo: on Paris' first pass, kneel onto left knee, on his second pass, thrust to the left outside of Paris' body outline at level of his stomach (note—sword edge makes contact with Paris' left side immediately following the thrusting action). Paris: stationary, right foot forward, react to stomach thrust. Paris: stationary, drop lantern and rapier (note—control release of weapons). Romeo: stationary, lift sword edge away from body and drop tip to the low outside well clear of Paris, as he slumps to floor.

HAMLET

What's his weapon?
Rapier and dagger.
That's two of his weapons—but well.

Hamlet vs. Laertes

The configuration of the final bloody duel in *Hamlet* has been an ardently contested subject for scholars and theatre professionals for generations. The arguments have come about because of discrepancies in the written stage directions between the quartos and first folio of the play and because stage conventions have changed over the centuries. Adding to the confusion, many scholars and theatre practitioners have been somewhat ignorant concerning the techniques of swordplay familiar to Shakespeare and his contemporary audiences and how that knowledge is reflected in this play.

No doubt, this is the most complex of all of Shakespeare's duels to choreograph; that there is little agreement how it should be staged is not surprising. Nor is it surprising that this is one of the most popular stage fights in all of dramatic literature. The structure of this "fencing match" is a masterful example of dramatic suspense spurred by the tightening threads of character and plot. To unravel the complexities, this conceptual framework will begin with those elements of the final duel that are fairly obvious.

First, the fight between Hamlet and Laertes is dangerously loaded against Hamlet. The audience knows that Laertes has a sharp sword whose tip is poisoned. Hamlet fights with a "foil," i.e., a sword whose tip has been bent over and flattened. (We can dismiss as theatrically ridiculous another type of sixteenth century fencing foil whose safety tip was wrapped as large as a tennis ball!) Unless one were to examine them closely, Hamlet's and Laertes' swords look quite identical. And to further galvanize the audience's anticipation, the wicked step-father has supplied a cup of poison to slack Hamlet's thirst!

Second, Hamlet believes this to be a friendly fencing match. Innocently, he assumes this to be a trial between two worthy opponents, who have reputations for being skillful with their weapons. Hamlet expresses his confidence in his skill with rapier and dagger to his friend in Act V, Scene ii, 209-211.

HORATIO.
You will lose my lord

HAMLET.
I do not think so; since he went into France
I have been in continual practice.
I will win at the odds.

Laertes, however, is in deadly earnest. He is fraught with tension and is bent, at least at the beginning of the bout, on murder. This difference in their attitudes towards the match will become very evident in the choreography.

Third, it is obvious that the fencing match changes after Hamlet is wounded by Laertes and turns into a deadly battle with tragic results. It is likely that some of Laertes' intense desire to wound Hamlet with the poisoned rapier is evident in the aggressive way in which he attacks Hamlet during each bout of the match. Hamlet, to hold his own and continue to score points against Laertes, must at least match Laertes' tempo and force. This in itself would create an exciting match to watch; even without the pernicious hidden agenda. Nevertheless, violence escalates immediately after Laertes' "Have at you now!" The change would be most palpable as Hamlet becomes ferociously aggressive and Laertes desperately defensive.

Finally, the pressure and pace of the scene steadily escalates as the bystanders act together to accelerate the dramatic tension. Claudius' reactions to events, and any others who might be in collusion with Claudius and are aware of the "pernicious hidden agenda" (such as Osric?), are as important to the dramatic pacing of this scene as are the reactions of the central combatants. The fight is carefully orchestrated to allow for the audience to observe the reactions of the guilty parties following each bout. Every time Laertes loses a bout, the likelihood of discovery increases and thus the tension increases. After Gertrude inadvertently drinks the poison, the stakes become unbearable. Shakespeare quickly concludes the "friendly" portion of the fight to take advantage of Laertes' acute anxiety and the queen's rapidly deteriorating condition.

The above points are fairly unanimously agreed upon; what has been less obvious to a number of Shakespearean scholars and stage directors is that there is a high probability that the original weapons used in the Hamlet/Laertes duel were rapier and dagger versus rapier and poniard. My opinion in this regard is supported by the history of Elizabethan weaponry, by an apparent Shakespearean device of presenting opposing fencing styles of the sixteenth century in several other plays, and by several textual references (not stage directions).

Hamlet was probably written in 1600-1. This is the period of popularity of rapier and dagger in London and rapier and poniard on the continent. The sword, at this time, was used primarily as an *offensive* weapon. A second weapon, such as a dagger or poniard, or *defensive* implement, like a buckler or a cloak, was used in the other hand. In the extant manuals of defense of the sixteenth century, the single rapier was taught to beginners to prepare them for the complexities of rapier and dagger. For two skilled fencers to use a rapier without a dagger, poniard, or second defensive weapon would have been an anomaly in a late sixteenth or very early seventeenth century fencing match.

Later, in the first quarter of the seventeenth century when the first folio was printed (1623), the use of the transition rapier (a lighter sword than the rapier although heavier than the small sword) was very popular as an offensive and defensive weapon. It would then be appropriate to stage the Hamlet/Laertes duel with a single weapon (as intimated in the stage directions in the folio of 1623).

Just as in *Romeo and Juliet*, for example, where fighting styles are contrasted in the persons of Tybalt and Mercutio, so too in *Hamlet* is Laertes a proponent of a Continental style of swordplay as opposed to Hamlet's English style.

Hamlet mentions that Laertes has been studying swordplay in France. In an earlier scene (VI, vii) Claudius suggests that Hamlet is jealous of Laertes' reputation as a French style swordsmen and has expressed a desire to personally test him. Reinforcing Laertes' French style of swordplay, Osric states that Laertes has wagered "six French rapiers and poniards." They are probably a portion of Laertes' private armory. (Laertes may also be making a subtle suggestion that Hamlet should adopt a more fashionable weapon.)

In contrast to Laertes' use of the poniard, Osric refers to the weapons to be used in the wager as rapier and dagger—in the celebrated little exchange between Laertes and Hamlet:

HAMLET.
What's his weapon?

OSRIC.
Rapier and dagger.

HAMLET.
That's two of his weapons—but well.

It seems that Shakespeare is again creating an empathetic connection for his audience, equating Hamlet with English custom and contrasting that with the "foreign" (in this case French) manners advocated by Laertes. Their differences in education will be reflected in the way they sword fight.

Their differences in sword fighting styles are further alluded to by Shakespeare's application of popular terminology for parrying weapons used by the Elizabethan Masters of Defence. "Dagger" was a term used by the English Masters of Defence to mean a short, (12–18 inches) weapon that had edges and a point. The "poniard" (poignard) was the classic term in sixteenth century England for Italian, Spanish or French parrying weapons of square or triangular cross-section, useful only for deflecting a light sword or for thrusting at close quarters. The poniard was introduced by foreign Masters of Defence.

Not wishing to stretch a point too far in advocating that, on one level, the Hamlet/Laertes duel is another example of Shakespeare's interest in presenting the contemporary controversies surrounding styles of swordplay in sixteenth and seventeenth century London, one may still appreciate that stressing such a difference would enliven the fencing match. Shakespeare's audience were very aware of the differences in fighting styles and they would quite naturally be cheering on their favorites during the bouts. It is yet another credit to his genius that Shakespeare could satisfy the groundlings and the nobility with the same dramatic actions!

How were these fencing matches usually conducted? We may take a cue from the fencing matches fostered by the sixteenth century English Masters of Defence. These public combats or fencing matches (referred to as "playing a prize" in the Minute Book of the English Masters of Defence), were designed to openly test a student's level of skill. They were often performed on a raised platform or theatre stage. The combatants could not retreat very far for fear of falling off the stage! Although the weapons were dull and blunt, they were of the type normally used in actual combat and could inflict injuries. Judges were present to decide the outcome. How many judges is unclear, but probably more than one. Targets below the waist were considered ungentlemanly. In addition to the torso, the face, head, and wrists were prime target areas. It was common to allow the combatants time to "breathe" between bouts and refresh themselves with stimulating drink. A pre-determined number of bouts and the types of weapons to be used was established before the event.

The use of hidden armor or mystic charms was not allowed.

A raucous audience was also a major part of the event. A certain amount of pompous posturing and speech making by the combatants was countenanced, so as to increase the audience's anticipation and incite largesse. The cheering crowd would encourage their chosen champion and hopefully throw money upon the stage.

The fencing match in *Hamlet* is a theatrical adaptation of a typical sixteenth century fencing match, both adhering to and departing from standard practices. The weapons are confined to rapiers, daggers and poniards. The combatants are without any protective clothing. The target areas would adhere to the gentlemanly agreement of confining attacks to above the waist. The playing area would be clearly defined and restrict the movements of the combatants. To focus on as few characters as possible, use only two judges—one of whom is Osric, who would silently defer to Claudius for any final decision. The number of agreed upon bouts —"A dozen passes"—is a rigorous test of strength and endurance.

The preparations for the match would be festive, with the court spectators vociferously supporting their favorite champion. No innocent bystander is expecting a tragedy. When all have assembled, the king begins the competition by introducing the mismatched weapons. (Is Osric in on the plot? The director must decide.)

KING.
Give them the foils, young Osric. Cousin Hamlet
You know the wager?

HAM.
Very well, my Lord.
Your Grace has laid the odds a' th' weaker side.

KING.
I do not fear it, I have seen you both;
But since he is [better'd], we have therefore odds.

LAER.
This is too heavy; let me see another.

HAM.
This likes me well. These foils have all a length?

[prepare to play]

OSR.
Ay, my good lord.

The King introduces the cup of wine that he will later use to try and poison Hamlet.

KING.
Come begin;
Trumpets the while.
And you, the judges, bear a wary eye.

HAM.
Come on, sir.

LAER.
Come, my lord.

[*They play and Hamlet scores a hit.*]

HAM.
One.

LAER.
No.

HAM.
Judgement.

OSR.
A hit, a very palpable hit.

LAER.
Well, again.

Hamlet and Laertes display the high level of their training in the very first exchange of "Come on, sir." "Come, my lord." Vincentio Saviolo, Henri de Sainct-Didier, and George Silver, fencing masters of the sixteenth century, cautioned that a combatant should not rush into an attack, but rather wait for an attack and launch a counter-attack. As they circle one another looking for an opening, it seems obvious that both fencers are attempting to induce his opponent to begin with a rash move. Naturally, given Laertes' intense need to quickly wound Hamlet, it is Laertes who launches the first attack.

In an exploratory way, Hamlet strikes Laertes' poniard with his rapier, in that instant Laertes, shouting "Hay!" leaps forward into a running attack with the point of his rapier fully extended towards Hamlet's chest. Hamlet lifts his dagger arm high in the air and pivots on his right foot, thus avoiding the thrust.

Laertes rushes by and turns to face Hamlet. Laertes' sudden rush has electrified the bystanders and for a moment there is a hushed, tense silence.

Hamlet, facing Laertes, extends the rapier fully out toward his opponent and begins to circle the tip of his rapier in a "universal parry," which was designed to cover all the lines of attack. Suddenly, Laertes passes forward and strikes Hamlet's rapier down with his poniard. He follows this with an immediate cut with his rapier to Hamlet's exposed shoulder. Hamlet passes back and parries the shoulder cut with his dagger.

Pressing his advantage, Laertes passes forward again and thrusts at Hamlet's hip. Hamlet passes back and parries the hip thrust with his rapier and lifts Laertes' rapier up over their heads and simultaneously advances at Laertes. Laertes retreats. Hamlet presses forward again and cuts at Laertes head with his rapier. Laertes protects his head with a rapier and poniard cross parry. Then Laertes drives Hamlet's rapier down toward the ground with his poniard, and passing forward, quickly snaps a cut to Hamlet's left hip with the sharpened back-edge of his rapier (often referred to as "false edge" cut). Hamlet passes back and parries the left hip with his dagger.

Laertes, determined to wound his enemy, passes forward and with his rapier thrusts at Hamlet's right hip, then passes forward again cutting at his left shoulder and left hip. Hamlet is being driven back to the edge of the fighting area. He alternately parries the thrust and cuts with his dagger and rapier.

Dipping his rapier below Hamlet's final dagger parry, Laertes lunges forward and thrusts at Hamlet's hip. Stationary, Hamlet circles his dagger and parries the thrust. Hamlet then lifts Laertes' rapier into the air with his dagger, and stepping beneath Laertes' lifted rapier, Hamlet strikes Laertes on the right flank with the flat of his rapier blade. Hamlet immediately continues by striking upwards with his rapier against Laertes' rapier, thus clearing the way for Hamlet to run beside and beyond Laertes.

In fury, Laertes advances upon Hamlet. Hamlet calls for a judgment. It is Osric's receiving of a nod from Claudius that determines the judgment and stops the eager Laertes.

Observing that Hamlet may win the match without a scratch, Claudius delays the proceedings by trying his poison device, but Hamlet thwarts the ploy.

KING.
Stay, give me drink. Hamlet, this pearl is thine.
Here's to thy health! Give him the cup.
Drums, trumpets [sound] flourish. Apiece goes off [within].

HAM.
I'll play this bout first, set it by a while. Come.

[*They play again.*] Another hit; what say you?

LAER.
[A touch, a touch,] I do confess't.

Instantly following "Come," Laertes steps to the side, mounts his rapier hand high overhead and thrusts savagely downwards towards Hamlet's left shoulder. Hamlet counter-steps and parries the shoulder thrust with his rapier. He then takes control of Laertes' rapier with two large enveloping circles and sweeps Laertes' weapon aside.

Warily they circle each other once again. Hamlet extends his rapier out towards Laertes, forcing him to keep his distance. Hamlet dips the point of his rapier back and forth, trying to evoke a rash response from his tense opponent.

Not waiting for that response, Hamlet passes forward and cuts down at Laertes' right shoulder with his rapier. Laertes passes backwards and parries the cut with his rapier. Forthwith, Hamlet cuts at Laertes hip, which Laertes dexterously parries with his rapier.

In an extremely fast riposte, Laertes passes forward, thrusting at Hamlet's left hip. Hamlet passes back, circles his dagger beneath Laertes' rapier, stops the rapier thrust and binds Laertes' rapier down and to the opposite side of his body—all in one continuous movement.

Lunging forward, Hamlet thrusts at Laertes' chest. Not retreating, Laertes parries the thrust with his poniard.

Passing forward, Hamlet feints with a rapier cut to Laertes' right shoulder and a dagger feint to his right hip. Laertes responds to the feinting moves by parrying both with his rapier. By responding to Hamlet's dagger feint, Laertes has exposed his left side to an attack and Hamlet quickly steps to the side and thrusts Laertes with considerable force in the left flank. The force of the thrust causes Laertes to grunt with the impact. He cannot deny the "touch."

Gertrude is proud of her son and drinks to his honor from the poisoned cup. Claudius and Laertes realize that time is running out and that all may be lost. When Laertes re-enters the fray, he is almost uncontrollable as he is torn between anxiety and guilt. Inadvertently, Hamlet's light hearted taunt that Laertes dallies masks Laertes' true desperation.

HAM.
Come, for the third, Laertes, you do but dally.
I pray you pass with your best violence;
I am sure you make a wanton of me.

LAER.
Say you so? come on.[*They play.*]

OSR.
Nothing, neither way.

Laertes has lost sight of his formal training and wildly advances upon Hamlet cutting at his shoulder, both flanks, and head. Hamlet gives ground from this furious attack and manages to defend himself, ending with a rapier parry protecting his head. From this position, Hamlet uses his rapier to envelop Laertes' rapier in a large circle and cast it aside. Then coming out of the envelopment, Hamlet leads into a head cut with his rapier.

Laertes parries the head cut with his poinard and binds Hamlet's rapier down to the side while simultaneously cutting at Hamlet's shoulder with his rapier. Hamlet parries the shoulder cut with his dagger and retorts with a rapier cut to Laertes' shoulder.

Laertes parries the cut with his dagger and passing forward, cuts at Hamlet's chest and thrusts at his exposed thigh. This attack below the waist causes the bystanders to gasp in shock, even while it angers Hamlet.

Hamlet passes back, protecting his shoulder with his dagger and leg with his rapier. Abruptly passing forward,

Laertes hooks Hamlet's sword with his poniard and binds it up over their heads. Passing in, Laertes again attempts to thrust Hamlet in his leading leg.

Hamlet passes back and parries the leg thrust with his dagger. Then, in an escalation of the violence, Hamlet thrusts in turn at Laertes' exposed thigh.

Standing firm, Laertes parries the leg cut with his dagger, and while maintaining control of Hamlet's rapier with his dagger, Laertes slashes downwards at Hamlet's shoulder with his rapier. Hamlet lifts his dagger high and parries the shoulder cut.

With all of their weapons now locked together, the combatants strain against each other in a corps a corps, trying to overpower each other by brute strength. Playing his role as judge at the King's silent bidding, Osric stops the struggle with, "Nothing neither way." The opponents reluctantly part with a shove.

Hamlet, somewhat piqued at Laertes' ungentlemanly behavior, turns his back upon him. Irrationally, Laertes wounds Hamlet in the back of the leg and all hell breaks loose.

LAER.
Have at you now!

[*Laertes wounds Hamlet; then, in scuffling, they change rapiers.*]

KING.
Part them, they are incens'd.

HAM.
Nay, come again.

[*Hamlet wounds Laertes. The Queen falls.*]

"Scuffling" is very difficult to execute safely. The tempo must be faster than anything seen thus far to convince the audience that "they are incens'd," and the characters' movements should *appear* more out of control. Any vestige of gentlemanly behavior is totally abandoned by both combatants. It is best, therefore, to keep this next sequence of the change of weapons short and furious.

In pain from his wound, Hamlet realizes that Laertes has been using a sharpened weapon all along. Hamlet believes that Laertes' probable intent is to exact revenge for the deaths of his father and sister. Thus far, Hamlet does not know that Laertes' sword is envenom'd. This infuriates Hamlet and he leaps upon Laertes with a thrust to his chest and a mighty slash at his head.

Backing up, Laertes parries the thrust to his chest with his rapier and avoids the cut to his head. Laertes then thrusts at Hamlet's right flank. Hamlet defends his right side with his rapier.

Performing a disarming technique by jamming the tip of his dagger beneath Laertes' sword near his hilt, and maintaining a stiff pressure with his rapier against Laertes' rapier, Hamlet pulls back on Laertes' rapier with his dagger and leverages the weapon out of Laertes' grasp. The poisoned rapier spins behind and to the side of Hamlet. Quickly covering Laertes with his rapier, Hamlet backs up, picks up Laertes' rapier, and for a moment observes the sharpened point of the offending weapon. Deliberately sliding his own blunted rapier over to Laertes, Hamlet uses Laertes' sharpened (and poisoned) weapon to launch an attack, shouting, "Nay, come again."

Before they can be parted by the King's guards, Hamlet executes a cross-step and thrusts upwards at Laertes' belly. Barely having enough time to pick up Hamlet's rapier from the floor, where it had slid to his feet, Laertes blocks the thrust to his stomach with a rapier and poniard cross parry.

Continuing his forward momentum, Hamlet drives his dagger downward atop Laertes' crossed blades and simultaneously drawing his own rapier back out of the way, Hamlet beats both of Laertes' weapons down toward the ground. Lifting the tip of his sharpened and "envenom'd" rapier above Laertes' lowered blades, Hamlet drives the rapier point deep into Laertes' lung.

The rest is chaos, clumsy vengeance, and farewells.

Hamlet vs. Laertes Choreography

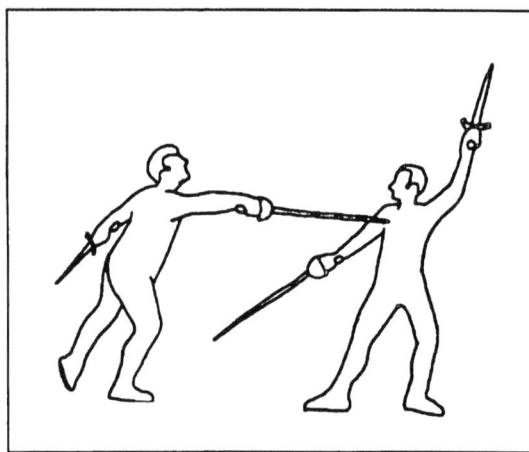

Fig. 231 In distance, Hamlet and Laertes circle each other 180 degrees. Hamlet (right): stationary, left foot forward, beat sword with dagger in pronation to Laertes' left side. Laertes: shout "Hay!", running attack (fleche), thrust to the left of Hamlet's body outline. Hamlet: demi volte pivoting on right foot, lift dagger arm over head to avoid thrust.

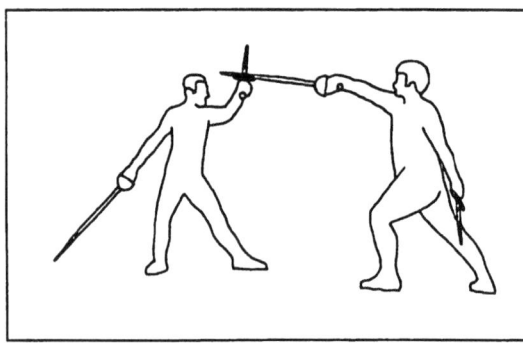

Fig. 232 Hamlet and Laertes pivot to face each other out of distance. Laertes (right): beat rapier to Hamlet's right side with poniard, pass forward onto left foot, cut to right shoulder. Hamlet: pass back onto right foot, dagger parry high four.

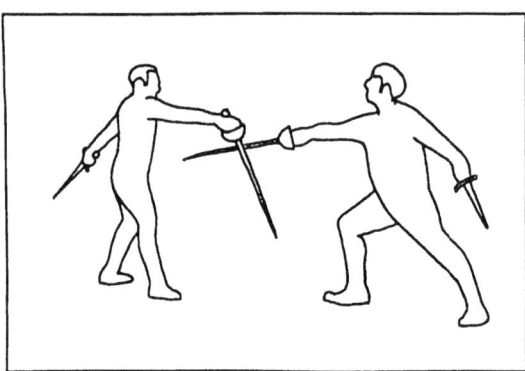

Fig. 233 Laertes (right): pass forward onto right foot, thrust left hip. Hamlet: pass back onto left foot, rapier parry one.

HAMLET

Fig. 234 Hamlet (left): advance with right foot leading and with rapier bind Laertes' sword to his high left side. Laertes: retreat, left foot leading.

Fig. 235 Hamlet (left): pass forward onto left foot, rapier cut to head. Laertes: pass back onto right foot, cross parry five.

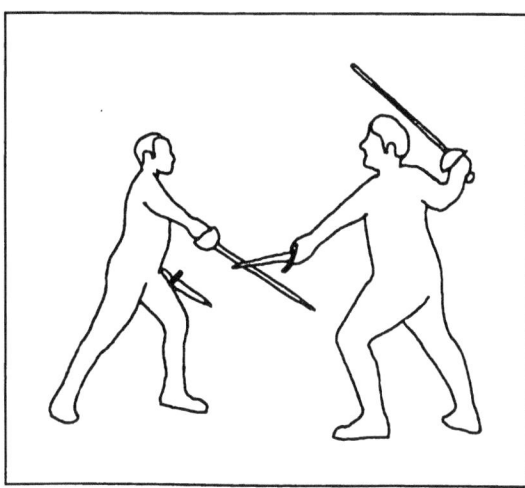

Fig. 236 Laertes (right): stationary, with poniard bind Hamlet's sword to his low right side.

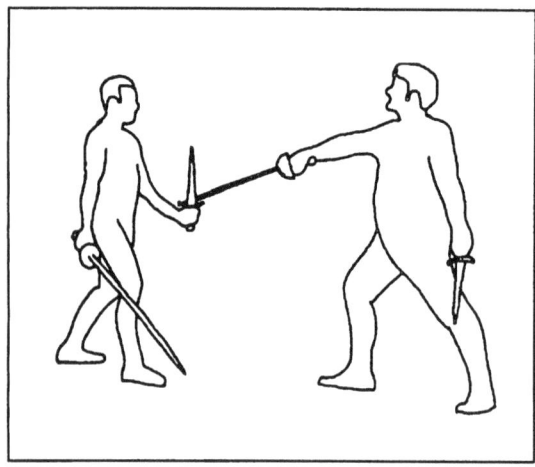

Fig. 237 Laertes (right): pass forward onto right foot, false edge cut with rapier to left hip. Hamlet: pass back onto left foot, dagger parry three.

Fig. 238 Laertes (right): pass forward onto left foot, rapier thrust to right hip. Hamlet: pass back onto right foot, rapier parry three.

Fig. 239 Laertes (right): pass forward onto right foot, rapier cut to left shoulder. Hamlet: pass back onto left foot, dagger parry high three.

HAMLET

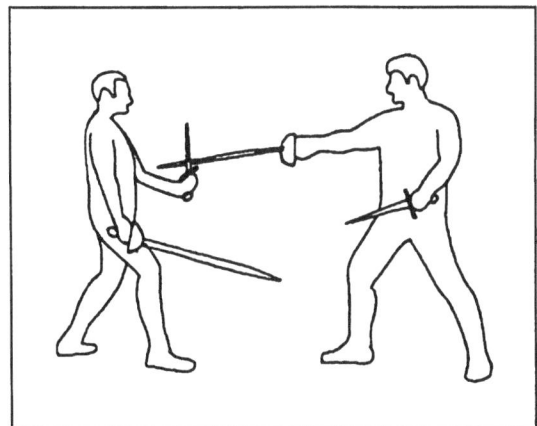

Fig. 240 Laertes (right): stationary, rapier cut to left hip. Hamlet: stationary, dagger parry three.

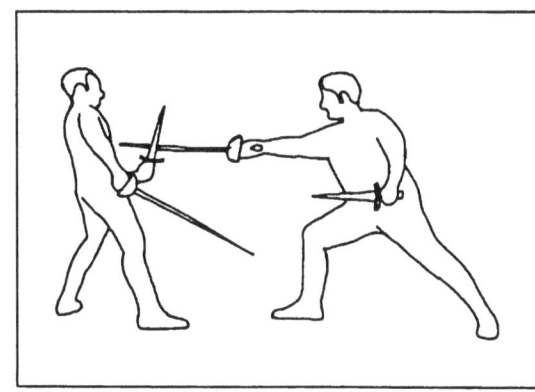

Fig. 241 Laertes (right): disengage under Hamlet's dagger hilt, lunge forward onto right foot, rapier thrust to left hip. Hamlet: stationary, counter parry three with dagger.

Fig. 242 Hamlet (left): croisé Laertes' rapier to his high right side with dagger, pass onto left foot beneath Laertes' rapier arm, strike right flank with edge of rapier (note—control force of contact to flank).

Fig. 243 Hamlet (left): rapier cut to Laertes' rapier, following cut to rapier continue running past Laertes' right side. Laertes: pivot to face Hamlet.

Fig. 244 Laertes (left): advance to the right side, right foot leading, thrust to left shoulder. Hamlet: advance to the right side, right foot leading, rapier parry high four.

Fig. 245 Hamlet (right): stationary, double envelopment to Laertes' low right side.

HAMLET 151

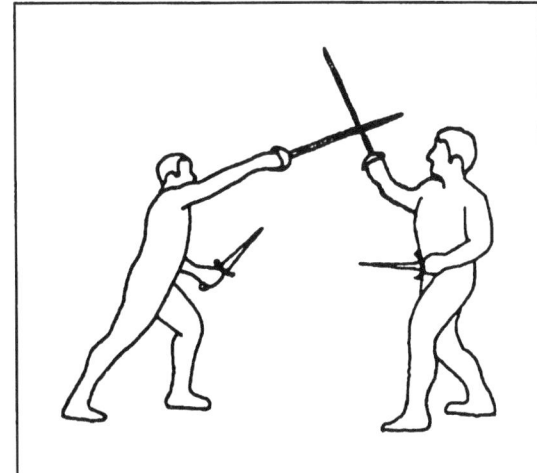

Fig. 246 Hamlet and Laertes circle each other in distance 180 degrees counter-clockwise. Hamlet (left): pass forward onto left foot, rapier cut to right shoulder. Laertes: pass back, rapier parry high three.

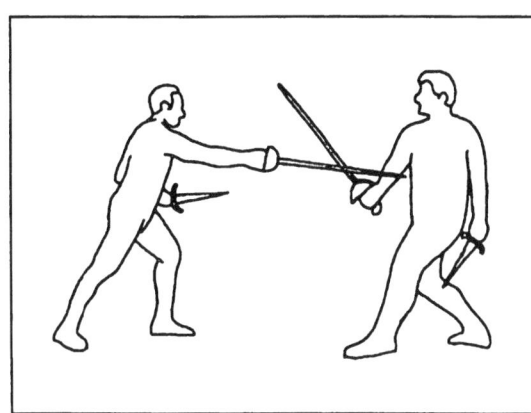

Fig. 247 Hamlet (left): stationary, rapier cut left hip. Laertes: stationary, rapier parry four.

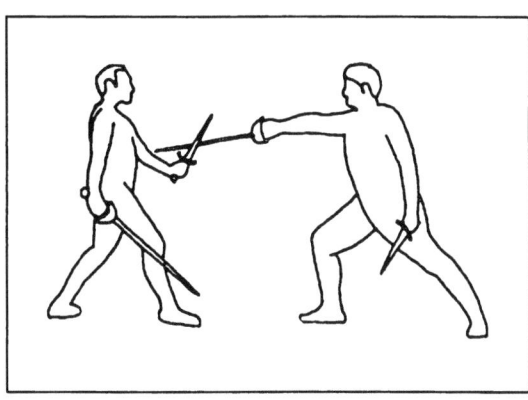

Fig. 248 Laertes (right): pass forward onto right foot, rapier thrust left hip. Hamlet: pass back onto left foot, dagger counter parry three.

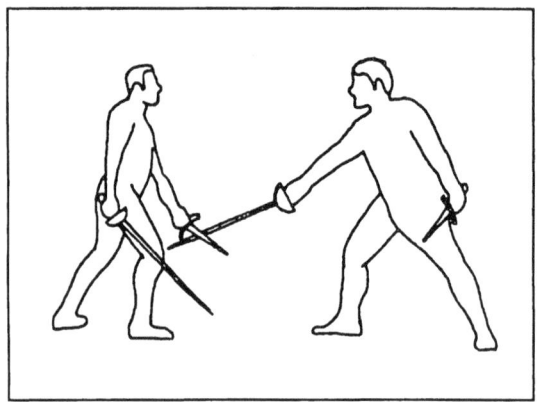

Fig. 249 Hamlet (left): stationary, croisé Laertes' rapier to your low left side with dagger.

Fig. 250 Hamlet (left): maintain control of Laertes' rapier with dagger as you lunge forward onto right foot, rapier thrust left hip. Laertes: stationary, poniard parry three.

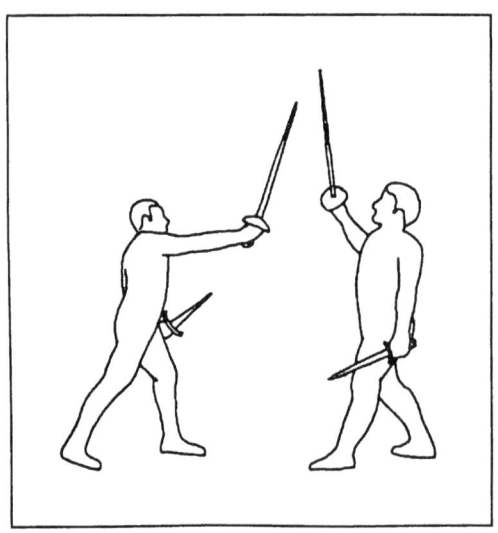

Fig. 251 Hamlet (left): pass forward onto left foot, feint right shoulder cut with rapier. Laertes: pass back onto right foot, respond to feint with rapier parry high three.

HAMLET 153

Fig. 252 Hamlet (left): stationary, feint right hip cut in supination with dagger. Laertes: stationary, respond to feint with dagger parry four.

Fig. 253 Hamlet (left): advance to the right side, right foot leading, thrust in supination and hit left flank at level of Laertes' chest (note—control contact with edge of foible). Laertes: stationary, vocalize reaction on impact of rapier to flank.

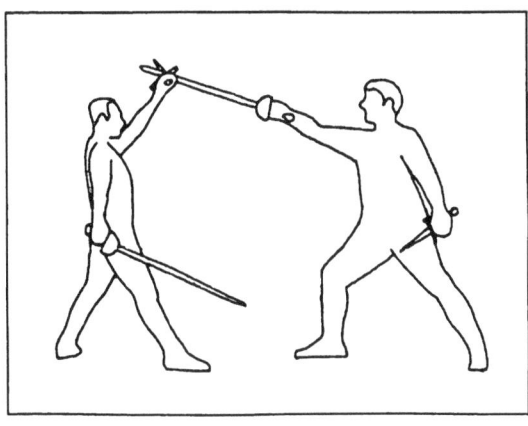

Fig. 254 Laertes (right): advance, right foot leading, rapier cut to left shoulder. Hamlet: retreat, left foot leading, dagger parry high three.

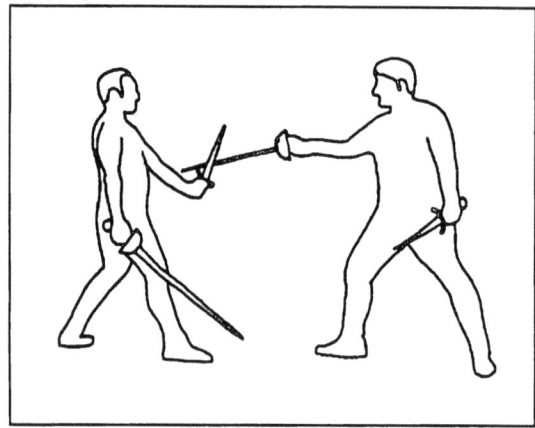

Fig. 255 Laertes (right): advance, rapier cut left hip. Hamlet: retreat, dagger parry three.

Fig. 256 Laertes (right): pass forward onto left foot, rapier cut right hip. Hamlet: pass back onto right foot, rapier parry three.

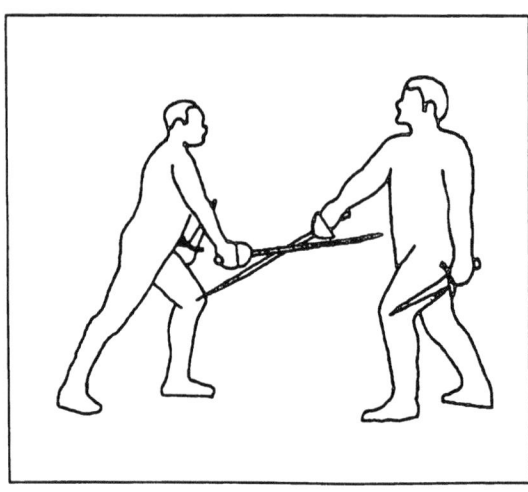

Fig. 257 Laertes (right): advance, left foot leading, left side molinello, rapier cut to head. Hamlet: retreat, right foot leading, rapier parry five. Hamlet: stationary, rapier envelopment of Laertes' rapier to his low left side (note—bring dagger to low left side to avoid path of envelopment).

Fig. 258 Hamlet (left): stationary, rapier cut head. Laertes: stationary, poniard parry five.

Fig. 259 Laertes (right): stationary, simultaneously bind Hamlet's rapier to his low right side with poniard, and rapier cut to left shoulder. Hamlet: stationary, dagger parry high three.

Fig. 260 Hamlet (left): stationary, rapier cut left shoulder. Laertes: poniard parry high three.

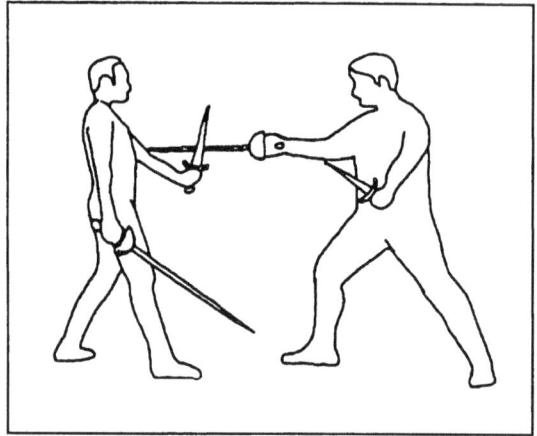

Fig. 261 Laertes (right): pass forward onto right foot, rapier cut left chest. Hamlet: pass back onto left foot, dagger parry three.

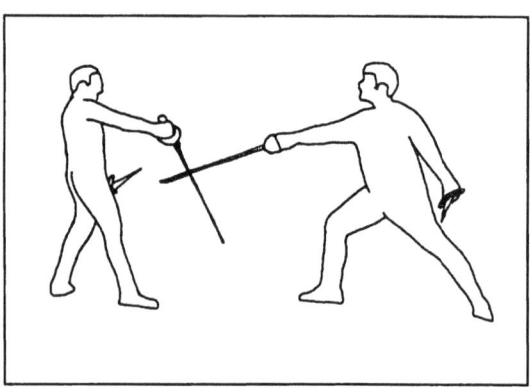

Fig. 262 Laertes (right): stationary, rapier thrust to left thigh. Hamlet: stationary, rapier parry one.

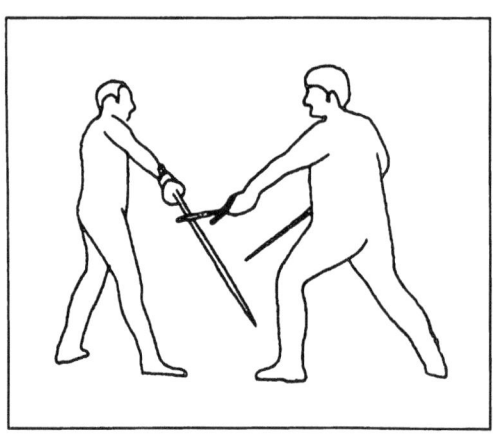

Fig. 263 Laertes (right): pass forward onto left foot, bind Hamlet's rapier overhead to his low right side with poniard.

HAMLET

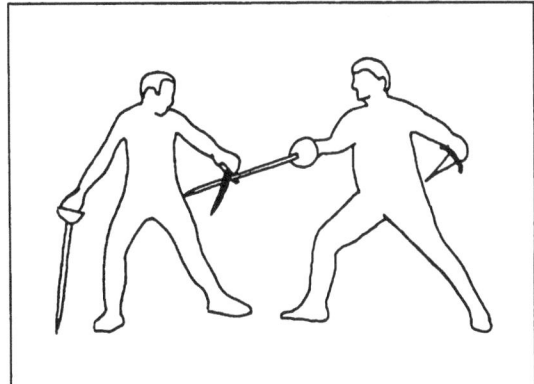

Fig. 264 Laertes (right): pass forward onto right foot, rapier thrust right thigh. Hamlet: pass back onto right foot, dagger parry one.

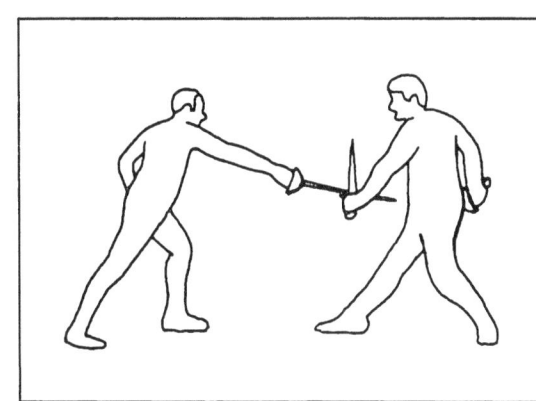

Fig. 265 Hamlet (left): stationary, rapier thrust to right thigh. Laertes: stationary, poniard parry low four.

Fig. 266 Laertes (right): stationary, maintain poniard parry low four, rapier cut to left shoulder. Hamlet: stationary, maintain rapier contact, dagger parry high three.

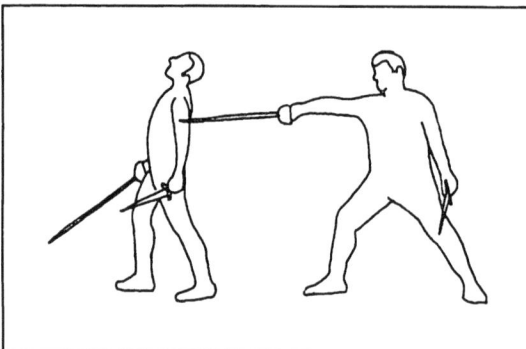

Fig. 267 Hamlet and Laertes struggle in a corps a corps until Osric stops the match with, "Nothing neither way." Laertes (right): "Have at you now!" lunge forward onto right foot, rapier cut to Hamlet's rear left upper arm (note—since Hamlet's back is turned, establish vocal cue for blade contact to body!). Hamlet: stationary, react to arm cut.

Fig. 268 Hamlet (left): slowly turn to face Laertes, Balestra, right foot leading, rapier thrust center chest (note—accurate fighting distance!). Laertes: retreat, left foot leading, rapier parry four.

Fig. 269 Hamlet (left): stationary, rapier slash to right side of Laertes' body outline. Laertes: pass to left side onto right foot avoidance (note—together create illusion of head cut and avoidance).

HAMLET

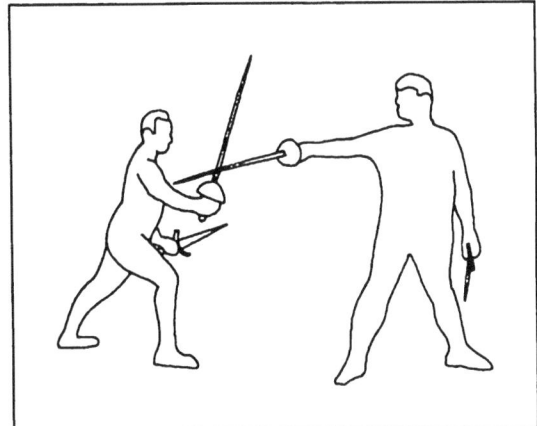

Fig. 270 Laertes (right): stationary, rapier thrust in supination to right chest. Hamlet: stationary, circle parry three with rapier.

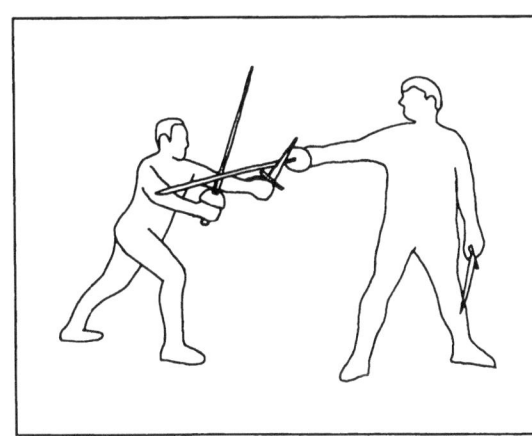

Fig. 271 Hamlet (left): stationary, maintain rapier parry three, place false edge of dagger beneath Laertes' forte.

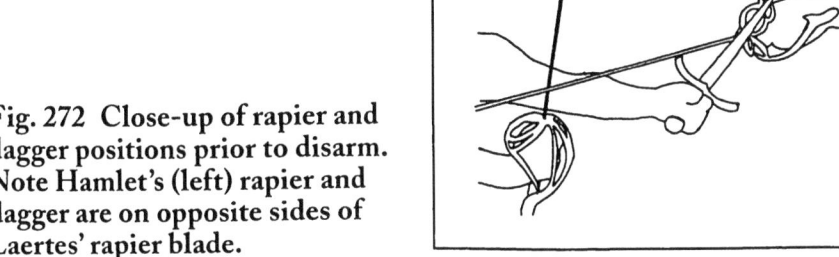

Fig. 272 Close-up of rapier and dagger positions prior to disarm. Note Hamlet's (left) rapier and dagger are on opposite sides of Laertes' rapier blade.

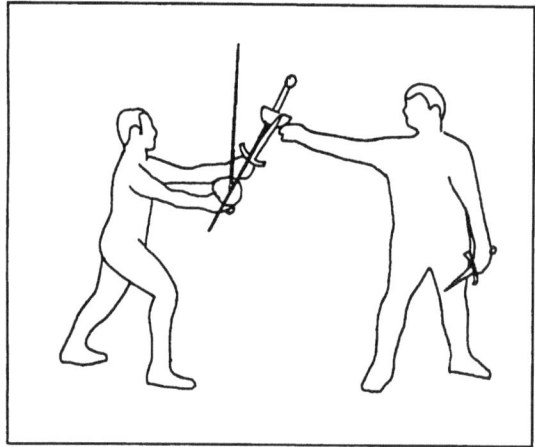

Fig. 273 Hamlet (left): pull Laertes' hilt back and to the far left side with dagger for disarm. Laertes: control disarm by throwing rapier at moment of release out and behind Hamlet's left side (caution—the rapier has a tendency to flip after release).

Fig. 274 Hamlet (left): cross to Laertes rapier and slide blunt rapier across floor to Laertes and pick up Laertes' sharpened rapier, close distance, pass to left side onto right foot, rapier thrust upward to center stomach (note—fighting distance!). Laertes: pick rapier up, cross parry low five.

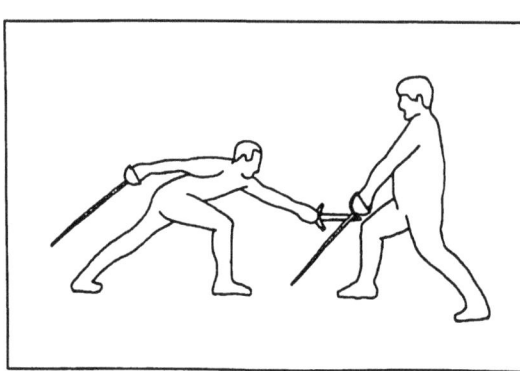

Fig. 275 Hamlet (left): stationary, downward beat attack to Laertes' crossed rapier and poniard with dagger (note—pull rapier out of the way immediately prior to beat attack). Laertes: open rapier and poniard out to the sides as reaction to Hamlet's beat attack.

Fig. 276 Hamlet (left): stationary, lift rapier hilt to high outside, thrust downward to the left of Laertes' body outline at chest level with rapier, contact left flank with false edge. Laertes: stationary, pain response to thrust in chest. Hamlet: following Laertes' pain response, lift sword away from body contact and withdraw blade to far right side. Laertes: following Hamlet's blade withdrawal, drop weapons and sink to floor (note—control positions of released weapons).

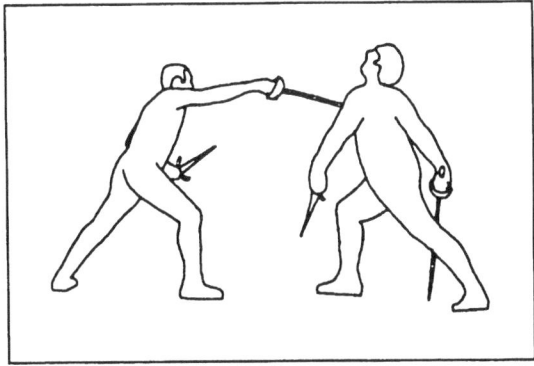

TROILUS AND CRESSIDA

Like or find fault, do as your pleasures are,
Now good or bad, 'tis but the chance of war.

A graceless war without heroes stumbles across the stage in this complex and morally distasteful play. Ironically, Shakespeare dramatizes one of the most heroic of classical sagas (the Trojan War) by depicting the principal characters as lazy, arrogant, greedy, spiteful, treacherous and lascivious.

Shakespeare's disgust with the coarse and brutal trappings of a pointless war are poignantly displayed by the fatuous behavior of the Trojan and Greek "Champions." After four acts of hypocrisy where the characters exhibit their baser instincts, petty political machinations, tragi-comic acts of pandered sexual betrayal and empty grandiloquent challenges, the closing duels in Act V are clumsy and pathetic.

Everyone gets what they deserve. Even Troilus, who at first glance appears to be the personification of the betrayed lover, on closer inspection reveals his libidinous nature and his superficial "love" for Cressida. He does not treat her with poetic respect as a courtly lover might. He values her as a sensuous piece of chattel or as an object of lust. Troilus is chiefly outraged that his "property" now belongs to another! The fact that he was betrayed offends his pride. His anguish, his anger, his need for vengeance, do not spring from the sense that he has lost the woman he loves, but rather that what had belonged to him was stolen.

Shakespeare's representation of Troilus and Cressida's relationship is a sad reflection and commentary upon the morality of the entire Trojan War. No parallel should be made between the innocent passion that Romeo harbors for Juliet, for example, with Troilus' appetite for Cressida. Nor should Cressida's infidelity be construed as tragic fate, but rather as a tragic flaw.

The other characters in the play are also not particularly contemplative or profound, nor are they overly concerned with the consequences of their actions. Viewed as a whole, the characters present a world that is all form and no substance. The glittering armor on the battlefield covers a "most putrified core"—Hector, Act V, Scene viii, line 1. Thus, the trappings of these soldiers of fortune should be splendid, even magnificent. Their arms and armor should shine and glitter under the stage lights. No bloody valor-streaked warriors here; instead, a host of dandys looking for the quick and painless victory—the easy road to fame.

The majority of modern productions of this play are costumed in classical

Greek period dress. It is likely that Shakespeare's company also used costume pieces to suggest the classical Greek period. This is an assumption based upon the costume renderings in a pen and ink sketch, circa 1594, depicting a scene from *Titus Andronicus*. In this sketch by an unknown author, there appears to be a mixture of Elizabethan and Roman period clothing.

Although period costume pieces might be incorporated to represent a foreign land or an ancient time, the weapons were not likely replicas of the classical Greek period. The weapons used on the English stage in the early seventeenth century would be those most familiar to the actors in their daily lives. They would use the weapons that they had been trained to use and that were familiar to their audience. It would be safe to assume that an Elizabethan audience was more interested in an entertaining battle, than in historical accuracy.

Most likely, the weapons used on Shakespeare's stage in his production of *Troilus and Cressida* would be the lighter sixteenth century double-edged broadsword and the circular target or small round shield. The broadswords may have been shortened to represent the Greek or Roman sword, but it is unlikely that the dramatists, actors or audiences in Shakespearean England cared much about such details. The important thing would be that the actors would be able to create rousing fights in the popular sword and buckler style.

Ajax vs. Hector

A formal duel in the "lists" (the medieval enclosure for officially sanctioned trials by combat before the king—rules for which were established by Thomas of Woodstock in 1385) is the first armed conflict the audience witnesses. All the pomp and spectacle cherished by these vainglorious combatants is present. The challenges have been sent and accepted and the champion of the Greeks, Ajax, faces the champion of the Trojans, Hector. The ornamented assemblage of both camps are present. This is a festive event with a party atmosphere, like a modern prize-fight, complete with heckling and cheering from the sidelines.

The champions look glorious in their polished helmets, breastplates and greaves (a type of shin guard). They each carry a double edged single-handed broadsword and a round shield of approximately 24 inches in diameter.

This duel could be viewed as a symbol for the entire Trojan War. The etiquette surrounding the duel is in many ways more important than the conflicts themselves.

Ajax' sole concern is to look good. He is in the business of maintaining his reputation. His interest is in winning at any cost. He confesses to Hector following this duel,

I came to kill thee, cousin, and bear hence
A great addition earned in thy death.

Later in the play, Ajax, with the help of several mercenaries, attacks a defenseless Hector and murders him. He then takes the credit for Hector's death. Ajax' cowardly and treacherous nature should be suggested in this duel.

Hector, although looking every inch like a magnificent warrior, is actually out of shape and in no condition to maintain a sustained sword fight. There are indications in the script that Hector frequently runs out of breath. He takes the first opportunity to conclude this duel and his later battle with Achilles as quickly as possible. The only fight Hector wins in the play occurs offstage with a nameless soldier. Hector kills the soldier because he covets the soldier's beautiful armor—not a very praiseworthy reason for killing a man in spite of a warrior's traditional privilege of confiscating a vanquished foe's arms and armor.

These anti-heroes face each other and strike picturesque poses. A hush falls over the crowd. Trumpets blare in an alarum and the battle begins (as though on a musical cue). The trumpets continue to sound throughout the ensuing combat, adding a quasi-chivalrous tone to a garish facade.

Alarum. [Hector and Ajax fight.]

AGAM.
They are in action.

NEST.
Now, Ajax, hold thine own!

TRO.
Hector, thou sleeps't,
Awake thee!

AGAM.
His blows are well dispos'd. There Ajax!
Trumpets cease.

DIO.
You must no more.

AENE.
Princes, enough, so please you.

AJAX.
I am not warm yet, let us fight again.

DIO.
As Hector pleases.

HECT.
Why then will I no more.

Ajax, eager to increase the coinage of his reputation by defeating the renowned Hector, inaugurates the first attack. Ajax, accompanied by a loud gasp from the crowd on stage, thrusts directly at Hector's groin. Hector leaps back and beats the thrust aside with the edge of his shield.

Ajax continues his attack with a mighty cut at Hector's helmeted head. Hector ducks, but the plume of feathers which rise up in a great arc from atop his helmet are cut off. There is laughter and jeering from the Greek faction. Ajax takes a moment to lift his weapons high and strut, basking in the adoration. In anger, Hector kicks the fallen plume lying on the ground.

Shamed into attacking by Troilus' criticism,

Hector, thou sleeps't, Awake thee!

Hector races towards Ajax, whose back is turned as he milks the crowd, and slams his shield into Ajax' back, throwing Ajax spread-eagle onto the ground. There is a triumphant roar from the Trojan faction this time, allowing Ajax time to scramble heavily to his feet. It is Hector's turn to strut.

Incensed at his ignominious fall to the ground, Ajax launches a vicious assault upon the unprepared Hector. Ajax alternates with crushing blows as he advances against the flaccid Hector, first with his sword and then with the hardened edge of his shield.

As best he can, Hector defends himself with his shield and sword, but he is driven backwards and almost knocked off balance with each powerful blow. It does not look good for Hector.

Exhausted, Hector is finally pinned against the railing encircling the lists and he thrusts desperately at Ajax. Ajax smashes Hector's sword aside with his shield.

Taking advantage of the fact that both of Hector's weapons are opened wide, fully exposing Hector's body, Ajax slams his knee upward into Hector's groin. The Trojans shout in outrage and the Greeks scream triumphantly. The Greek General, Agamemnon, yells,

There Ajax!

Hector lets fall his sword and drops to his knees in agony. Ajax casts his shield aside to grip his sword with both hands for the coup de grâce. Just then the Greek Commander, Diomedes, and the Trojan Commander, Aeneas, rush forward to stop the fight. The trumpets cease their blaring. Ajax throws a tantrum at being stopped just at the moment of his victory. Meanwhile, Hector's helmet is removed and he gasps for breath.

Ajax vs. Hector Choreography

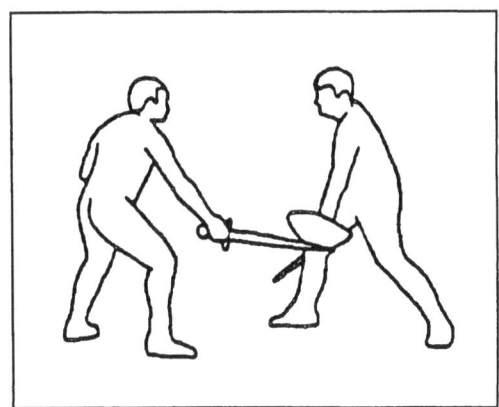

Fig. 277 Ajax (left): advance, right foot leading, thrust crotch. Hector: leap back, land right foot forward, shield parry low five.

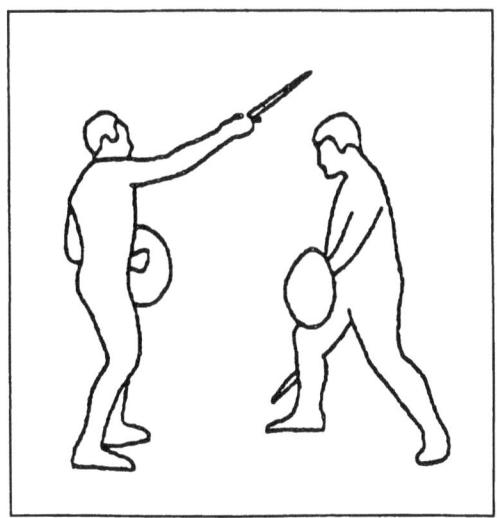

Fig. 278 Ajax (left): pass forward onto left foot, slash in pronation from inside to outside above Hector's head (cut off tip of feathered plume from helmet). Hector: stationary, duck head slash.

Fig. 279 Ajax (right): strut 180 degrees with both weapons stretched triumphantly above head, end up facing away from Hector. Hector: pick up feathers from ground in disgust and throw them back onto ground out of combat area. Hector: close fighting distance, with left foot forward slam shield onto Ajax' center back (note—top edge of shield must be below Ajax' neck). Ajax: react forward two steps, front fall (note—control weapons on fall).

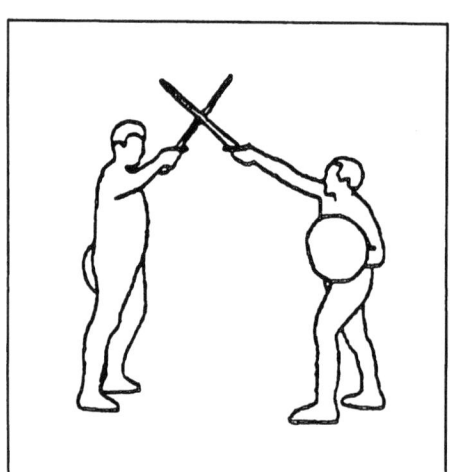

Fig. 280 Hector (left): strut in circle 360 degrees with weapons held overhead. Ajax: rise, close distance, pass forward onto left foot, cut right shoulder. Hector: pass back onto right foot, sword parry high three.

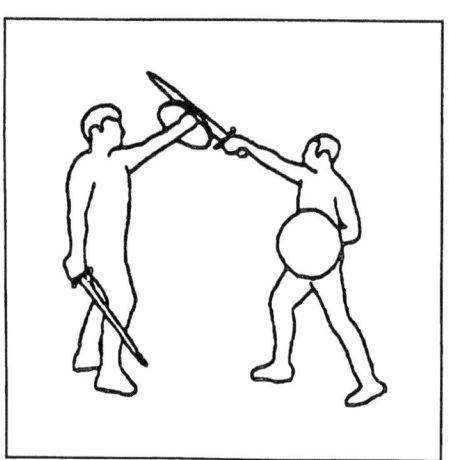

Fig. 281 Ajax (right): pass forward onto right foot, cut left shoulder. Hector: pass back onto left foot, shield parry high three.

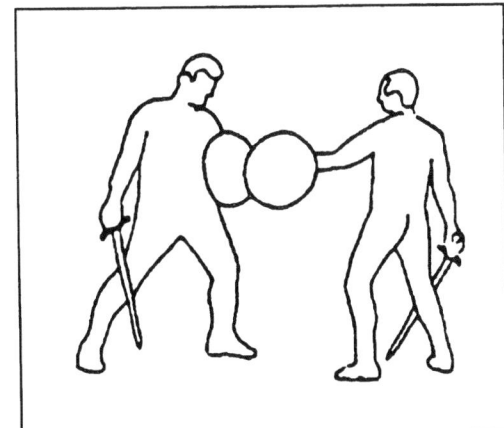

Fig. 282 Ajax (right): pass forward onto left foot, strike with inside edge of shield to right flank. Hector: pass back onto right foot, shield parry four.

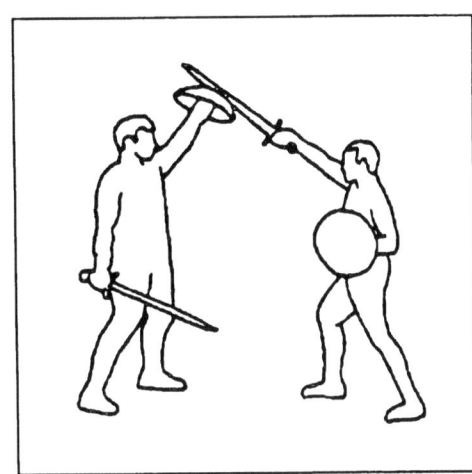

Fig. 283 Ajax (right): pass forward onto right foot, cut center head. Hector: pass back onto left foot, shield parry five.

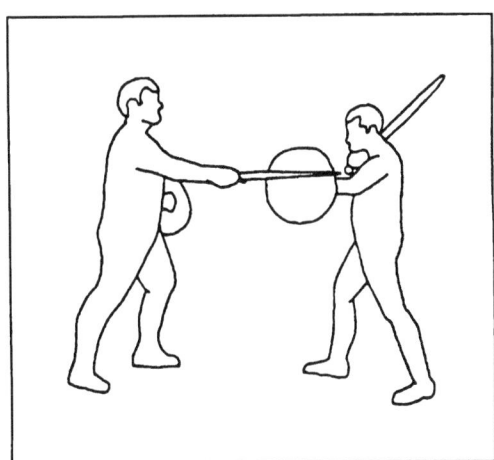

Fig. 284 Hector (left): stationary, thrust left chest. Ajax: stationary, shield parry three.

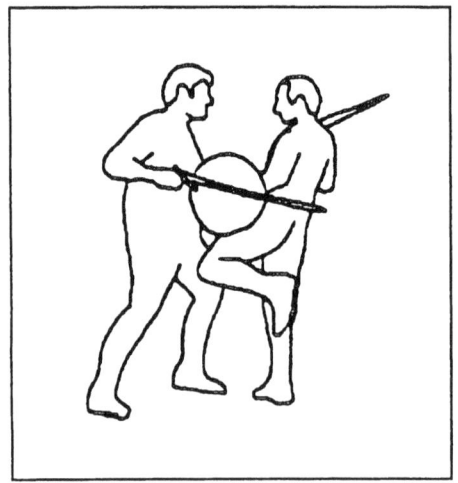

Fig. 285 Ajax (right): balance on right foot, left knee to groin. Hector: stationary, react in pain, drop sword and shield to far outside and inside.

Fig. 286 Hector (left): kneel onto both knees and clutch groin. Ajax: stationary, toss shield aside, grasp sword with both hands and lift hilt high in preparation for head cut. Fight is stopped at this point by Diomedes and Aeneas.

Troilus vs. Diomedes

Following Ajax and Hector's display of facile vain glory, Shakespeare presents a bout between a jealous bachelor-cuckold and a gloating philanderer.

Earlier, in Act IV, Scene iv, Troilus and Cressida exchanged love tokens in order to seal their undying fidelity to each other. He gave her his sleeve (both men and women's sleeves could be untied from a late sixteenth century garment) and she gave him a glove.

However, in Act V, Scene ii, Cressida proves false and gives Troilus' sleeve to her new love interest, Diomedes. To add insult to injury, Troilus is hiding and observes Cressida giving his sleeve away to his hated Greek enemy. Naturally, Troilus swears vengeance on Diomedes.

In this scene, during the thick of battle, Troilus overtakes his detested rival. Diomedes is flagrantly wearing the sleeve on his helm (helmet). A running commentary on this fight is provided by that carping cynic, Thersites.

[*Enter* Diomed *and* Troilus *following.*]

(THER.)
Soft, here comes sleeve and t'other.

TRO.
Fly not, for shouldst thou take the river Styx,
I would swim after.

DIO.
Thou dost miscall retire.
I do not fly, but advantageous care
Withdrew me from the odds of multitude.
Have at thee!

THER.
Hold thy whore, Grecian!—now for thy whore, Troyan!—now the sleeve, now the sleeve!

[*Exeunt Troilus and Diomedes fighting.*]

Diomedes is accoutred with the typical armor and colors of the Trojan faction. He wears an open-faced helmet with Troilus' sleeve attached in lieu of a plume, breastplate, greaves, short broadsword and round shield. Troilus is similarly armored and weaponed, except he sports the colors of the Greeks.

Diomedes runs onstage and pivots to face Troilus, who is in hot pursuit. When Diomedes turns, he thrusts his sword forward threateningly. The rivals begin to circle and taunt each other.

Diomedes, stung by Troilus' intimation that he is a coward, initiates the first attack with a running thrust at Troilus' groin. Troilus sidesteps the attack and smashes the thrust aside with his shield.

Troilus immediately slashes at Diomedes' back. Diomedes arches his back and avoids the attack. Troilus rushes after Diomedes and cuts at his head and legs. Diomedes backs away from the furious attack and parries the head cut with his shield and the leg cuts with his sword.

Diomedes then retorts with another thrust at Troilus' groin. Troilus parries the groin thrust with his sword, then steps in towards Diomedes and slams his shield against Diomedes' shield.

Troilus, maintaining shield contact, attempts to strike Diomedes over his shield with a head cut. Diomedes parries the head cut with his sword and slams his shield against Troilus' shield in an attempt to drive Troilus backwards. Troilus stands his ground.

Diomedes then thrusts at Troilus from beneath his shield. Troilus avoids the thrust by twisting his body out of the way. Unexpectedly, Troilus drops his own sword and grasps Diomedes' sword-wrist, and with a violent blow of his shield against the pummel of Diomedes' sword, Troilus manages to knock Diomedes' sword from his grasp. Both warriors are now armed only with shields.

Without the slightest hesitancy, Troilus reaches up and grasps the sleeve attached to Diomedes' helmet and yanks Diomedes' head to the side. Diomedes grabs Troilus' wrist. Locked together and scrabbling for possession of the sleeve, they struggle off stage.

Troilus vs. Diomedes Choreography

Fig. 287 Out of distance, Diomedes and Troilus circle each other counter-clockwise 360 degrees during their dialogue. Diomedes (left): running attack (fleche), thrust to the left of Troilus' body outline at level of Troilus' crotch. Troilus: pass to left side onto left foot avoidance, shield parry three.

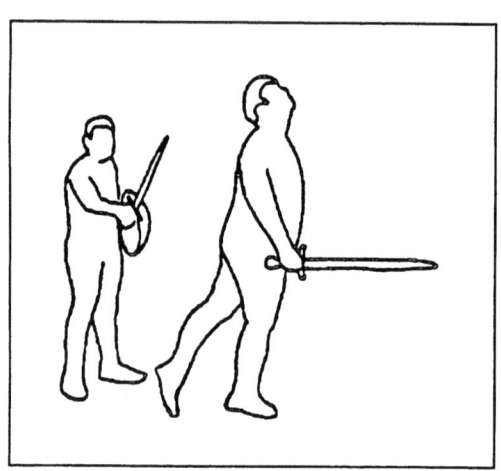

Fig. 288 Troilus (left): stationary, verticle slash to left side after Diomedes passes by. Diomedes: running avoidance of slash (arch back to accentuate avoidance).

Fig. 289 Troilus and Diomedes pivot 180 degrees to face each other. Troilus (left): close distance, right foot forward, cut head. Diomedes: stationary, shield parry five.

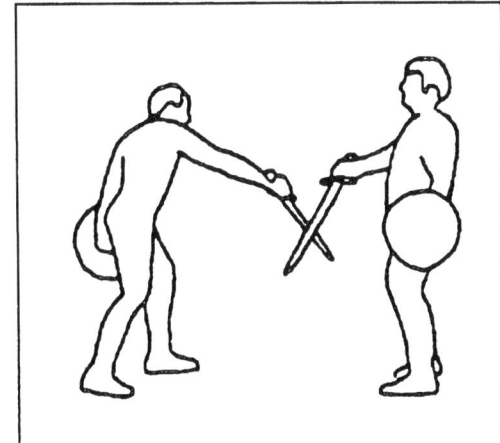

Fig. 290 Troilus (left): pass forward onto left foot, cut right knee. Diomedes: pass back onto right foot, sword parry two.

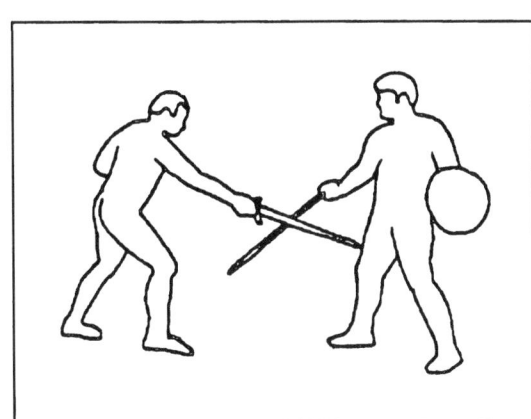

Fig. 291 Troilus (left): pass forward onto right foot, cut left knee. Diomedes: pass back onto left foot, sword parry seven.

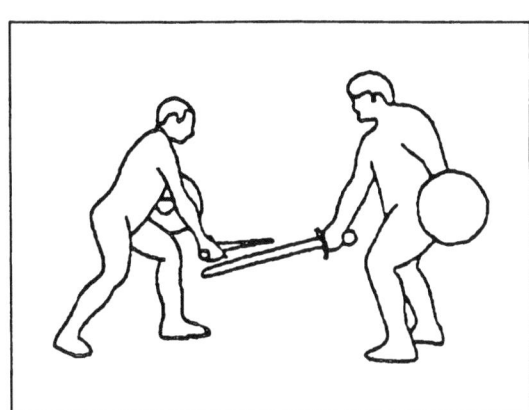

Fig. 292 Diomedes (right): pass forward onto left foot, thrust crotch. Troilus: pass back onto right foot, sword parry low five.

THE SWORDS OF SHAKESPEARE

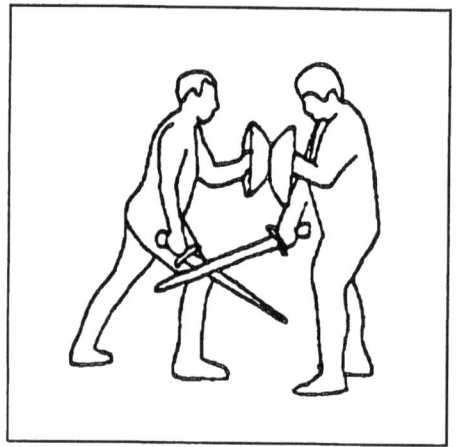

Fig. 293 Troilus (left): maintain sword parry low five and pass forward onto right foot, shield strike to center chest. Diomedes: stationary, shield parry center chest.

Fig. 294 Troilus (left): maintain shield contact, sword cut center head. Diomedes: stationary, sword parry five.

Fig. 295 Diomedes (right): stationary, maintain sword parry five, slam shield against Troilus' shield.

Fig. 296 Diomedes (right): stationary, maintain shield contact, bind Troilus' sword to his left side.

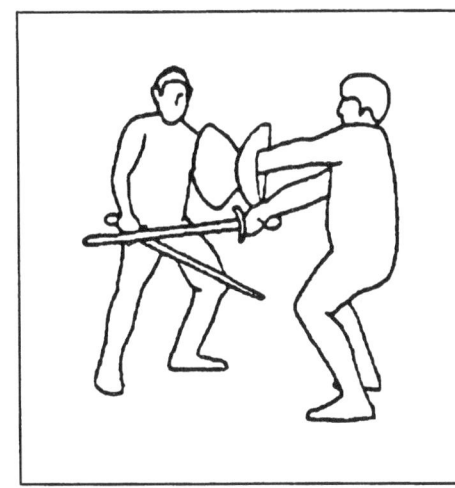

Fig. 297 Diomedes (right): stationary, maintain shield contact, pull sword hilt to low outside and thrust below shield to the left of Troilus' body outline at groin level. Troilus: lunge to left side onto left foot avoidance.

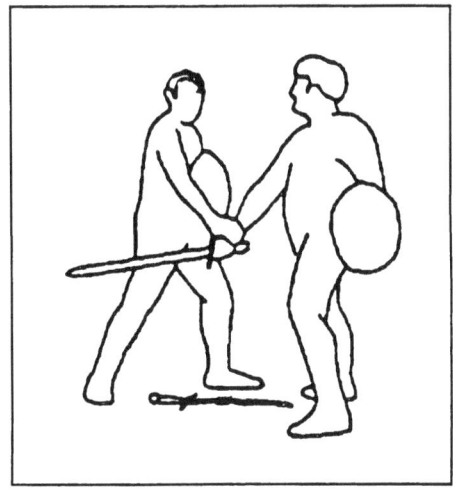

Fig. 298 Troilus (left): stationary lunge position, drop sword (note— control release of sword), grab right sword wrist with right hand in pronation.

174   THE SWORDS OF SHAKESPEARE

Fig. 299 Troilus (left): shift weight onto right foot, shield strike to Diomedes' sword pummel. Diomedes: stationary, release sword (note—control disarm).

Fig. 300 Troilus (left): stationary, release wrist and grab sleeve atop Diomedes' helmet with right hand. Diomedes: stationary, grab Troilus' right wrist with right hand in pronation. Diomedes and Troilus support illusion of struggling over sleeve as they exit.

Troilus vs. Ajax and Diomedes

The Trojan War continues unabated and a series of running duels now ensue. We hear that the Trojans are getting the worst of it. Reports from Ulysses are that Troilus has proven himself a valiant mad-man on the field. Troilus has killed a friend of Ajax and Ajax is pursuing Troilus for vengeance.

Ajax meets Diomedes, who has somehow become separated from his hated rival. When Troilus enters, Ajax and Diomedes are shouting Troilus' name and arguing over who will fight with him. Troilus is splattered with grime and mud and has a wild look in his eye. It is obvious that reason has fled this impetuous jilted lover.

Ajax and Diomedes are armed with sword and shield, but Troilus has only a sword.

Enter Troilus

TRO.
O traitor Diomed! turn thy false face, thou traitor,
And pay thy life thou owest me for my horse.

DIO.
Ha, art thou there?

AJAX.
I'll fight with him alone. Stand, Diomend.

DIO.
He is my prize, I will not look upon.

TRO.
Come both you cogging Greeks, have at you both!
[*Exeunt fighting.*]

Troilus furiously swings his sword in an arc and charges both Ajax and Diomedes. Raining blows left and right in a ferocious attack, he takes both Ajax and Diomedes by surprise and drives them backwards.

Neither Ajax nor Diomedes are allowed to respond with an attack of their own. They can only parry and defend themselves against this berserker.

In a matter of moments, Troilus drives the Trojans backwards off stage. One wonders how long Troilus can keep up his tempestuous pace. Yet later in the play, we see that neither Troilus, Ajax, nor Diomedes have been injured. There is no explanation forthcoming from Shakespeare how Troilus or his adversaries managed to escape unharmed.

Troilus vs. Diomedes and Ajax Choreography

Fig. 301 Troilus (center): close distance with Diomedes on right side and Ajax on left side, right foot forward, cut Diomedes left shoulder (note—tempo is twice that of Diomedes and Ajax). Diomedes: stationary, shield parry high three.

Fig. 302 Troilus (center): pass forward onto left foot, cut to Ajax' right shoulder. Ajax: stationary, sword parry high three.

176 THE SWORDS OF SHAKESPEARE

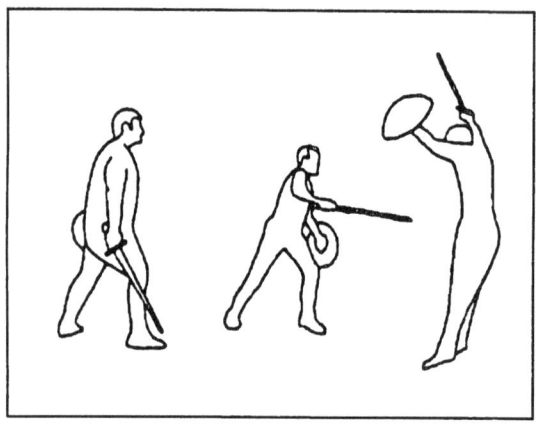

Fig. 303 Troilus (center): stationary, sword slash in pronation from inside to outside at level of Ajax' stomach (note—fighting distance!) Ajax: leap back avoidance.

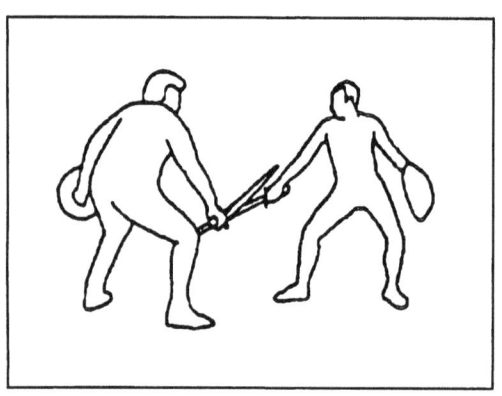

Fig. 304 Troilus (right): pass forward onto right foot, thrust to Diomedes' center groin. Diomedes: pass back onto left foot, sword parry low five.

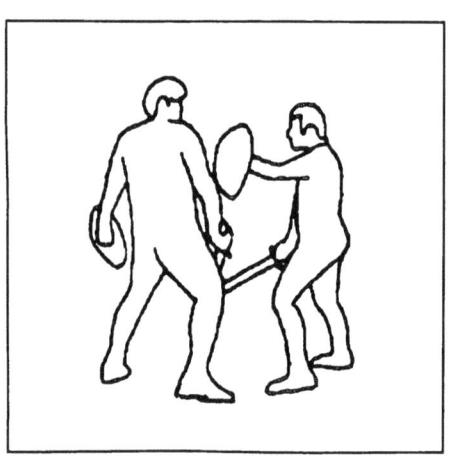

Fig. 305 Troilus (right): pass forward onto left foot, shield strike to Diomedes' right shoulder. Diomedes: react backwards.

TROILUS AND CRESSIDA

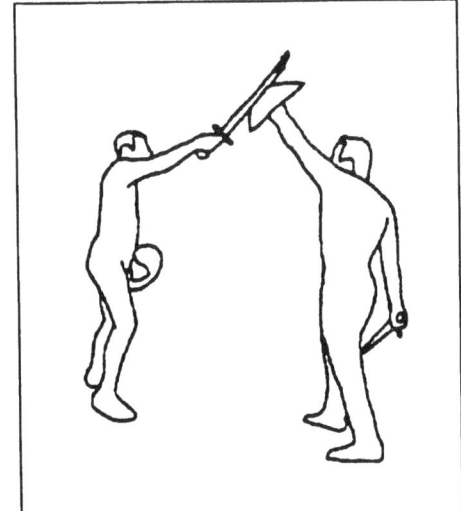

Fig. 306 Troilus (left): pass to left side onto right foot, cut Ajax' center head. Ajax: stationary, shield parry five.

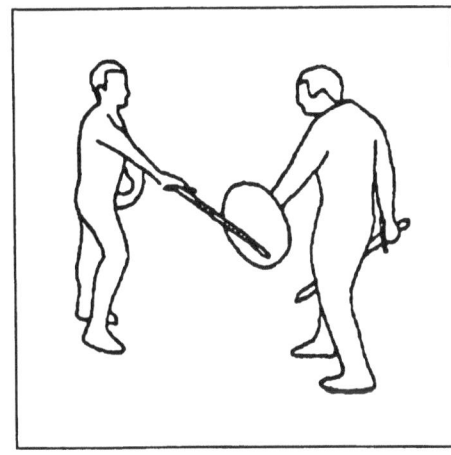

Fig. 307 Troilus (left): stationary, cut left knee. Ajax: stationary, shield parry two.

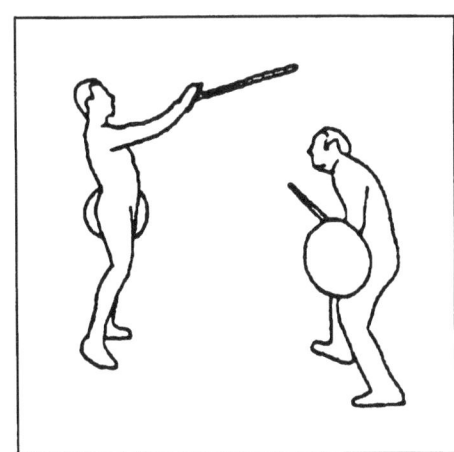

Fig. 308 Troilus (left): stationary, slash diagonally upwards from low outside to high inside to Ajax' left shoulder. Ajax: leap to the right side avoidance.

Fig. 309 Troilus (right): pass forward onto left foot toward Diomedes, cut to Diomedes' right shoulder. Diomedes: pass back onto right foot, sword parry high three.

Fig. 310 Troilus (right): pass forward onto right foot, cut to Diomedes' left shoulder. Diomedes: pass back onto left foot, shield parry high three.

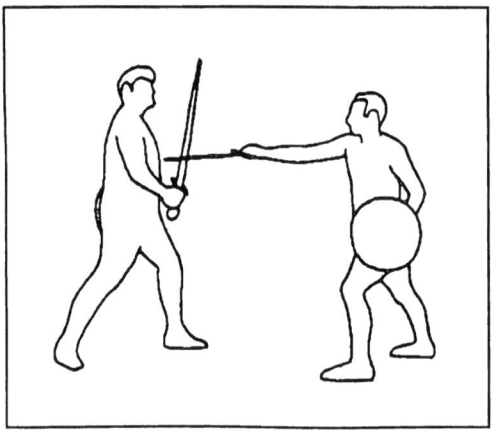

Fig. 311 Troilus (right): pass forward onto left foot, cut to Diomedes' right chest. Diomedes: pass back onto right foot, sword parry three.

TROILUS AND CRESSIDA 179

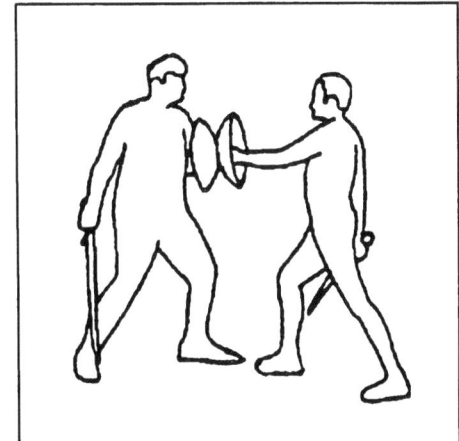

Fig. 312 Troilus (right): pass forward onto left foot, shield strike to center chest. Diomedes: stationary, shield parry center chest.

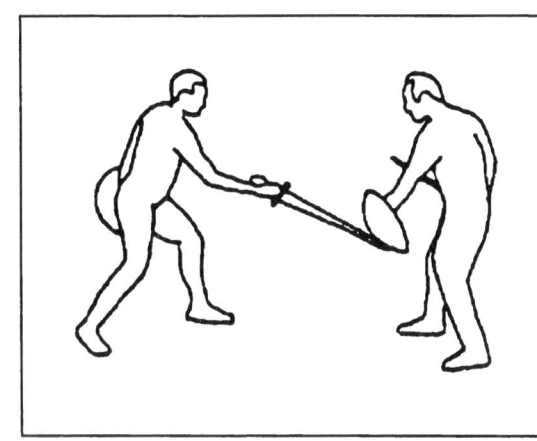

Fig. 313 Troilus (left): push Diomedes off stage with shield and close distance with Ajax, left foot forward, cut center groin. Ajax: stationary, shield parry low five.

Fig. 314 Troilus (left): pass forward onto right foot, cut center head. Ajax: pass back onto left foot, shield parry five.

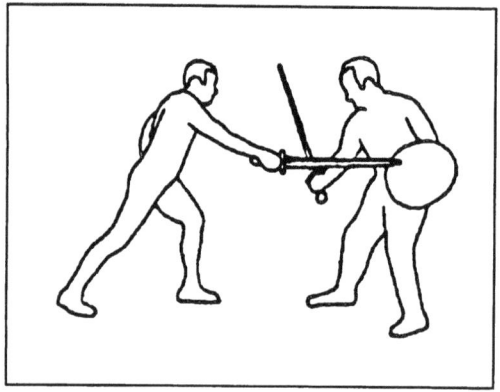

Fig. 315 Troilus (left): pass forward onto left foot, thrust center stomach (note—fighting distance!). Ajax: pass back onto left foot, sword parry four.

Fig. 316 Troilus (left): pass onto right foot, sword slash in pronation from high inside to high outside above Ajax' head. Ajax: stationary, duck slash and run off stage pursued by Troilus.

Hector vs. Achilles

The next duel segues directly from the fight between Troilus, Diomedes and Ajax. The trumpets and drums of war are thundering in the background as Hector enters. Hector has been performing heroic feats upon the field of battle. Nestor laments that,

There is a thousand Hectors in the field: ...
... And there the strawy Greeks, ripe for his edge,
Fall down before him like a mower's swath.

Judging from Hector's willingness to take a pause in his fight with Achilles, Hector is probably a bit fatigued from his earlier exploits. Hector's fatigue is fortuitous for Achilles, who admits that he is out of shape.

This is a lackluster duel between a couple of tired, if beautiful, champions. Although Hector has been fighting all day, his armor gleams and shines. He reminds one of the film actor who emerges from a rousing barroom brawl with every coiffured hair in place! Achilles has not lifted a finger in exertion in the day's battle and he looks as though he has just stepped out of a fashion plate from a magazine devoted to advertising best-dressed warriors of the age.

Both erstwhile warriors are armed

with short swords and round shields. Their armor consists of magnificent helmets, breastplates and greaves. They also sport wrought metal wrist guards.

[*Enter* Hector.]

HECT.
Yea, Troilus? O, well fought, my youngest brother!

[*Enter* Achilles]

[ACHIL.]
Now do I see thee, ha! Have at thee, Hector!

[*They fight.*]

Achilles has been seeking Hector to avenge the wounding of Patrocles and thus plunges directly into an attack. With an overly-formal style, Achilles cuts at Hector's head. Hector steps back and parries the head cut with his shield.

Achilles presses the attack with a chest thrust and a cut to Hector's leading knee. Hector retreats and protects himself with his shield and sword.

Achilles is already beginning to breathe heavily from his exertions, but he presses his attack by passing forward and once again cutting at Hector's head. Hector raises his shield to protect his head.

Continuing the attack, Achilles strides forward and pushes Hector's sword aside with his shield long enough to drive his knee upward into Hector's groin. Hector groans and staggers back. He is in pain and incensed that Achilles would stoop to so base a trick.

Not quite recovered from the pain, Hector nevertheless retorts with a thrust at Achilles' stomach, and a thrust at his knee. Achilles parries the stomach thrust and the knee cut with his shield.

Achilles exposes his head when he lowers his shield to protect his knee and in that instant Hector strikes upwards with the edge of his shield and strikes a ringing blow upon the side of Achille's helmet. Achilles reels backwards from the force of the blow.

Separated for the moment, both warriors lower themselves onto one knee to cope with fatigue and lingering pain. Here they begin to negotiate and Achilles backs out of the fair fight.

HECT.
Pause if thou wilt.

ACHIL.
I do disdain thy courtesy, proud Troyan.
Be happy that my arms are out of use;
My rest and negligence befriends thee now,
But thou anon shalt hear of me again;
Till when, go seek thy fortune.

Exit.

HECT.
Fare thee well.
I would have been much more a fresher man,
Had I expected thee.

Later, Achilles will return with his mercenaries to take advantage of a vulnerable Hector and to murder him—a reminder that not far beneath the requisite courtesies lies the untutored face of ambition and treachery.

Achilles vs. Hector Choreography

Fig. 317 Achilles (left): close distance, right foot forward, cut center head. Hector: pass back onto left foot, shield parry five.

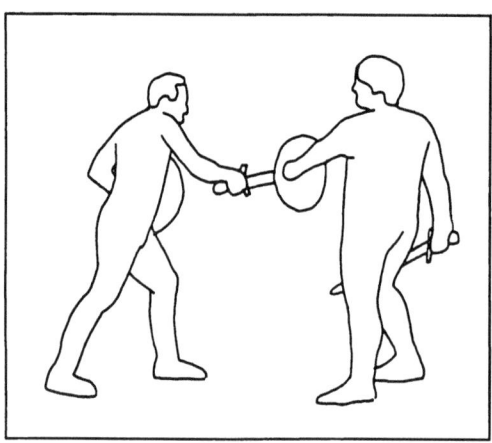

Fig. 318 Achilles (left): pass forward onto left foot, thrust center chest (note—fighting distance!). Hector: pass back onto right foot, shield parry four.

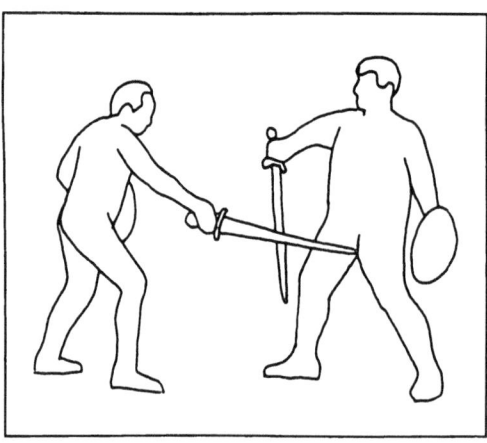

Fig. 319 Achilles (left): pass forward onto right foot, thrust left knee. Hector: pass back onto left foot, sword parry one.

TROILUS AND CRESSIDA 183

Fig. 320 Hector (right): pass forward onto left foot, cut center head. Achilles: stationary, shield parry five.

Fig. 321 Achilles (left): stationary, balance onto right foot, left knee to groin. Hector: pain reaction and pass backwards two steps.

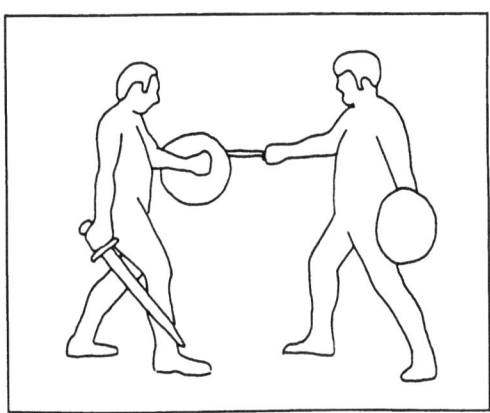

Fig. 322 Hector (right): close distance, right foot forward, thrust center stomach (note—fighting distance!). Achilles: stationary, shield parry three.

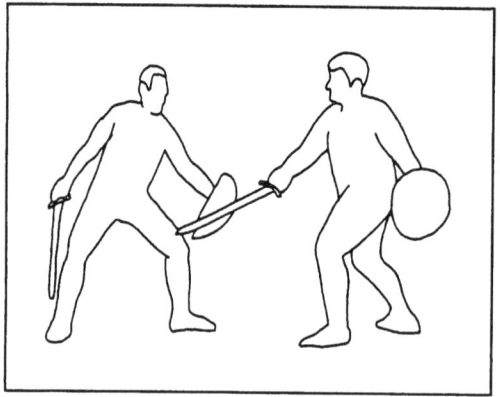

Fig. 323 Hector (right): pass forward onto left foot, thrust in supination to right knee. Achilles: pass back onto right foot, shield parry low one.

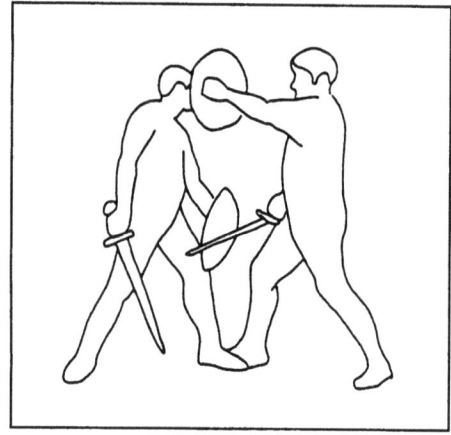

Fig. 324 Hector (right): pass forward onto right foot, strike right side of Achilles' helmet (note—control force of blow and turn shield to the right so that flat not edge of shield makes contact with helmet). Achilles: react backwards. Achilles and Hector kneel down facing each other out of distance.

Menelaus vs. Paris

The last fight that the audience is privy to represents Shakespeare's vision of the Trojan War. It is fitting and ironic that the closing duel pits Helen of Troy's husband, Menelaus, against her lover, Paris.

One would expect this to be a climactic duel, a contest worthy of so great a mythic battle; however, nothing of the kind is presented. Instead, a decidedly anti-climactic fight is staged between two relatively minor characters.

What could have been a decisive conclusion to the many conflicts seen, ends up being ridiculed and demeaned by the scathing banter of the play's gadfly, Thersites. The audience is left strangely dissatisfied by this impotent and unresolved skirmish between the "Cuckold and cuckold-maker."

Presumably, the war continues to be waged between the Trojans and Greeks. Off stage, the trumpets blare and the drums pound. Perchance a few soldiers cross the stage running in retreat and pursuit. Perhaps the war has begun to dwindle down. The whole affair is taking on a pallid and spiritless tone.

When Menelaus and Paris are first seen, they are already fighting. To vaguely represent the Troyan rout, Paris enters the stage retreating from Menelaus' attack. But one needn't be overly concerned with the inherent symbolism in this final duel of the play.

After all, Shakespeare left the ultimate consequences of his play in a peculiar state of limbo. We are left with a cloying discontent and the emptiness of immoral appetite. Whatever messages there are in this enigmatic and brilliant play, they are certainly not dependent upon the outcome of the Trojan War.

Menelaus and Paris are peacocks squabbling over a hen. Their plumage (armor), swords and shields are likewise magnificent and displayed to best advantage. They are not soiled from previous battles. Indeed, one receives the distinct impression that they are not very eager to be fighting at all. Taking a cue from the brevity of Thersites' accompanying dialogue, this duel lasts only a few moments as it travels across the stage. They are lovers, not fighters.

The imagery that Thersites uses to describe the fight is borrowed from the Elizabethan Bear Garden, where bears were baited and attacked by dogs for sport. The implication is that this duel is merely for show; an empty, pointless display of aggression for the benefit of an idle voyeur.

Enter Thersites; Menelaus [*and*] Paris [*fighting.*]

THER.
The cuckold and the cuckold-maker are at it. Now, bull! now dog! 'Loo, Paris, 'loo! Now my double-henn'd Spartan! 'Loo, Paris, 'loo!
The bull has the game, ware horns ho!

Exeunt Paris and Menelaus.

Paris backs out onto the stage while defending himself against Menelaus' tepid series of cuts and thrusts. In fact, Menelaus' succession of cuts and thrusts are rather mechanical and predictable. Paris is having little trouble defending himself, but he continues to retreat, as it is better to be cautious when one's precious person is at stake.

Menelaus concludes his advancing attack with a slash at Paris' head. Paris ducks the slash and riposte with a thrust at Menelaus' groin.

Menelaus parries the groin thrust with his sword and ineffectually swipes his shield in front of Paris' face. Paris avoids the shield swipe and inaugurates an advancing series of attacks of his own.

Paris cuts at Menelaus' leg and head, and then drives Menelaus backwards off stage with a series of thrusts to chest, stomach and groin. Paris' attack is no more virile than was Menelaus' initial gambit, but Menelaus is taking no chances. He cautiously gives ground as he methodically parries Paris' measured attacks.

The "Cuckold and Cuckold-Maker" are evenly matched. As they drift from the stage, one wonders what Helen saw in either one of them!

Menelaus vs. Paris Choreography

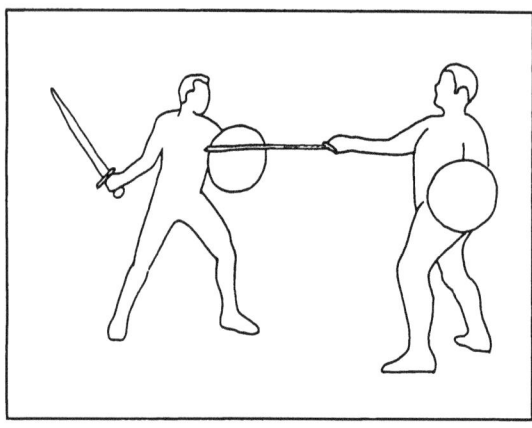

Fig. 325 Menelaus (right): pass forward onto left foot, thrust in supination to right chest. Paris: pass back onto right foot, shield parry four.

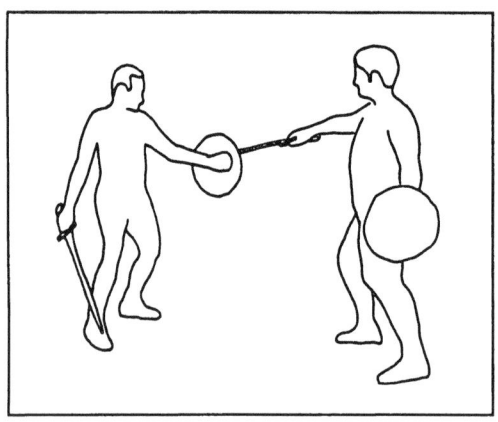

Fig. 326 Menelaus (right): pass forward onto right foot, thrust left chest. Paris: pass back onto left foot, shield parry three.

Fig. 327 Menelaus (right): pass forward onto left foot, cut right shoulder. Paris: pass back onto right foot, sword parry high three.

TROILUS AND CRESSIDA

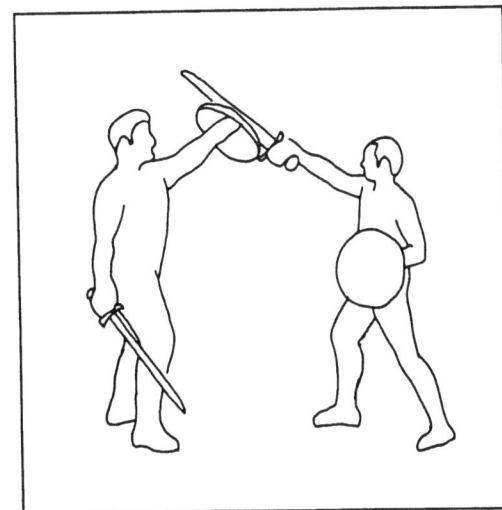

Fig. 328 Menelaus (right): pass forward onto right foot, cut left shoulder. Paris: pass back onto left foot, shield parry high three.

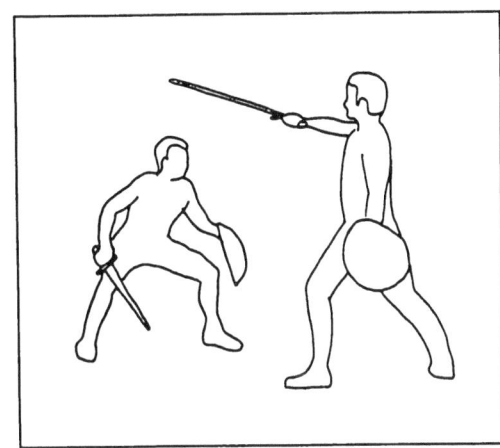

Fig. 329 Menelaus (right): pass forward onto left foot, sword slash from high inside to high outside above Paris' head. Paris: pass back onto right foot, duck slash.

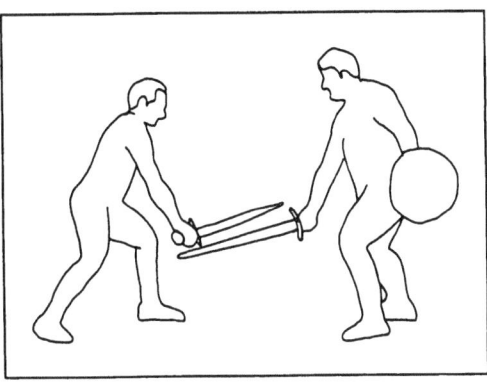

Fig. 330 Paris (right): rise from crouch, pass forward onto left foot, thrust groin (note—fighting distance!). Menelaus: pass back onto right foot, sword parry low five.

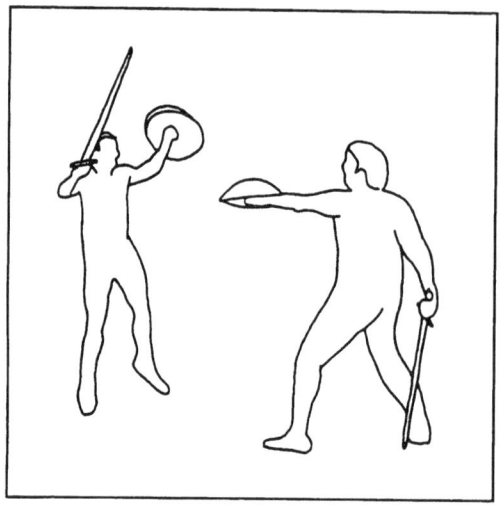

Fig. 331 Menelaus (right): stationary, sweep shield in pronation from inside to outside below the level of Paris' head. Paris: leap back avoidance.

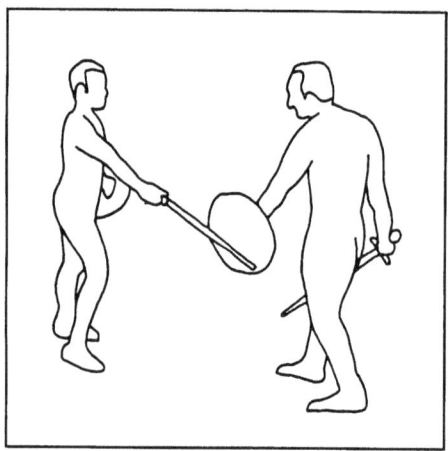

Fig. 332 Paris (left): close distance, right foot forward, cut left knee. Menelaus: pass back onto left foot, shield parry two.

Fig. 333 Paris (right): stationary, cut head. Menelaus: stationary, shield parry five.

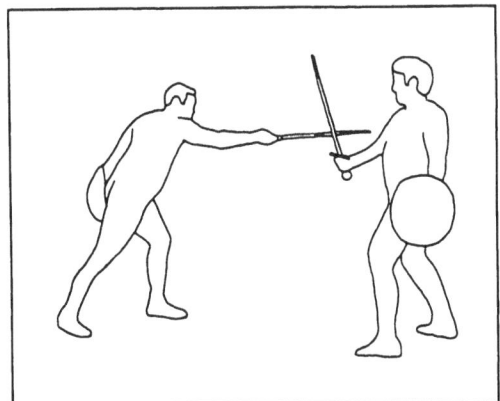

Fig. 334 Paris (left): pass forward onto left foot, thrust in supination to right chest (note—fighting distance!). Menelaus: pass back onto right foot, sword parry three.

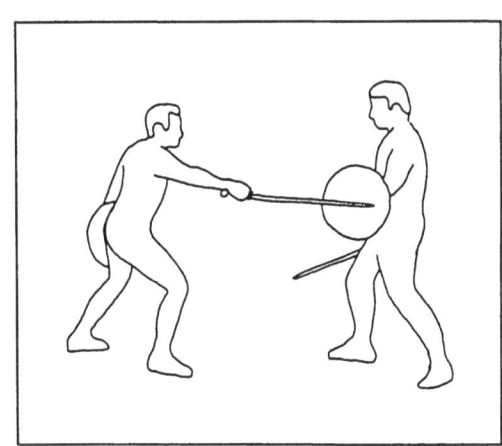

Fig. 335 Paris (left): pass forward onto right foot, thrust in pronation to center stomach (note—fighting distance!). Menelaus: pass back onto left foot, shield parry three.

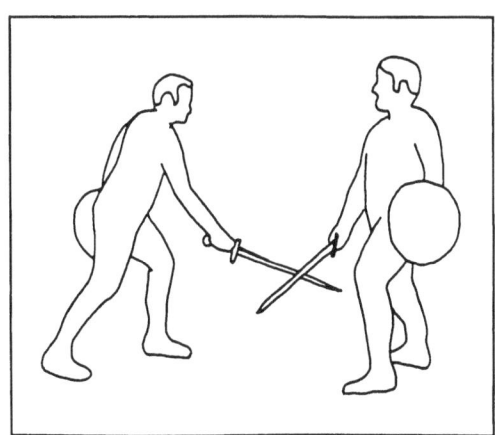

Fig. 336 Paris (left): pass forward onto left foot, thrust groin. Menelaus: pass back onto right foot, sword parry low five.

Fig. 337 Paris (left): pass forward onto right foot, sword slash in supination from inside to outside at level of Menelaus stomach (note—fighting distance!). Menelaus: leap back avoidance and exit off stage with Paris in pursuit.

OTHELLO

Why, how now ho? From whence ariseth this?

Montano vs. Cassio

Oh, that crafty, villainous Iago! For his own nefarious reasons Iago has managed to pit two equally noble gentlemen against each other in deadly combat!

By playing upon the carnival atmosphere of celebration established by Othello in the previous scene, Iago induces the honorable Lieutenant Cassio to drink wine; even though Cassio is reluctant and admits that he doesn't have a head for alcohol, "I am infortunate in the infirmity." In addition, Iago knows that Cassio is somewhat hot-headed and touchy when it comes to issues of honor and duty. Iago therefore persuades the dull witted Roderigo to insult Cassio about his drinking on duty, with the assurance that Iago will stand behind Roderigo if events turn to violence.

The final ingredient in Iago's machinations, which leads to this most unfortunate duel, is the poisoning of Cassio's character in the eyes of the former Governor of Cyprus, Montano. Iago convinces Montano that Cassio is a drunkard and not to be trusted.

Here then is Iago's successful recipe for chaos.

Enter Cassio *pursueing* Roderigo

CAS.
['Zounds,] you rogue! you rascal!

MON.
What's the matter, lieutenant?

CAS.
A knave teach me my duty? I'll beat the knave into a twiggen bottle.

ROD.
Beat me?

CAS.
Dost thou prate, rogue? *[Striking Roderigo.]*

MON.
Nay, good lieutenant; I pray you, sir, hold your hand. *[Staying him.]*

CAS.
Let me go, sir, or I'll knock you o'er the mazzard.

MON.
Come, come—you're drunk.

CAS.
Drunk? *[They fight.]*

IAGO.
[Aside to Roderigo.] Away, I say; go out and cry a mutiny.

[Exit Roderigo.]

Nay, good lieutenant—[God's will], gentlemen—
Help ho!—sir—Montano—[sir] -
Help, masters!—Here's goodly watch indeed!

[A bell rung.]

Who's that which rings the bell? Diablo, ho!
The town will rise. [God's will], lieutenant, [hold]!
You'll be asham'd for ever.

Enter Othello *and* [gentlemen *with weapons*].

OTH.
What is the matter here?

MON.
['Zounds] I bleed still,
I am hurt to th' death. He dies.
[assailing Cassio again.]

OTH.
Hold, for your lives!

IAGO.
Hold ho! Lieutenant—sir—Montano—gentlemen—
Have you forgot all place of sense and duty?
Hold! the general speaks to you; hold, for shame!

OTH.
Why, how now ho? From whence ariseth this?
Are we turn'd Turks, and to ourselves do that
Which heaven hath forbid the Ottomites?
For Christian shame, put by this barbarous brawl.
He that stirs next to carve for his own rage
Holds his soul light; he dies upon his motion.
Silence that dreadful bell, it frights the isle
From her propriety.

Given the social standing of the combatants, and the urban setting (Venice; a sea port in Cyprus), rapier and dagger would be the fashionable weapons of theatrical choice for the Elizabethans in 1604, when *Othello* was written. Further evidence for choosing the rapier, rather than the early seventeenth century broadsword, is Iago's comment that the combatants were engaged in using both the edge and the point of their weapons;

I found them close together
At blow and thrust,

It can be assumed, after garnering clues from the text about this fight, that Iago's description of the fight is at least partially truthful. Iago has a vested interest in appearing honest and it can also be assumed that there may have been other witnesses to the duel.

Iago relates that the action begins with Cassio, sword drawn, in hot pursuit of Roderigo. Cassio ignores Montano's, "What's the matter, lieutenant?," and strikes Roderigo across the face.

Montano then steps in to grasp Cassio's sword arm. Further incensed by Montano's inference that Cassio is drunk, Cassio violently pushes Montano backwards.

Montano draws his rapier and dagger in angry self defense and launches a thrusting attack at Cassio's arm to disable him. Cassio quickly draws his weapons and parries the arm thrust with his dagger. Cassio reposts with a snapping cut to Montano's knee, which Montano avoids by leaping backwards.

At this point both combatants are inflamed by passions beyond their control. Their full fighting instincts are aroused. They are now deadly enemies. This escalation into madness is vintage Shakespeare. He often depicts the folly of violence piqued by wounded pride.

The fault for this duel, therefore, cannot be laid solely at the feet of Iago. The intemperate natures of the combatants must share some of the blame. One of the themes of this great play is being played out in this deplorable duel—i.e., without civility man is no better than a beast.

Cassio leaps toward Montano, circling his rapier like a windmill and lets fly a cut to Montano's head. Montano protects his head with both sword and dagger, slides his sword back (the audience hears the sound of steel grating on steel) and slashes at Cassio's stomach. Cassio leaps back, narrowly avoiding the stomach slash.

Montano, passing forward, presses his advantage with a series of lightening-quick thrusts at Cassio's chest, at his knee, again at his chest, and follows up with a broad slash at Cassio's ankles.

Cassio, passing backward, parries the attacks with his rapier, then dagger, then rapier and vaults over the slashing blade aimed at his ankles.

The clamor of alarum bells begins to ring out, heightening the chaotic turmoil. Iago continues to shout out his dialogue in a false attempt to stop the combatants. Blades are clashing against blades and the combatants are grunting with effort. The din is almost overwhelming!

With a full lunge forward, Montano thrusts at Cassio's chest. Cassio parries the chest thrust with his rapier, quickly steps forward and with his dagger, slashes deeply into the flesh beneath Montano's outstretched sword arm. Montano reacts in pain as Othello enters.

Ignoring Othello, the wild-eyed Montano screams, "I am hurt to th' death. He dies," and springs in fury at Cassio.

Montano cuts wildly at Cassio's chest, legs and head with insane vigor. The effects of Montano's wound are visible on his pain-wracked face.

Cassio defends himself against Montano's onslaught and finally is able to bind Montano's rapier and dagger with his own two weapons. As the combatants are locked together in this struggle, Othello steps in and physically parts the combatants, sending them reeling to opposite sides of the stage, as he bellows,

OTHELLO.
He that stirs next to carve for his own rage
Holds his soul light; he dies upon his motion.

Montano vs. Cassio Choreography

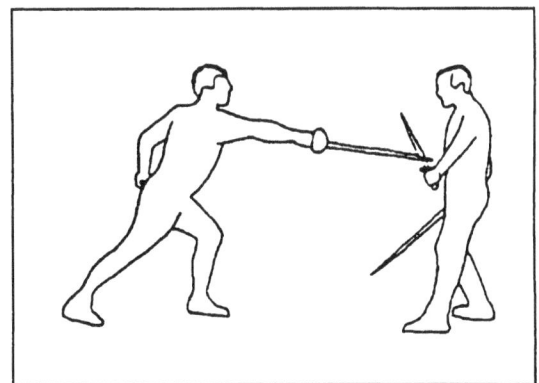

Fig. 338 Montano (left): close distance, left foot forward, rapier thrust to left wrist. Montano: pass backward onto right foot, dagger parry three.

Fig. 339 Cassio (right): pass forward onto right foot, rapier cut right knee. Montano: leap backwards avoidance.

Fig. 340 Cassio (right): leap forward, right foot forward, right side molinello, rapier cut head. Montano: stationary, cross parry five.

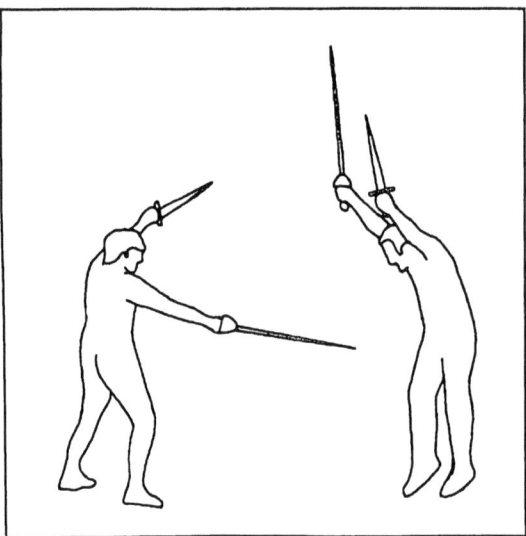

Fig. 341 Montano (left): stationary, stomach slash in supination from outside to inside (note—fighting distance!). Cassio: leap back avoidance.

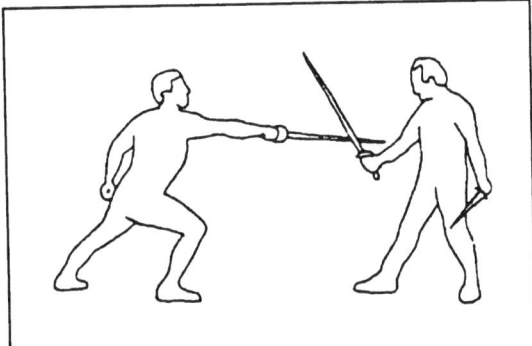

Fig. 342 Montano (left): close distance, lunge forward onto right foot, rapier thrust center chest (note—fighting distance!). Cassio: stationary, rapier parry three.

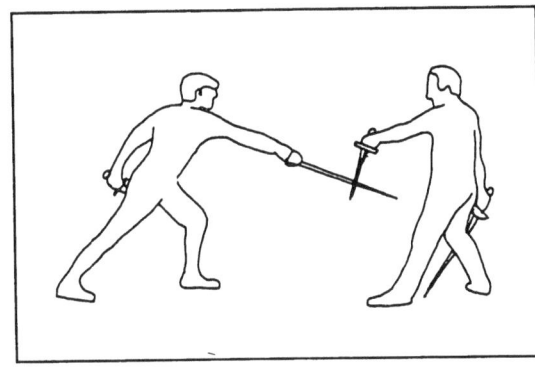

Fig. 343 Montano (left): pass forward onto left foot, rapier thrust right knee. Cassio: pass back onto right foot, dagger parry seven.

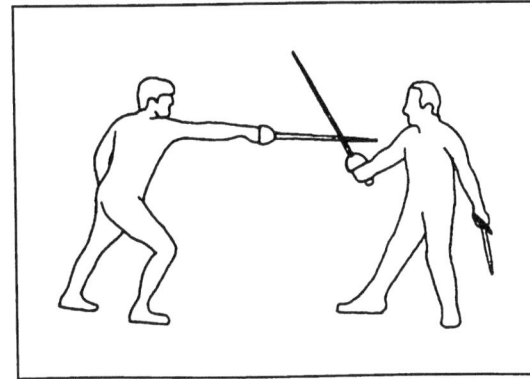

Fig. 344 Montano (left): pass forward onto right foot, rapier thrust center chest (note—fighting distance!). Cassio: pass back onto left foot, rapier parry three.

196 THE SWORDS OF SHAKESPEARE

Fig. 345 Montano (left): stationary, rapier slash in pronation from inside to outside at level of Cassio's ankle (caution—fighting distance!). Cassio: vault avoidance.

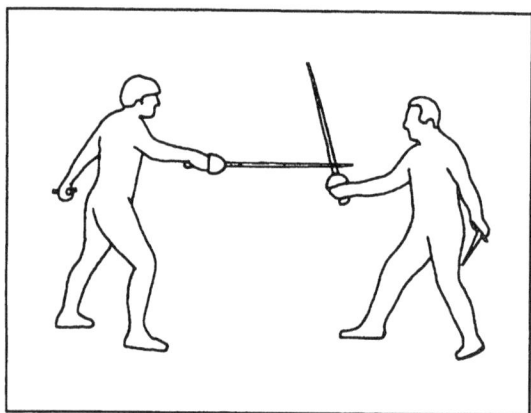

Fig. 346 Montano (left): right foot forward, thrust center chest. Cassio: right foot forward, rapier parry three.

Fig. 347 Cassio (right): lift Montano's sword up overhead, pass forward onto left foot, upward diagonal cut to Montano's right armpit (note—control force of contact), lift blade from body contact and withdraw blade to low left side. Montano: stationary, react to wound, following blade withdrawal react backward two steps.

OTHELLO

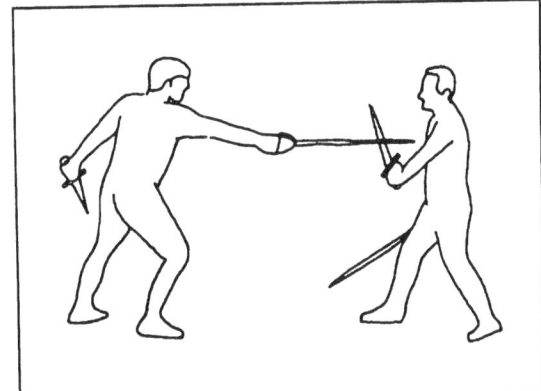

Fig. 348 Montano (left): close distance, right foot forward, rapier cut left chest. Cassio: pass back onto left foot, dagger parry three.

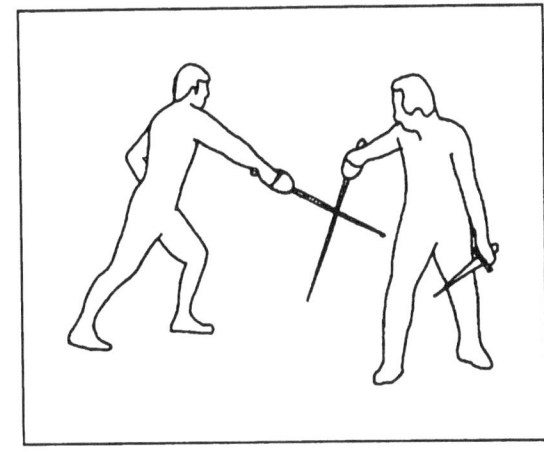

Fig. 349 Montano (left): pass diagonally forward to the left side onto the left foot, rapier cut right knee. Cassio: advance diagonally to the left side with the right foot leading, rapier parry two.

Fig. 350 Montano (left): pass forward toward Cassio onto the right foot, rapier cut head. Cassio: pass forward onto left foot and pivot to face Montano, dagger parry five.

Fig. 351 Montano (left): stationary, maintain rapier blade contact, dagger thrust to right hip. Cassio: stationary, maintain dagger parry five, rapier parry two. Cassio and Montano are locked in a corp a corps when Othello intervenes to part them.

KING LEAR

O untimely death! Death!

Cornwall and Regan vs. Servant

A more macabre scene for a duel cannot be imagined than this in Act V, Scene vii. It is the dining hall within the Earl of Gloucester's castle. The gentle white-haired Gloucester is tied to a chair and one of his eyes has just been gouged out by the villainous Duke of Cornwall. Regan, Cornwall's wife (daughter to Lear), has been encouraging the horrible torture.

Several of Cornwall's servants who have assisted in tying up the vulnerable Gloucester, remain to witness the barbarous blinding. One of the servants can bear the cruelty no longer and he rebels against his lord. His mutiny is all the more courageous when one considers the bonds of loyalty forged between lord and vassal in the sixteenth century.

The brave servant pays dearly for acting upon his conscience.

[1.] SERV.
Hold your hand, my lord!
I have serv'd you ever since I was a child;
But better service have I never done you
Than now to bid you hold.

REG.
How now, you dog?

[1.] SERV.
If you did wear a beard upon your chin,
I'ld shake it on this quarrel. What do you mean?

CORN.
My villain! [*Draw and fight.*]

[1.] SERV.
Nay then come on, and take the chance of anger.
[*Cornwall is wounded.*]

REG.
Give me thy sword. A peasant stand up thus?

[*She takes a sword and runs at him behind; kills him.*]

[1.] SERV.
O, I am slain! My lord, you have one eye left
To see some mischief on him. O!

[*He dies.*]

The Duke of Cornwall carries a rapier, as befits his station. The servant suggests that he has been an intimate member of the Duke's household, *I have serv'd you ever since I was a child;* and therefore would be allowed to carry a rapier as well. The personal servants of the nobility often aped the manners of their betters and sought the fashionable weapons of the day.

Cornwall cannot bear this affront to his dignity by a minion expected to remain loyal. It is essential in the politically turbulent atmosphere of the play to demand loyalty. Rebellion gone unpunished would set a dangerous precedent. Most importantly, Cornwall is mindful that Regan is watching and he would never show weakness in front of her.

Cornwall draws his rapier and lunges, thrusting at the servant's chest. The servant avoids the lunge by throwing himself to the side. He then reluctantly draws his own sword.

[1.] SERV.
Nay then come on, and take the chance of anger.

The Duke lunges again, thrusting at the servant's stomach. With a circular parry, the servant deflects the Duke's blade and returns a thrust at Cornwall's leading knee. The servant hopes to merely wound or disarm his master.

Cornwall deflects the thrust and passing forward, launches a series of attacks at the servant's chest, stomach and legs. The servant desperately parries the skillful attacks while retreating in a circle.

Cornwall halts the servant's retreat with a diagonal slash, which the servant narrowly avoids. Cornwall's ferocious diagonal slash, however, throws him off balance and his sword arm sweeps out to the side, exposing his chest. In an instant, without premeditation, the servant lunges forward and thrusts through Cornwall's chest. Cornwall groans and writhing in pain drops his sword to the floor.

The servant sheathes his own sword and immediately crosses to Gloucester to untie the suffering old man. Regan rushes to Cornwall and picks up his sword.

REG.
Give me thy sword. A peasant stand up thus?

Regan runs up to the servant, whose back is turned while attempting to untie Gloucester. She stabs the luckless servant though the back. The servant clutches at the chair and slides to the floor at Gloucester's feet. His final utterance, before death puts an end to his heroic gesture, is a plea for justice.

Cornwall and Regan vs. Servant Choreography

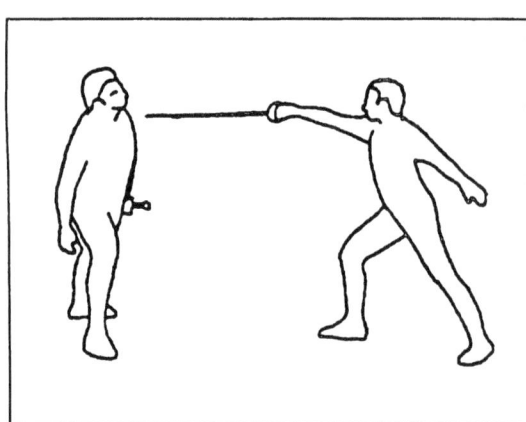

Fig. 352 Cornwall (right): close distance, lunge forward onto right foot, thrust to left outside of servant's body outline. Servant: avoid to right side with right foot leading.

KING LEAR   201

Fig. 353 Servant (left): "Nay then come on, and take the chance of anger," draw sword. Cornwall: close distance, lunge forward onto right foot, thrust left chest. Servant: stationary, circle parry four.

Fig. 354 Servant (right): advance, thrust right knee. Cornwall: pass back onto right foot, parry two.

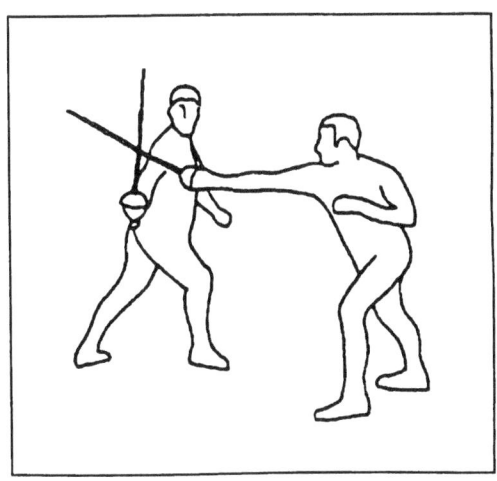

Fig. 355 Cornwall (right): pass to left side onto left foot, thrust in supination to right chest. Servant: pass to left side onto right foot, parry three.

Fig. 356 Cornwall (right): pass and lunge to left side onto right foot, thrust to left knee. Servant: pass to left side onto left foot, parry one.

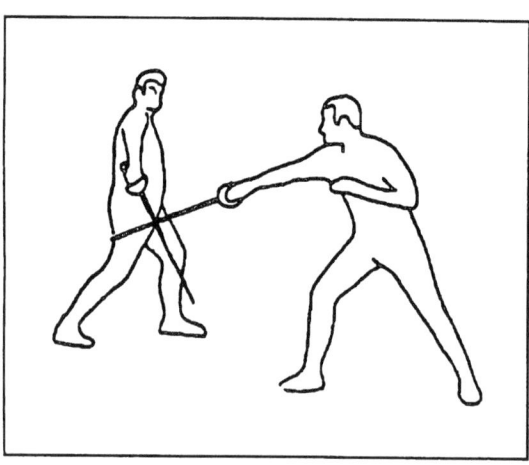

Fig. 357 Cornwall (right): advance to left side, right foot leading, cut right knee. Servant: advance to left side onto left foot, parry two.

Fig. 358 Cornwall (right): stationary, diagonal slash from high left to low right toward the left outside of servant's body out line. Servant: stationary, lean torso over right knee avoidance.

Fig. 359 Servant (left): pass forward into lunge onto right foot, thrust in pronation to left of Cornwall's body outline at chest level, contact left flank with false edge (note—hide blade contact from audience). Cornwall: stationary, react to chest wound, drop rapier. Servant: sheath rapier, cross to Gloucester. Regan: pick up Cornwall's rapier, cross to servant, right foot forward, thrust to the right of servant's body outline (note—hide thrust from audience).

Kent vs. Edmund

With a wonderful, characteristic, quicksilver shift of mood, Shakespeare turns the following comic chase scene into a fight for life.

The Earl of Kent is one of those robust and noble characters which Shakespeare's forthright English audiences must have loved! In the beginning of the play, Lear threatens Kent's life for opposing him when Lear turns against his loving daughter, Cordelia. Kent responds to the threat by saying, "*My life I never held but as [a] pawn To wage against thine enemies.*"

In the following scene, Kent is vigorously renewing an acquaintance with that sniveling coward, Oswald. Kent, recognizing Oswald as a traitor to Lear, is determined to teach Oswald a lesson he will never forget, or to kill him in the process. What ensues is a slapstick beating of Oswald. (Since the altercation with Oswald includes no swordfighting, choreography for that portion of the scene has not been included.)

The mood abruptly shifts when the bastard, Edmund, interrupts the lesson.

KENT.
What a brazen-fac'd varlet art thou, to deny
Thou knowest me? Is it two days since I tripp'd up thy
heels, and beat thee before the King?
Draw, you rogue, for though it be night, yet the moon shines;

[*Drawing his sword*]

I'll make a sop o' th' moonshine of you, you whoreson cullionly barber-monger, draw!

Osw.
Away, I have nothing to do with thee.

KENT.
Draw, you rascal! You come with letters
against the King, and take Vanity the puppet's part
against the royalty of her father. Draw, you rogue, or
I'll so carbonado your shanks! Draw, you rascal!
Come your ways.

Osw.
Help ho! murther, help!

KENT.
Strike, you slave! Stand, rogue, stand, you neat slave! Strike! [*Beating him.*]

Osw.
Help ho! murther, murther!

Enter Bastard [Edmund, *with his rapier drawn*].

EDM.
How now, what's the matter? Part!

KENT.
With you, goodman boy, [and] you please!
Come, I'll flesh ye, come on, young master.

[*Enter*] Cornwall, Regan, Gloucester, Servants.

GLOU.
Weapons? arms? What's the matter here?

CORN.
Keep peace, upon your lives!
He dies that strikes again. What is the matter?

Edmund, the bastard ("bastard" in the sense of "illegitimate"), is accustomed to violence. He has a violent nature and appears willing to stop at nothing in order to further his ends. For example, in Act II, Scene i, Edmund wounds his own arm to create a favorable impression! Kent is facing a dangerous opponent.

As befitting his station, Edmund carries a rapier. Kent is fighting with an English broadsword of the early seventeenth century. While his social status is above the rank and file, the Earl of Kent behaves like an honest soldier and could very well favor a military weapon, such as the broadsword. In addition, Kent is disguised as a common man (Caius by name) and a broadsword would fit the disguise.

Although there is no stage direction indicating that Edmund and Kent actually fight, the lines spoken by Cornwall strongly indicate that he is interrupting a duel in progress. Besides, a fight between Edmund and Kent (aborted by the entrances of Cornwall, Regan and Gloucester), seems inevitable.

Kent, in a stubborn mood, firmly stands his ground and invites Edmund to attack. Edmund obliges with a fearless, full frontal assault.

Edmund, passing forward, thrusts at Kent's chest and then at his thigh. Kent strongly parries both thrusts as he gives ground.

Following the second parry, Kent returns a powerful thrust at Edmund's chest. Edmund skillfully parries the thrust. The noise of battle begins to rouse the castle (ostensibly this fight takes place at night).

[*Enter*] Cornwall, Regan, Gloucester, Servants.

GLOU.
Weapons? arms? What's the matter here?

Edmund then binds Kent's sword down and to the side, following up this deflecting tactic with a lunge and thrust at Kent's exposed chest.

Leaping back, Kent parries the chest thrust. He then shouts and begins an assault of his own, running directly at Edward and delivering a volley of powerful cuts at Edmund's shoulders and head. Edmund scrambles backwards as he defends himself against Kent's vigorous attack.

Edmund manages to halt Kent's assault by fending off Kent's final head cut and quickly stepping in to grasp Kent's sword arm with his left hand. Kent immediately responds by grasping Edmund's sword arm.

The two warriors struggle for a moment in a corps a corps, before Kent's superior strength dominates and he flings Edmund aside. Between them steps the furious Duke of Cornwall.

CORN.
Keep peace, upon your lives!
He dies that strikes again.

Kent vs. Edmund Choreography

Fig. 360 Edmund (right): close distance, lunge forward onto right foot, thrust left chest. Kent: stationary, parry four.

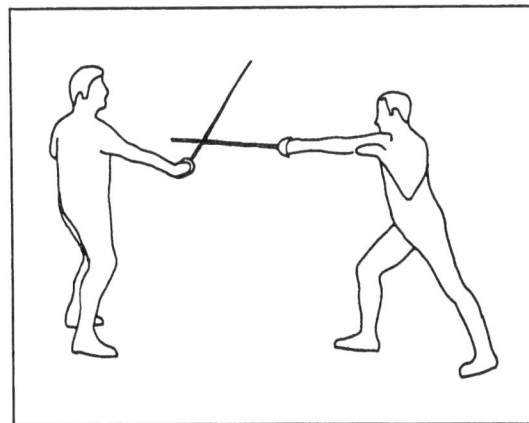

Fig. 361 Edmund (right): pass forward into lunge onto left foot, thrust right knee. Kent: pass back onto right foot, parry two.

Fig. 362 Kent (left): pass forward, right foot leading, thrust left chest. Edmund: pass back onto left foot, parry four.

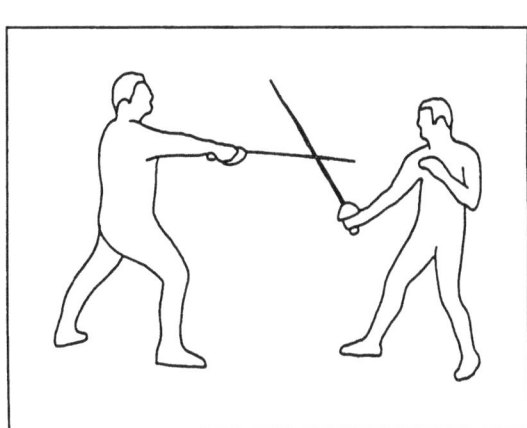

206　THE SWORDS OF SHAKESPEARE

Fig. 363 Edmund (right): stationary, croisé to Kent's low right side.

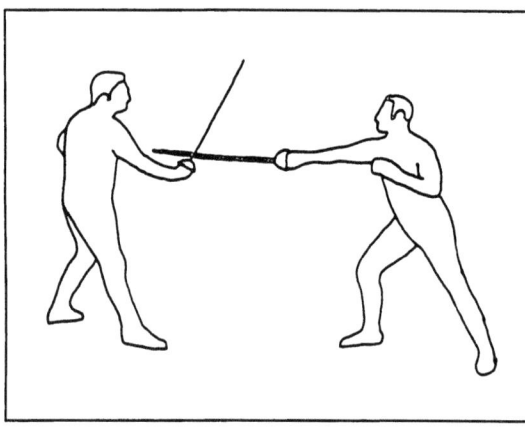

Fig. 364 Edmund (right): lunge forward onto right foot, thrust left chest. Kent: leap backwards, parry four.

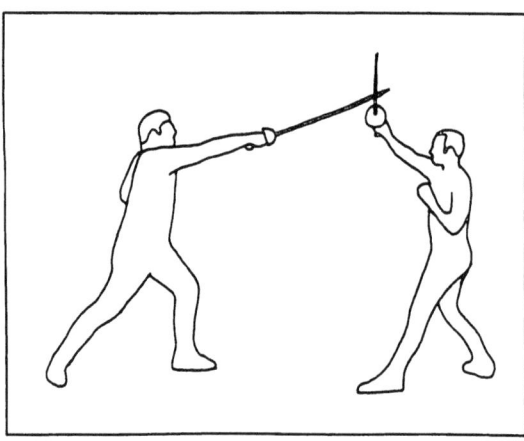

Fig. 365 Kent (left): pass forward onto left, cut right shoulder. Edmund: pass back onto right foot, parry high three.

Fig. 366 Kent (left): pass forward onto right foot, cut head. Edmund: pass back onto left foot, parry five.

Fig. 367 Edmund (right): maintain parry five, pass forward onto left foot, grab right wrist with left hand. Kent: stationary, grasp right wrist with left hand. Kent grasps Edmund's right wrist and as they struggle in a corps a corps, Kent throws Edmund backwards. Cornwall steps in between combatants and stops fight.

Edgar vs. Oswald

The ensuing tragi-comic scene of combat in *King Lear* opens with poor, blind Gloucester being lead by his loving son, Edgar. Edgar has disguised himself as a peasant (he uses a delightful Somerset dialect) to avoid detection by the minions of Lear's evil daughters.

They are overtaken by that miscreant Oswald, Goneril's steward. Oswald is the very worst kind of sycophant. He is an opportunistic, amoral villain—the kind of petty sneak that thrives in Lear's kingdom-gone-mad. The audience will not likely shed many tears over Oswald's deserved demise.

Enter Steward [Oswald]

Osw.
A proclaim'd prize! Most happy!
That eyeless head of thine was first fram'd
    flesh

To raise my fortunes. Thou old unhappy traitor,
Briefly thyself remember; the sword is out
That must destroy thee.

GLOU.
Now let thy friendly hand
Put strength enough to't. [*Edgar interposes.*]

OSW.
Wherefore, bold peasant, [Durst] thou support a publish'd traitor?
Hence, Lest that th' infection of his fortune take
Like hold on thee. Let go his arm.

EDG.
Chill not let go, zir, without vurther [cagion].

OSW.
Let go, slave, or thou di'st!

EDG.
Good gentleman, go your gait, and let poor voke pass. And chud ha' been zwagger'd out of my life, 'twould not ha' bin zo long as 'tis by a vortnight. Nay, or Ice try whither your costard or my ballow be the harder. Chill be plain with you.

OSW.
Out, dunghill! [*They fight.*]

EDG.
Chill pick your teeth, zir. Come, no matter vor your foins.

OSW.
Slave, thou hast slain me.
Villain, take my purse:
If ever thou wilt thrive, bury my body,
And give the letters which thou find'st about me
To Edmund Earl of Gloucester; seek him out
Upon the English Party. O untimely death!
Death!

[*He dies.*]

To complete his disguise, Edgar is armed only with a "ballow" or "cudgel"—a stout stick about as long as a sword; often with a woven basket attached to protect the hand. The cudgel was used for sword practice. However, in this instance a stout walking stick, without a basket hilt, was likely intended by Shakespeare. A walking stick the length of a cudgel would be more consistent with Edgar's disguise.

Oswald is not a soldier, but a steward, a manager of Goneril's large household. Normally, Oswald would never be called upon to do battle. He is acting as a messenger bearing letters from Goneril and Regan to Edmund. He wears no armor, nor helmet. He carries the courtly rapier.

In spite of the cudgel being a poor defense against a rapier, the scales are tipped in Edgar's favor, because Edgar is a skilled warrior. In addition, Oswald is overly confident and enraged by this lowly peasant. Oswald expects to dispatch the arrogant dolt with ease.

Anger is the worst defense in battle, and Oswald is seething with it as he rushes towards Edgar. Oswald clumsily slashes at Edgar's head, which Edgar easily ducks.

Edgar, in a low crouch, steps to the side and strikes Oswald on the back of the thigh. Oswald reacts in pain and turns to face the amused Edgar.

EDG.
Chill pick your teeth, zir.

Oswald lifts his blade high and slashes diagonally at shoulders. Edgar dodges the slash.

Oswald lunges and thrusts at Edgar's stomach. With his cudgel, Edgar beats the thrust off to the left. Stepping forward, Edgar strikes Oswald in the pit of the stomach with the tip of the cudgel. The air is knocked out of Oswald. He staggers back a few paces and kneels to catch his breath, glaring at Edgar.

EDG.
Come, no matter vor your foins.

KING LEAR

This insolent arrogance, not to mention the ignominious beating he is receiving from this peasant, is too much for Oswald's pride. Rising and running forward, Oswald slashes at Edgar's stomach, which Edgar avoids by leaping backward. Oswald continues to press forward with another stomach slash, which Edgar evades as before.

Oswald passes forward and slashes at Edgar's legs. Edgar leaps up into the air, avoiding the leg slash.

Oswald passes forward and thrusts at Edgar's chest. Edgar steps to the side, and driving his cudgel down upon Oswald's extended blade, succeeds in driving the tip of Oswald's sword into the ground.

Discarding his cudgel and quickly stepping forward, Edgar, with his left hand, grasps Oswald's sword hilt, and with the back of his right fist, strikes Oswald in the face.

Oswald releases his grip upon his sword and staggers backward from the force of the blow. With grim design, Edgar grasps the hilt of Oswald's rapier. All humor has left Edgar's face as he steps forward and drives the point of the sword through Oswald's body. For a long moment, the shock and horror of violence are etched in a painful tableau.

Edgar withdraws the sword from Oswald's body, and with a pitiable moan, Edgar sinks to the ground.

Osw.
Slave, thou hast slain me.

Edgar vs. Oswald Choreography

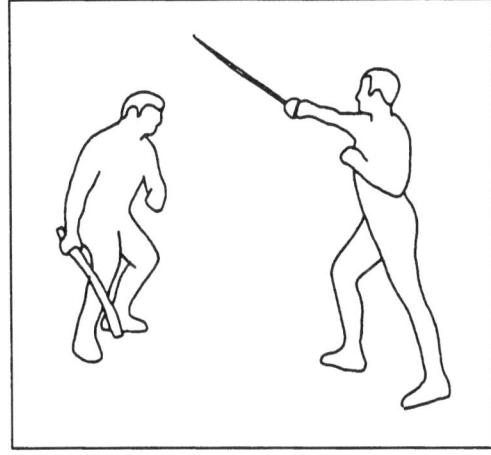

Fig. 368 Oswald (right): close distance, right foot forward, diagonal slash in pronation from high inside to low outside above Edgar's head. Edgar: stationary, duck head slash.

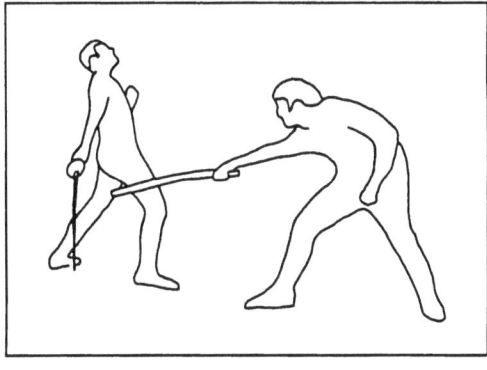

Fig. 369 Edgar (right): diagonal advance to left side, right foot leading, strike rear of right thigh (note — control force of contact), "Chill pick your teeth, zir." Oswald: react in pain.

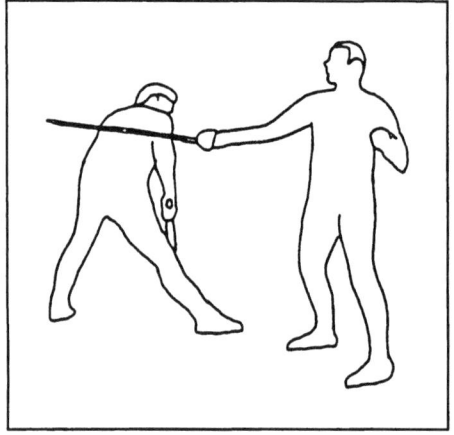

Fig. 370 Oswald (right): stationary, diagonal slash in supination from high outside to low inside above Edgar's head. Edgar: stationary, lean torso over left knee avoidance.

Fig. 371 Oswald (right): lunge forward onto right foot, thrust left chest. Edgar: stationary, parry four.

Fig. 372 Edgar (left): pass forward onto left foot, strike center stomach (note—no body contact! Allow vocal reaction to support illusion), "Come, no matter vor your foins." Oswald: kneel on both knees for reaction.

Fig. 373 Oswald (right): rise, run at Edgar, right foot forward, slash in supination from outside to inside at level of Edgar's stomach (caution—accurate fighting distance!). Edgar: leap back avoidance.

Fig. 374 Oswald (right): pass forward onto left foot, slash in pronation from inside to outside at level at Edgar's stomach. Edgar: leap back avoidance.

Fig. 375 Oswald (right): pass forward onto right foot, slash in supination from low outside to low inside at level of Edgar's ankle. Edgar: vault ankle slash.

Fig. 376 Oswald (right): pass forward onto left foot, thrust to right outside of Edgar's body outline at level of hip. Edgar: stationary, lean torso over left knee avoidance.

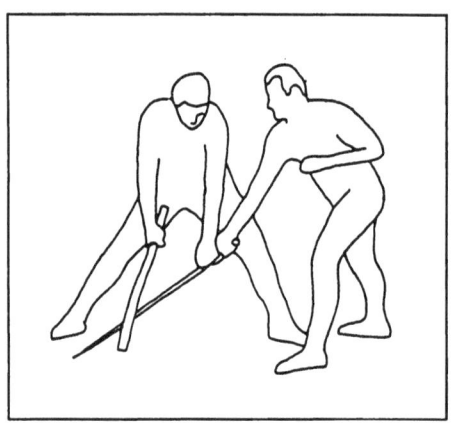

Fig. 377 Edgar (left): croisé Oswald's rapier to ground on his low outside.

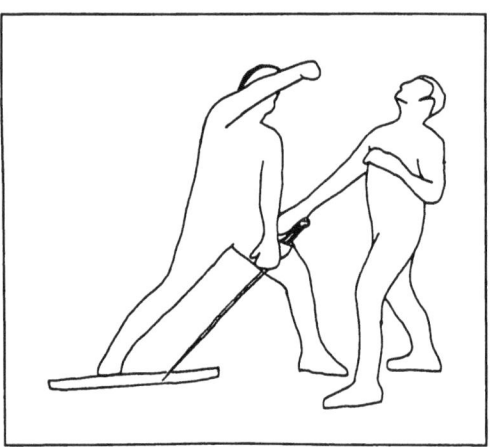

Fig. 378 Edgar (left): pass forward onto left foot, grasp Oswald's rapier hilt with left hand in pronation. Drop cudgel, backhand punch to face with right hand. Oswald: release rapier, react backwards three steps.

KING LEAR

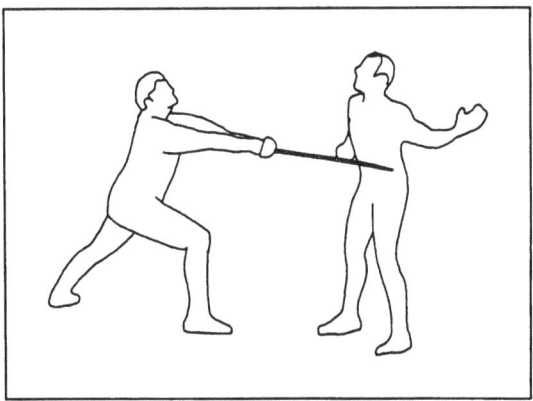

Fig. 379 Edgar (left): close distance, right foot forward, change rapier to right hand, thrust in pronation to left side of Oswald's body outline and contact left side with false edge (note—hide contact from audience). Oswald: stationary, react to wound. Edgar: lift rapier from left flank and withdraw rapier to low outside. Oswald: following rapier withdrawal sink to ground.

Edgar vs. Edmund

The closing duel between Edgar, the son of the Earl of Gloucester, and Edgar's half-brother, the bastard Edmund, is perhaps the most formally structured of all of Shakespeare's staged duels. It is obvious from the entrance of the herald in Act V, Scene iii, that a ritualized battle of champions will be witnessed.

The Duke of Albany begins this portion of the fateful encounter between the virtuous Edgar and the traitorous Edmund by summoning the herald.

ALB.
Come hither, herald, Let the trumpet sound,
And read out this.

[Capt. sound, trumpet] A trumpet sounds.

HER. [READS]
"If any man of quality or degree within the lists of the army will maintain upon Edmund, supposed Earl of Gloucester, that he is a manifold traitor, let him appear by the third sound of the trumpet. He is bold in his defense."

[Edm. Sound!] First trumpet.

HER.
Again Second trumpet.

HER.
Again! Third trumpet.
Trumpet answers within.

Enter Edgar [at the third sound,] armed, [A trumpet before him].

ALB.
Ask him his purposes, why he appears
Upon this call o' th' trumpet.

HER.
What are you?
Your name, your quality? and why you answer
This present summons?

EDG.
Know, my name is lost,
By treason's tooth bare-gnawn and canker-
    bit,
Yet am I noble as the adversary
I come to cope.

ALB.
Which is that adversary?

EDG.
What's he that speaks for Edmund Earl of
    Gloucester?

EDM.
Himself; what say'st thou to him?

EDG.
Draw thy sword,
That if my speech offend a noble heart,
Thy arm may do thee justice; here is mine:
Behold, it is my privilege,
The privilege of mine honors,
My oath, and my profession. I protest,
Maugre thy strength, place, youth, and emi-
    nence,

[Despite] thy victor-sword and fire-new eminence,
Thy valor and thy heart, thou art a traitor;
False to thy gods, thy brother, and thy father,
Conspirant 'gainst this high illustrious prince,
And from th' extremest upward of thy head
To the descent and dust below thy foot,
A most toad-spotted traitor. Say thou "No,"
This sword, this arm, and my best spirits are bent
To prove upon thy heart, whereto I speak,
Thou liest.

EDM.
In wisdom I should ask thy name,
But since thy outside looks so fair and warlike,
And that thy tongue some say of breeding breathes,
What safe and nicely I might well delay
By rule of knighthood, I disdain and spurn.
Back do I toss these treasons to thy head,
With the hell-hated lie o'erwhelm thy heart,
Which for they yet glance by, and scarcely bruise,
This sword of mine shall give them instant way
Where they shall rest for ever. Trumpets, speak!

Alarms. [They fight, Edmund falls.]

ALB.
Save him, save him.

GON.
This is practice, Gloucester.
By th' law of war thou wast not bound to answer,
An unknown opposite. Thou art not vanquish'd,
but cozen's and beguiled.

The rules governing an appeal of treason through trial by combat, such as presented impromptu on the field of battle between Edmund and Edgar, were established by Thomas of Woodstock, sixth son of Edward III, in 1385. The weapons to be used in trial by combat were specified as being the battle axe, the long sword, the short sword, the dagger and the shield.

An area, called the "lists," was set apart and surrounded by ropes or a wooden fence. Guards were placed strategically around the area to prevent any interference. In fact it was often announced prior to a trial by combatant, that anyone entering the "lists" would be immediately punished by death! The guards traditionally carried white staffs to discourage intruders. According to the Woodstock Code, special canopied seating arrangements were also built for the many officials who were required to witness the event.

Since an appeal of treason through a trial of combat was a privilege generally reserved for the aristocracy, Goneril is correct when she belatedly complains to Edmund that he was not required by law to, "Answer an unknown opposite." Assuming that Edgar's face is covered by a war helmet of some sort, it might be plausible that Edmund recognized his half-brother's voice and therefore Edmund chose to ignore his right to deny a trial by combat in order to settle once and for all the threat posed by a living brother and rightful heir.

When Edmund accepts Edgar's challenge, the atmosphere is suddenly charged with expectation. The formal ritual of a trial by combat is immediately begun. Marching to the four corners of the battle ground, four guards, carrying white battle staves, rigidly establish the area of the "lists." Attendants rush to help Edmund don his war helmet.

Of the weapons included as appropriate by Thomas of Woodstock for this occasion, the single hand short sword and shield are selected. Both combatants are in full body armor and they each carry a large dagger at their side called a misericorde, designed to pierce between the joints of body armour. They have been engaged in mortal combat upon the field of battle all that day. Their armor is soiled and blood stained. Fierce and warlike, they are both trained soldiers versed in the arts of war since boyhood. In his challenge to Edmund, Edgar speaks of his right to bear a sword, a right preserved for nobleman, and that the use of arms is his "profession."

here is mine:
Behold, it is my privilege,
The privilege of mine honors,
My oath, and my profession.

Both champions enter the lists and kneel for a short prayer, for it was believed that trial by combat was a judgment by God of guilt or innocence. Edmund finishes his prayer more quickly than Edgar and then treacherously attacks Edgar while he is kneeling! There is an audible gasp from the assembled witnesses at this dastardly beginning to what should have been a chivalrous match.

Edgar lifts his shield above his head just in time to protect himself from Edmund's precipitous attack and he retorts by slashing at Edmund's leading leg. Edmund throws his weight back, drawing back his leading leg and narrowly avoiding Edgar's slash. Edgar rises from his knee, and the two combatants warily circle each other.

Edmund swings his sword above his head to gain momentum and slashes at Edgar's head. Edgar ducks the powerful blow and simultaneously delivers a swordcut at Edmund's exposed lower leg, which Edmund protects with his shield. Edgar then follows with an attack above Edmund's shield, which Edmund parries with his sword. Edgar renews his attack with a head cut, and Edmund successfully parries the crushing downward blow with his shield and quickly retreats, circling Edgar and looking for an opening in his defenses.

Edmund again wildly loops his sword above his head to gain force for a mighty cut at Edgar's flank, which Edgar parries with his sword. Immediately, Edmund steps into close distance and delivers a head cut. Edgar stands his ground and again parries with his sword. Without removing his sword, Edmund crashes his shield against Edgar's shielded flank and for a few moments the combatants are locked in a struggle of strength.

Breathing heavily, Edgar manages to push Edmund backwards and, taking advantage of Edmund's momentary loss of balance, he drives his knee against Edmund's flank. Edmund falls heavily to the ground onto his back, his sword and shield splayed to either side of his body on his outstretched arms. Quickly tossing aside his sword, Edgar kneels upon Edmund's shield arm and also pins Edmund's sword arm to the ground. As Edmund helplessly struggles to free himself, Edgar draws his heavy dagger and pierces Edmund's armour at the vulnerable armpit joint, driving his dagger deeply into Edmund's chest.

A pitiful groan is heard behind Edmund's closed visor. Edgar then grasps Edmund's sword and tosses it aside. Edgar rips off his own helmet and raises Edmund's visor, exposing Edmund's pain-racked face. For a moment they stare into each other's eyes. Then Edgar raises his bloody dagger, with the intent of thrusting the terrible point of the weapon into Edmund's eyes, to blind him forever in death, as his own father was blinded by Edmund's treachery. Edgar pauses when Albany shouts,

"Save him, save him!"

Stepping away from the prostrate Edmund, Edgar allows Goneril, who has burst through the restraining grip of a guard, to kneel beside Edmund and gently remove his helmet.

Edgar vs. Edmund Choreography

Fig. 380 Edgar (left): stationary from kneeling position, sword slash in supination from low outside to low inside at level of Edmund's ankle. Edmund: leap back avoidance (note—draw leading leg backward on leap).

Fig. 381 Edmund (right): close distance, sword cut to head. Edgar: kneeling on left knee, shield parry five.

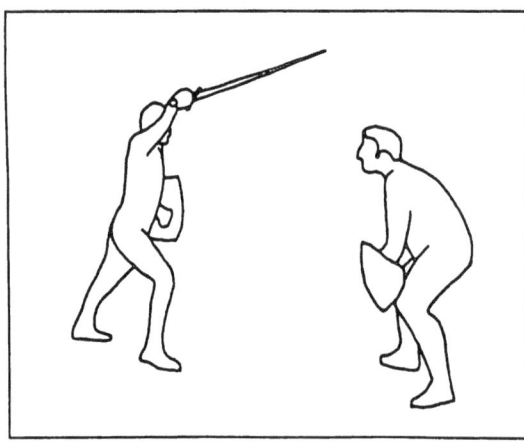

Fig. 382 Edgar and Edmund circle each other out of distance counter clockwise 180 degrees. Edmund (left): close distance, right foot forward, overhead molinello, sword slash in pronation from high inside to high outside above Edgar's head. Edgar: stationary, duck head slash.

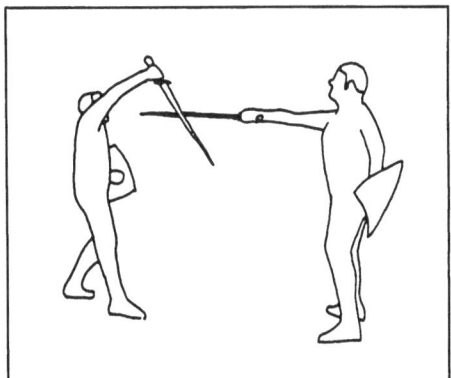

Fig. 383 Edgar (right): stationary, rise, sword cut left shoulder. Edmund: stationary, sword parry high one.

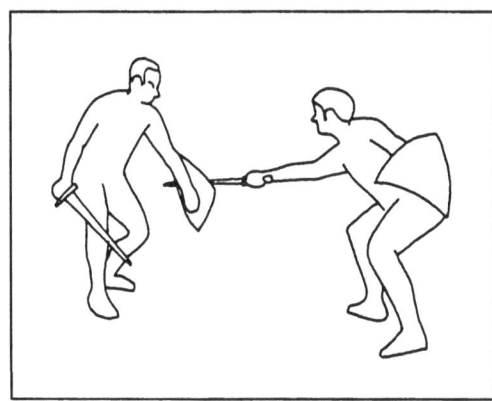

Fig. 384 Edgar (right): stationary, from crouched position, sword cut left knee. Edmund: stationary, shield parry two.

Fig. 385 Edgar (right): pass forward onto left foot, sword cut to head. Edmund: pass back onto right foot, shield parry five.

Fig. 386 Edmund (left): out of distance, circle clockwise around Edgar 360 degrees. Edgar: pivot to face Edmund. Edmund: close distance with right foot forward, overhead molinello, cut to left hip below shield. Edmund: stationary, sword parry four.

Fig. 387 Edmund (left): pass forward onto left foot, sword cut to head. Edgar: stationary, sword parry five.

Fig. 388 Edmund (left): maintain sword contact, stationary, shield strike to center chest. Edgar: stationary, shield parry center chest.

KING LEAR

Fig. 389 Edmund and Edgar struggle in a corps a corps. Edgar (right): maintain corps a corps, pass forward onto left foot. Edmund: maintain corps a corps, pass back onto right foot.

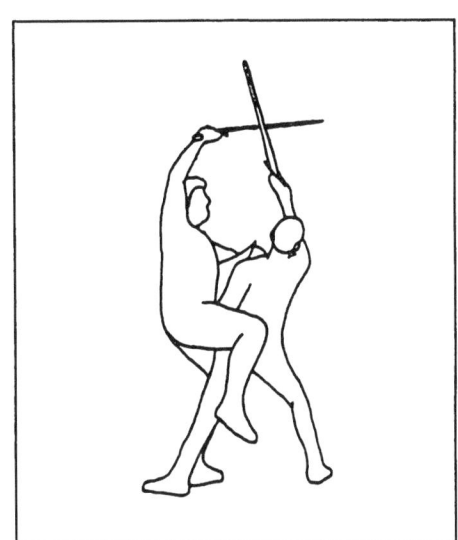

Fig. 390 Edgar (left): maintain corps a corps, balance on left foot, right knee blow to left flank (note— use right thigh, *not knee*, for body contact). Edmund: backfall, shield and sword out to each side.

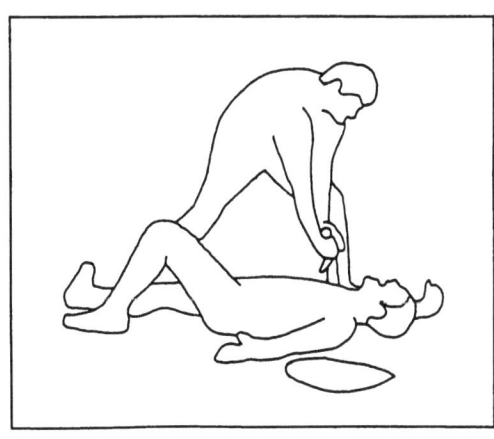

Fig. 391 Edgar (left): draw dagger with right hand, place left hand on pummel of dagger and thrust to right side of Edmund's body outline at armpit level (hide thrust from audience). Edmund: vocal reaction on wound.

MACBETH

They have tied me to a stake; I cannot fly,
But bear-like I must fight the course.

"The Scottish Play," as *Macbeth* is religiously referred to by superstitious theatre people, has always been an enormous challenge for the brave actor who has assumed the title role. Following an exhausting emotional and physical tour-de-force for over two hours, Shakespeare demands that the actor portraying Macbeth conclude the evening with several climactic battles! Little wonder that this play has contributed its fair share of accidental injuries over almost four centuries. (Supporting the myth that speaking the play's title aloud in a theatre brings bad luck!)

Macbeth vs. Young Siward

The Macbeth/Young Siward duel in Act V, Scene vii, is short and morbid. Young Siward is woefully inferior to the seasoned warrior, Macbeth. In a graphic depiction of Macbeth's cruelty, young Siward is terribly wounded several times before Macbeth contemptuously murders him.

The image which characterizes the offstage battles, prior to the tragic duel between Macbeth and young Siward, arises from the opening lines of the scene. They allude to the Elizabethan bear garden, where dogs were tossed into a ring with a chained bear for an audience's savage amusement. The bear garden would have been very familiar to Shakespeare's contemporaries.

Enter Macbeth

MACB.
They have tied me to a stake; I cannot fly,
But bear-like I must fight the course.
What's he
That was not born of woman? Such a one
I am to fear, or none.

Enter Young Siward

Y. SIW.
What is thy name?

MACB.
Thoul't be afraid to hear it.

Y. SIW.
No; though thou call'st thyself a hotter name
Then any is in hell.

MACB.
My name's Macbeth.

Y. SIW.
The devil himself could not pronounce a title
More hateful to mine ear.

MACB.
No; nor more fearful.

Y. SIW.
Thou liest, abhorred tyrant, with my sword
I'll prove the lie thou speaks't.

Fight, and Young Siward slain.

Both young Siward and Macbeth carry single hand broadswords and shields. Young Siward wears a war helmet, but Macbeth is bare headed.

Young Siward screams a battle-cry and races with naive abandon towards Macbeth. With a huge molinello, Siward gathers momentum and delivers a head cut at the "abhorred tyrant."

Macbeth protects his head with his shield and cuts at young Siward's chest. Young Siward defends his chest with his shield and strikes again at Macbeth's head.

Macbeth beats the head cut aside with his broadsword, and again cuts at young Siward's chest. Young Siward parries the chest cut with his shield.

Suddenly dropping to one knee, Macbeth sweeps his sword beneath young Siward's shield and cuts the tendons in the back of young Siward's leading leg. With a groan of pain, young Siward drops to one knee.

Rising, with a mighty sweep of his own shield, Macbeth smashes young Siward's shield out of his hand. Then with a savage downward cut, Macbeth wounds young Siward across his exposed shoulder. Writhing in pain, young Siward falls to the ground.

Weakly, lying on his back, young Siward raises his sword to defend himself. Macbeth laughs in scorn and kicks the sword out of young Siward's grasp.

Stepping in, Macbeth raises his broadsword and thrusts it down into the body of young Siward, pinning him to the earth. There is a piteous moan from the victim. Macbeth withdraws his sword and thrusts home again. This time young Siward mercifully dies.

Macbeth places his foot on young Siward's chest, and withdraws his sword. Wiping the blood from his broadsword on the body of his victim, Macbeth gloats to end this mournful scene.

Thou wast born of woman.
But swords I smile at, weapons laugh to
   scorn,
Brandish'd by man that's of woman born.

Exit

Macbeth vs. Young Siward Choreography

Fig. 392 Siward (right): close distance, right foot forward, right side molinello, cut head. Macbeth: stationary, shield parry five.

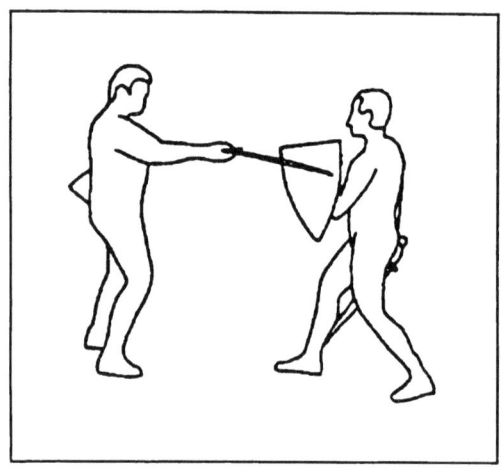

Fig. 393 Macbeth (left): stationary, cut left chest. Siward: stationary, shield parry three.

Fig. 394 Siward (right): stationary, cut head. Macbeth: stationary, beat parry high three with sword.

Fig. 395 Macbeth (left): pass forward onto left foot, cut right chest. Siward: pass back onto right foot, shield parry four.

Fig. 396 Macbeth (left): drop to right knee, cut to rear left knee and follow-through to low inside (note—control contact to muscle with flat of blade).

Fig. 397 Siward (right): following Macbeth's follow-through drop to left knee in pain reaction. Macbeth: rise, sweep inside edge of shield left to right, strike Siward's inside edge of shield for disarm. Siward: kneeling on left knee, release shield on contact for disarm (note—control release of shield to left side). Macbeth: stationary, sword cut left shoulder (note—contact left deltoid muscle with flat of blade). Siward: following blade withdrawal, fall to ground onto back.

Fig. 398 Siward (right): from prone position lift sword to parry five. Macbeth: balance on left foot, kick sword with right foot. Siward: release sword to right side. Macbeth: stationary, thrust to left outside of Siward's body outline (note—thrust tip of sword into stage floor and hide from audience). Siward: lift right arm in pain reaction. Macbeth: stationary repeat thrust to left outside of body outline. Young Siward: expire.

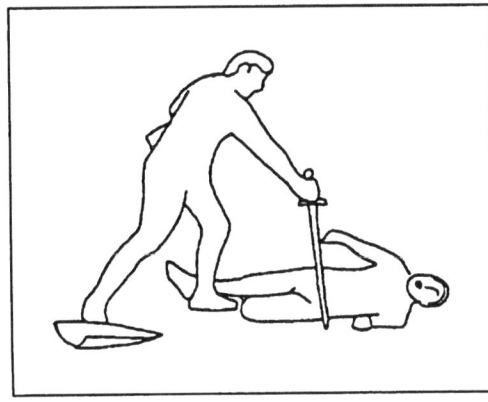

Macbeth vs. Macduff

It would appear, from the butchery of young Siward, that Macbeth is completely without conscience, certainly without mercy. However, when confronted by Macduff in Act V, Scene viii, Macbeth is reluctant to fight, because he feels something like remorse at the slaughter of Macduff's wife and children,

Of all men else I have avoided thee.
But get thee back, my soul is too much charg'd
With blood of thine already.

Macduff ignores Macbeth's warning and, seething with the desire for revenge, he attacks furiously. Macbeth repels Macduff's several charging attacks. The reason for Macbeth's apparent ease at repelling Macduff's attacks is not so much Macbeth's superiority in skill, but rather Macduff's irrational thirst for vengeance which makes him wild and incautious.

Guilt ridden, Macbeth does not take advantage of Macduff, he merely defends himself by avoiding Macduff's erratic slashes with the broadsword and parries with his sword or shield only when necessary.

After the third furious attack, Macbeth knocks Macduff to the ground and warns him,

"Thou losest labor.
As easy mayst thou the intrenchent air
With thy keen sword impress as make me bleed.
Let fall thy blade on vulnerable cress,
I bear a charmed life, which must not yield
To one of woman born."

Here the tide of battle changes dramatically with Macduff's bitter rejoinder.
"Despair thy charm,
And let the angel whom thou still hast serv'd
Tell thee, Macduff was from his mother's womb
Untimely ripp'd."

There is a pause in the fight. Macbeth perhaps drops to one knee as he realizes that he has been betrayed by the weird sisters. For a short time his will to fight leaves him, until Macduff, wishing to taunt Macbeth into continuing the fight so that he may destroy his hated enemy then and there, stings Macbeth into defiance. Macbeth, rising from the ground, heroically bellows,

"Before my body
I throw my warlike shield. Lay on, Macduff,
And damn'd be him that first cries, "Hold, enough!"

Macbeth allows Macduff to once again begin the attack, but this time Macduff is more cautious and Macbeth has become desperate. As a warrior born, Macbeth is now seen to be very dangerous and powerful and beats Macduff back.

At one point, Macbeth flings his shield at Macduff and attacks him ferociously with his broadsword alone. This is Macbeth's rash mistake, or we could argue that Macbeth is deliberately evening the odds with Macduff in a guilt-ridden hope that Macduff will win this battle and end Macbeth's cursed life!

With a huge cut to the head, which Macduff parries with his shield, Macbeth has left himself wide open. Macduff drops to one knee and cuts Macbeth across the stomach. Macbeth reels off stage with Macduff in hot pursuit. The end is inevitable and the classic entrance of Macduff with Macbeth's severed head

Macbeth vs. Macduff Choreography

quickly follows to end the play.

Fig. 399 Macduff (left): close distance, right foot forward, cut left shoulder. Macbeth: stationary, beat parry high three with shield.

Fig. 400 Macduff (right): circle Macbeth clockwise out of distance 90 degrees, close distance, sword cut right shoulder. Macbeth: pivot to face Macduff, stationary, sword parry high three.

Fig. 401 Macbeth (left): stationary, sword bind to Macduff's low right side. Macduff: circle, out of distance, 90 degrees clockwise around Macbeth.

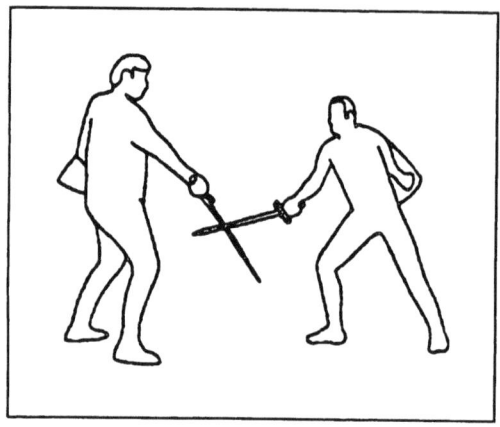

Fig. 402 Macduff (left): close distance, sword thrust to center groin (note—accurate fighting distance!). Macbeth: stationary, counter cut sword parry two.

Fig. 403 Macbeth (left): stationary, shield strike to right deltoid. Macduff: backfall reaction.

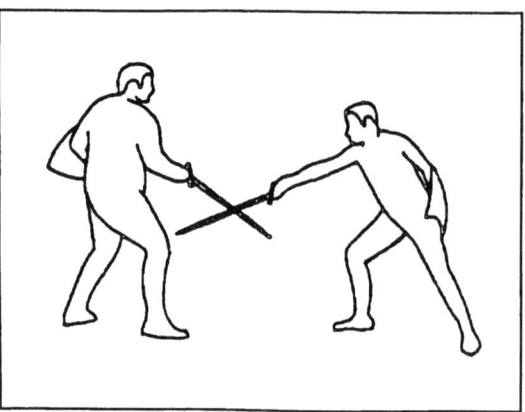

Fig. 404 Macduff (right): close distance, pass to right side, right foot leading, sword thrust to right knee. Macbeth: stationary, beat parry seven with sword.

MACBETH 227

Fig. 405 Macbeth (left): pass forward onto left foot, left side molinello, sword cut to head. Macduff: pass back onto right foot, sword parry five.

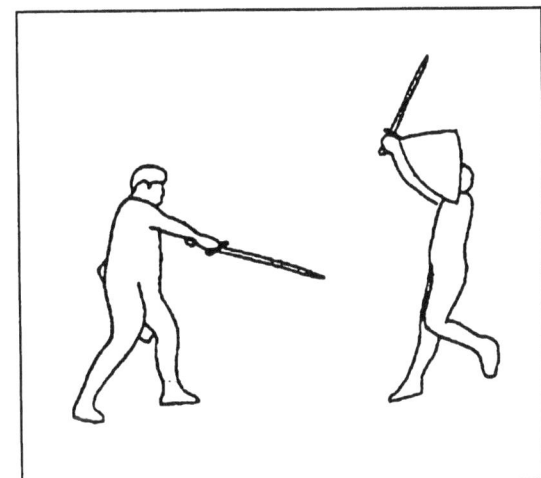

Fig. 406 Macbeth (left): stationary, sword slash in pronation from left to right at level of Macduff's stomach (caution—fighting distance!). Macduff: leap back avoidance.

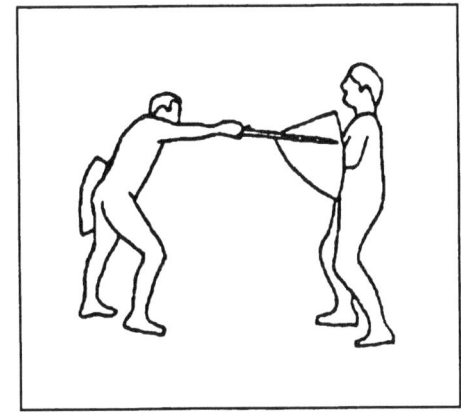

Fig. 407 Macduff (left): circle Macbeth 90 degrees counter clockwise around Macbeth, advance, right foot leading, sword thrust to left chest. Macbeth: pivot to face Macduff, stationary, beat parry three with shield.

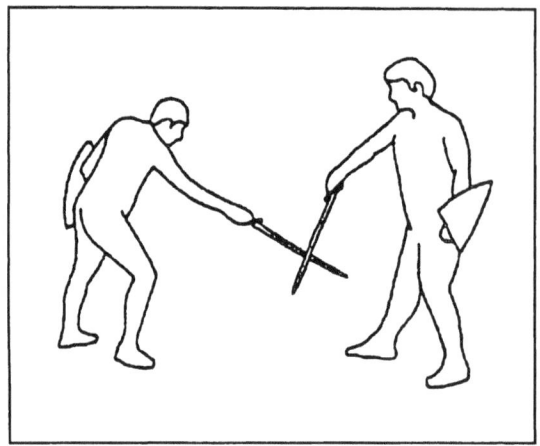

Fig. 408 Macduff (left): stationary, sword cut to inside right knee. Macbeth: stationary, circle parry two with sword.

Fig. 409 Macbeth (right): stationary, throw shield left to right above Macduff's head. Macduff: stationary, duck shield.

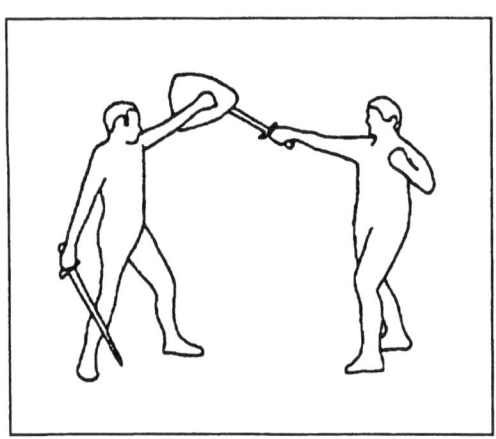

Fig. 410 Macbeth (right): pass forward onto left foot, right side molinello, sword cut to head. Macduff: pass back onto right foot, shield parry five.

Fig. 411 Macduff (right): pass forward onto right foot, sword slash (wound) in supination from right to left at Macbeth's stomach level below shield (note—fighting distance!). Macbeth: pass back onto left foot and attempt right shoulder cut (stop sword momentum immediately upon feeling sword contact on stomach), vocal reaction to stomach wound. Macbeth staggers off stage with Macduff in pursuit.

CORIOLANUS

...for thy revenge wrench up thy power to th' highest.

Coriolanus vs. Aufidius

Caius Martius Coriolanus could be the most disagreeable of all of Shakespeare's "heroes." He is a fierce warrior whose heroic passions are offensive in times of peace. He is brash, unreasonable, contemptuous of any weakness in others and immune to compromise. On the other hand, what a glorious warrior he is!

In a pivotal scene, Shakespeare depicts Coriolanus single-handedly entering a hostile city in hot pursuit of his enemies' army. The defenders' city gates close upon Coriolanus, trapping him behind enemy lines, "To answer all the city." Coriolanus' soldiers fear to follow and think him dead. Titus Lartius, a fellow Roman general who also believes that Coriolanus has died behind the enemy's gates, delivers this revealing eulogy:

...Thou wast a soldier
Even to [Cato's] wish, not fierce and terrible
Only in strokes, but, with thy grim looks and
The thunder-like percussion of thy sounds,
Thou mad'st thine enemies shake, as if the world
Were feverous and did tremble.

Suddenly the gates burst open!

Enter Martius *bleeding, assaulted by the enemy.*

[1.] SOLD.
Look, Sir.

LART.
O, 'tis Martius!
Let's fetch him off, or make remain alike.

They fight, and all enter the city.

Balancing the dramatic scale is Tullus Aufidius, Coriolanus' arch-enemy. Aufidius is a general of a rival city-state and sworn to destroy Coriolanus. Aufidius is not able to best Coriolanus on the battlefield, but he has other, craftier means of wreaking vengeance on his nemesis. Aufidius encapsulates his relationship with Coriolanus in Act I, Scene x, lines 7–16, and sets the tone for the entire action of the play that follows:

...Five times, Martius,
I have fought with thee; so often hast thou beat me;
And wouldst do so, I think, should we encounter
As often as we eat. By th' elements,
If e'er again I meet him beard to beard,
He's mine, or I am his. Mine emulation
Hath not the honor in't it had; for where
I thought to crush him in an equal force,
True sword to sword, I'll potch at him some way,
Or wrath or craft may get him.

Here then in Act I, Scene viii, upon the field of battle is the martial encounter between these sworn enemies, or rather the encounter that Shakespeare allows us to witness. In this duel, Aufidius has yet to be defeated "five times" and he remains committed to meeting Coriolanus, "True sword to sword." Around them the Roman and Volscian Armies wage war, but Coriolanus and Aufidius are completely intent upon their private vendetta.

Alarum as in battle. Enter Martius and Aufidius at several doors.

MAR.
I'll fight with none but thee, for I do hate thee
Worse than a promise-breaker.

AUF.
We hate alike:
Not Afric owns a serpent I abhor
More than thy fame and envy. Fix thy foot.

MAR.
Let the first budger die the other's slave,
And the gods doom him after!

AUF.
If I fly, Martius,
Hollow me like a hare.

MAR.
Within these three hours, Tullus,
Alone I fought in your Corioles walls,
And made what work I pleas'd. 'Tis not my blood
Wherein thou seest me mask'd; for thy revenge
Wrench up thy power to th' highest.

AUF.
Wert thou the Hector
That was the whip of your bragg'd progeny
Thou shouldst not scape me here.

Here they fight, and certain Volsces come in aid of Aufidius. Martius fights till they be driven in breathless.

Officious, and not valiant, you have sham'd me
In your condemned seconds. [*Exeunt*]

A reference by Coriolanus to the use of shields during the protracted battle before the duel with Aufidius in Act I, Scene iv, lines 23-24, supports the choice of the use of sword and shield in this duel.

...Now put your shields before your hearts, and fight
With hearts more proof than shields.

Later in this same speech, Martius Coriolanus makes reference to his sword.

He that retires, I'll take him for a Volsce,
And he shall feel mine edge.

Since Coriolanus threatens to use the "edge" of his sword to *cut*, rather than the point of his sword to *thrust* at retreating soldiers, it can be surmised that Shakespeare intended that Coriolanus use a double edged English broadsword, rather than the more fashionable rapier of the early seventeenth century when *Coriolanus* was probably written (1607-8).

Therefore it is safe to assume that both Coriolanus and Aufidius carry a small round shield and a stout double edged sword (the classic sword and buckler of the Elizabethan era). The use of the sword and buckler in this scene could serve a traditional "Elizabethan style" staging or (with some modification of the sword) a "Roman-period style" staging of the play.

Coriolanus is covered in blood. Although he says, "Tis not my blood," this is just a noble boast. There has been an earlier stage direction and several line references to Coriolanus' wounds. Aufidius has also been fighting before this encounter with Coriolanus, but any references to Aufidius being wounded are conspicuously absent. There is, however, an equally notable reference to Aufidius being *bloody* after his narrow escape from Coriolanus. Can it be that Shakespeare wanted the audience's sympathies to lie with the wounded Coriolanus at the beginning of this duel? Shakespeare may have also intended to emphasize Coriolanus' extraordinary vitality as a warrior by demonstrating his valor despite his wounds.

Aufidius and Coriolanus slowly move toward each other from opposite sides of the stage as they speak. They continue to close their distance until the phrase, "fix thy foot." At this point they are closer than normal fighting distance; so close as to be able to strike without advancing.

After, "Thou should not scape me here," there is a long tense pause of absolute stillness. They are playing a game of "chicken" (i.e., who will make the first move?). They resemble gunfighters fixing to draw. Aufidius "cracks" first and attacks Coriolanus with a lightning-quick series of stationary cuts. Coriolanus stands his ground and parries with his sword and shield. Coriolanus performs a particularly powerful parry and follows up with a tremendous blow with his shield against Aufidius' body which sends Aufidius reeling backwards.

Making a horrid noise by banging his shield with his sword ("the thunder-like percussion of thy sounds"), Coriolanus closes in upon Aufidius. Circling, they exchange cuts, thrusts and parries. By chance, Aufidius wounds Coriolanus on the shield arm and Coriolanus drops his shield. (This wound is suggested by the stage direction at the top of Act I, Scene ix, "*Martius with his arm in a scarf.*")

With his shield, Aufidius smashes Coriolanus' wounded arm. The pain merely serves to enrage Coriolanus. Using only his sword, Coriolanus drives Aufidius backwards with a furious attack and succeeds in wounding Aufidius on the leg.

Wounded, Aufidius drops his shield guard for a moment. Coriolanus smashes Aufidius across the face with his left fist, knocking Aufidius to the ground unconscious. Just then, three Volscian soldiers enter.

Two of the soldiers attack Coriolanus, while the third soldier picks Aufidius up from the ground and drags him, semi-conscious, behind a barricade and into the Volscian camp.

Meanwhile, Coriolanus is driving both soldiers backwards. He picks up his shield by the rim and uses it as an offensive weapon against the soldiers. He beats the retreating soldiers back behind their barricade. The soldiers manage to close the barricade against Coriolanus.

In anger and frustration, Coriolanus beats upon the barricade with the pommel of his sword and with the rim of his shield. Then, contemptuously, he exits.

Aufidius regains consciousness, extricates himself from the soldiers who have come to his aid and pushes open the barricade in order to do battle with Coriolanus once again. When Aufidius manages to open the barricade, amid the protests of his soldiers, Coriolanus is already gone. A bitterly disappointed Aufidius strikes one of the soldiers across the face and verbally lashes out with,

Officious, and not valiant, you have sham'd
   me
In your condemned seconds.

Coriolanus vs. Aufidius Choreography

Fig. 412 Aufidius (left): stationary, right foot forward, sword cut right shoulder. Coriolanus: stationary, right foot forward, sword parry high three.

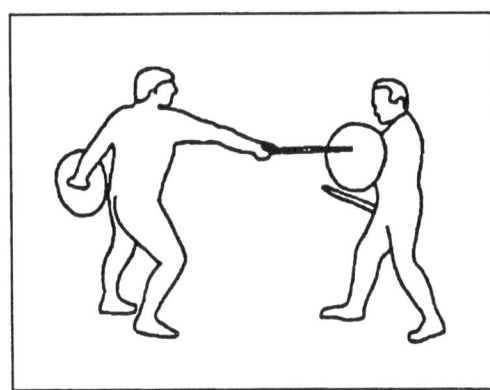

Fig. 413 Aufidius (left): stationary, sword cut left chest above shield. Coriolanus: stationary, shield parry three.

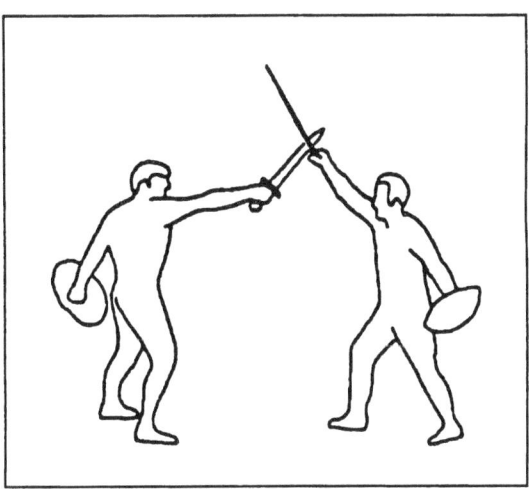

Fig. 414 Aufidius (left): stationary, sword cut to head. Coriolanus: sword parry five.

234 THE SWORDS OF SHAKESPEARE

Fig. 415 Coriolanus (right): stationary, shield strike to right chest (control force of impact). Aufidius: react backwards two steps.

Fig. 416 Coriolanus (right): close distance, advance to right side, right foot leading, sword cut to head. Aufidius: advance to right side, right foot leading, shield parry five.

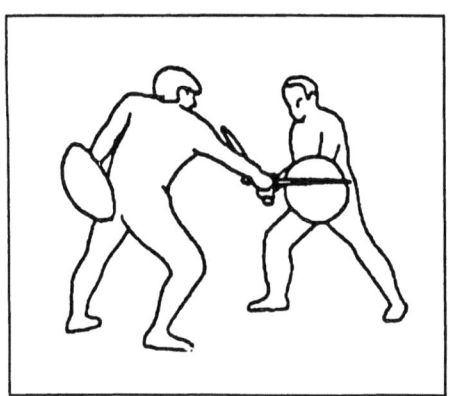

Fig. 417 Aufidius (left): advance to right side, right foot leading, sword cut to the inside of right knee. Coriolanus: advance to right side, right foot leading, shield parry two.

CORIOLANUS

Fig. 418 Coriolanus (right): advance to right side, right foot leading, sword thrust in pronation to center chest. Aufidius: advance to right side, right foot leading, shield parry four.

Fig. 419 Coriolanus (right): pass to the left side onto left foot, shield slash from right to left above Aufidius' head. Aufidius: duck shield.

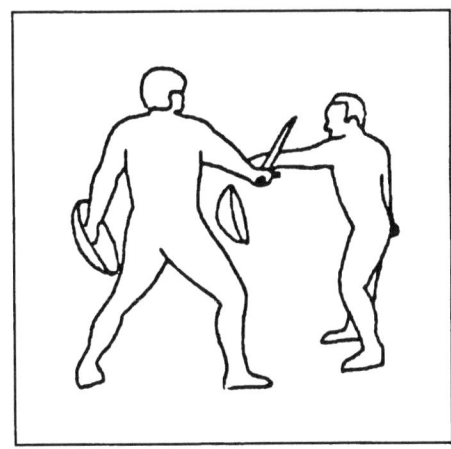

Fig. 420 Aufidius (left): quickly rise, diagonal sword slash from high outside, across path of Coriolanus' shield arm, to low inside (accurate fighting distance!). Coriolanus: react to wound on shield arm by dropping shield.

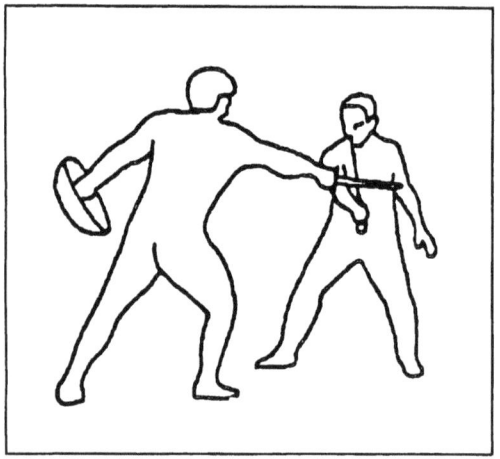

Fig. 421 Aufidius (left): advance forward, right foot leading, sword thrust left chest. Coriolanus: pass back onto left foot, sword parry four.

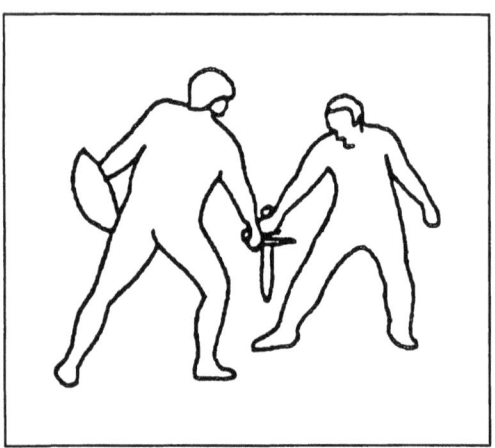

Fig. 422 Coriolanus (right): stationary, bind Aufidius' sword to his low left side.

Fig. 423 Aufidius (left): pass forward onto left foot, shield strike to Coriolanus' wounded shield arm. Coriolanus: pass back two steps, pain reaction.

CORIOLANUS

Fig. 424 Coriolanus (right): pass forward onto left foot, cut right shoulder. Aufidius: stationary, sword parry high four.

Fig. 425 Coriolanus (right): pass forward onto right foot, cut left shoulder. Aufidius: pass back onto left foot, shield parry high three.

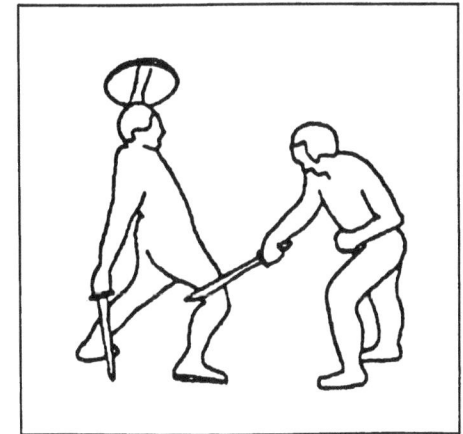

Fig. 426 Coriolanus (right): stationary, cut to outside of Aufidius' right knee (flat of blade contact to above knee). Stationary, lift sword away from contact and to low inside. Aufidius: drop to right knee.

238   THE SWORDS OF SHAKESPEARE

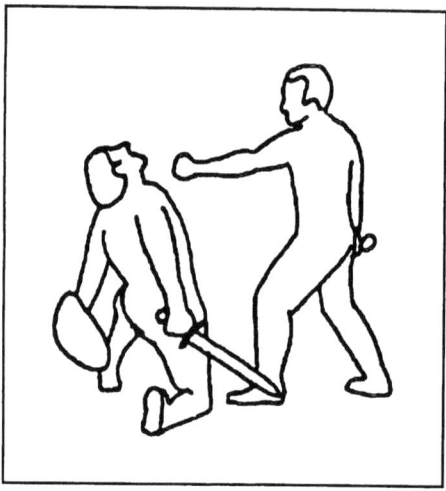

Fig. 427 Coriolanus (right): stationary, left hand cross jab to face. Aufidius: back fall. Three Volscian soldiers enter to come to Aufidius' aid.

CYMBELINE

... to the face of peril
Myself I'll dedicate

Cloten vs. Guiderius

It is easy enough for the audience to choose sides in this mismatched duel. Albeit of royal blood (son of the Queen by a previous marriage), Cloten is a fool, a boor, a vain degenerate rascal, and a bully. Throughout the play he has terrible luck and loses every game he plays. The indications are that he is not a very good warrior either. The very first time we see him he is soundly thrashed by his rival, Posthumus.

Everyone ridicules Cloten behind his back. One almost feels sorry for him. It is obvious that his fate is sealed even before the first blow is struck.

Guiderius, on the other hand, is a noble youth, brave by nature, a warrior born, and equal in birth to Cloten. Unbeknownst to either Guiderius or Cloten, Guiderius is actually the son of the king, Cymbeline, and therefore a half-brother to Cloten. Although Cloten is well dressed and Guiderius wears the simple cloth of a mountain peasant, it is Guiderius who appears the more royal of the two.

Act IV, Scene ii, takes place in the mountains of Wales. Cloten has come in the hope of overtaking his rival. It is Cloten's typically rotten luck that he encounters Guiderius instead.

Enter Cloten

CLO.
I cannot find those runagates, that villain
Hath mock'd me. I am faint.

BEL.
"Those runagates"?
Means he not us? I partly know him, 'tis
Cloten, the son o' th' Queen. I fear some
 ambush.
I saw him not these many years, and yet
I know 'tis he. We are held as outlaws.
 Hence!

GUI.
He is but one. You and my brother search
What companies are near. Pray you away,
Let me alone with him.
[Exeunt Belarius and Arviragus.]

CLO.
Soft, what are you
That fly me thus? Some villain mountainers?
I have heard of such. What slave art thou?

GUI.
A thing
More slavish did I ne'er than answering
A slave without a knock.

CLO.
Thou art a robber,
A law-breaker, a villain. Yield thee, thief.

GUI.
To who? to thee? What art thou? Have not I
An arm as big as thine? a heart as big?
Thy words I grant are bigger; for I wear not
My dagger in my mouth. Say what thou art;
Why I should yield to thee.

CLO.
Thou villain base,
Know'st me not by my clothes?

GUI.
No, nor thy tailor, rascal,
Who is thy grandfather! he made those
   clothes,
Which (as it seems) make thee.

CLO.
Thou precious varlet,
My tailor made them not.

GUI.
Hence then, and thank
The man that gave them thee. Thou art some
   fool,
I am loath to beat thee.

CLO.
Thou injurious thief,
Hear but my name, and tremble.

GUI.
What's thy name?

CLO.
Cloten, thou villain.

GUI.
Cloten, thou double villain, be thy name,
I cannot tremble at it. Were it Toad, or
   Adder, Spider,
'Twould move me sooner.

CLO.
To thy further fear,
Nay, to thy mere confusion, thou shalt know
I am son to th' Queen.

GUI.
I am sorry fo't; not seeming
So worthy as thy birth.

CLO.
Art not afeard?

GUI.
Those that I reverence, those I fear—the
   wise:
At fools I laugh, not fear them.

CLO.
Die the death!
When I have slain thee with my proper hand,
I'll follow those that even now fled hence,
And on the gates of Lud's-Town set your
   heads.
Yield, rustic mountaineer. *Fight and exeunt.*

Cloten refers to a singular "sword," in Act IV, Scene i, line 22. This generic reference to a sword is not much help in deciding what actual type of sword he carries. There are also no textual references as to what kind of weapon Guiderius might be using in this battle. An educated guess is in order.

The historic milieu for this play is ostensibly pre–Christian Britain. However, Shakespeare was not one to confine his genius within the bounds of historic accuracy. It is generally agreed that the Elizabethan theatre practitioners often used their contemporary clothing, with added bits of fancifully historic garments, to establish the period or locale of a scene. So, too, the weapons of Elizabethan and Jacobean England were freely used in place of more historically accurate period weaponry.

1609-10, when Cymbeline was composed, is the early age of the transition rapier. Side by side with the rapier and dagger, the well-to-do and the nobility of England would be engaged in the practice of both cut and thrust with a single blade—the more versatile transition rapier. Given Cloten's royal station it would not be amiss to arm him with a transition rapier of the early seventeenth century.

Since this encounter with Cloten sidetracks Guiderius on his way to go hunting, it is possible that he would be armed with a bow and arrows, single edged hunting sword (akin to the backsword), and knife. Given Guiderius' current lowly station, a rapier is out of the question. Gruesomely, Guiderius does reappear with Cloten's severed head. It would require little labor to cut off a head with an early seventeenth century English broadsword.

This duel is a quick one, with Cloten getting the worst of it. Guiderius is reluctant to fight as he rightly recognizes Cloten as a fool. Traditionally, those of noble nature are reluctant to take advantage of fools. Foolishly, Cloten begins the first attack by rushing forward and thrusting at Guiderius' stomach. Guiderius steps nimbly to the side, avoiding the thrust, and with the flat of his blade lands a resounding thwack on Cloten's rear end. Cloten howls, spins and futilely slashes the air between them. Guiderius steps back and awaits Cloten's next gambit.

Enraged, Cloten advances and savagely thrusts several times at Guiderius' chest. Guiderius, with his heavier blade, easily parries the thrusts, and with a particularly powerful final parry, beats Cloten's rapier aside, causing Cloten to lose his balance and stumble.

Taking advantage of Cloten's imbalance, Guiderius begins to powerfully advance with an inexorable series of cuts to Cloten's head, chest and legs. Cloten is driven backwards, desperately parrying the onslaught of cuts threatening targets all over his body. Cloten is not given the chance to retaliate.

Just before Cloten is driven off stage, he attempts a thrust to Guiderius' leading knee. Guiderius parries the cut and, taking control of Cloten's blade with a large circling envelopment, whips Cloten's rapier off to the side. Cloten barely manages to hang on to his sword.

Beginning to demonstrate a bit of hard won wisdom, Cloten turns and runs off stage. Guiderius follows in close pursuit.

I have already mentioned that, a few lines later, Guiderius enters with Cloten's bloody severed head; a harsh lesson, even for a fool.

Cloten vs. Guiderius Choreography

Fig. 428 Cloten (left): close distance, right foot forward, thrust to center stomach. Guiderius: advance to right side avoidance, right foot leading.

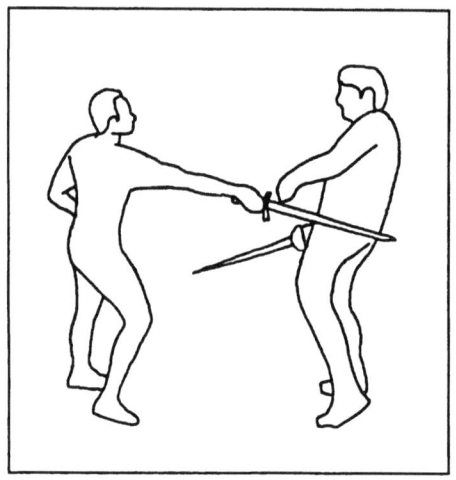

Fig. 429 Guiderius (left): stationary, flat of blade strike to left buttock. Cloten: react in pain to rear end strike.

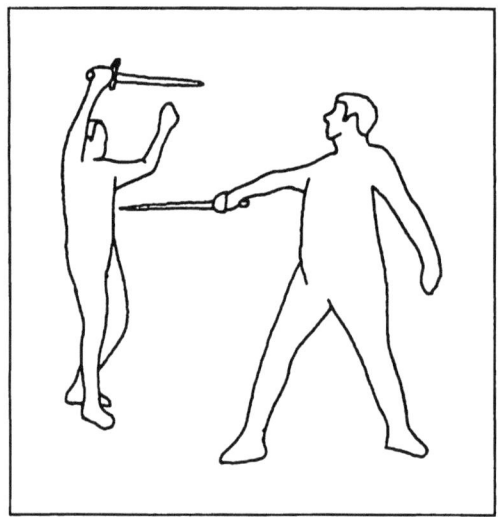

Fig. 430 Cloten (right): spin 180 degrees counter-clockwise, rapier slash in pronation from right to left at level of Guiderius' stomach. Guiderius: retreat avoidance.

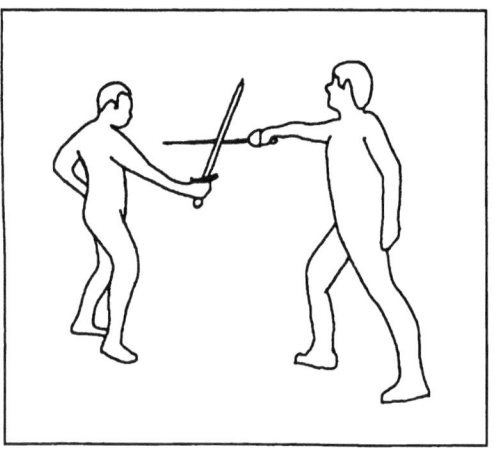

Fig. 431 Cloten (right): advance, right foot leading, thrust left chest. Guiderius: parry four.

CYMBELINE

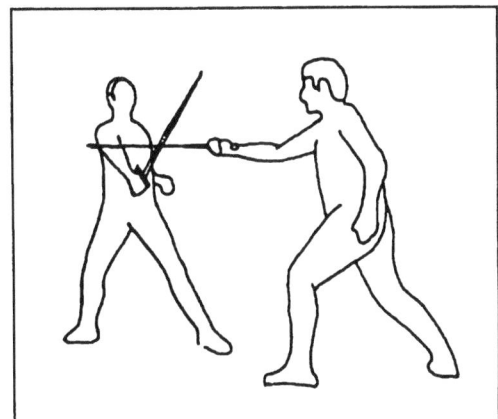

Fig. 432 Cloten (right): pass forward onto left foot, thrust right chest. Guiderius: pass back onto right foot, beat parry three.

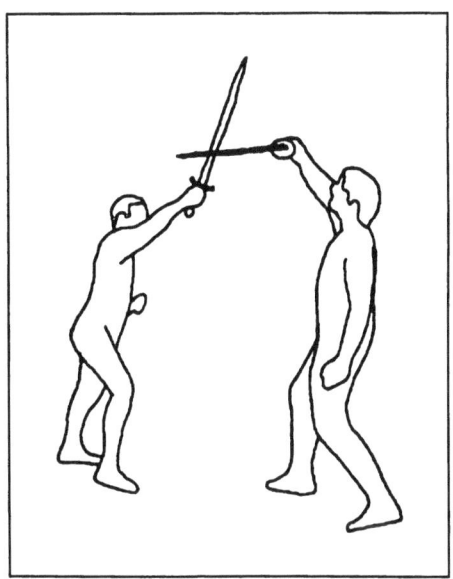

Fig. 433 Guiderius (left): pass forward onto right foot, cut head. Cloten: pass back onto left foot, parry five.

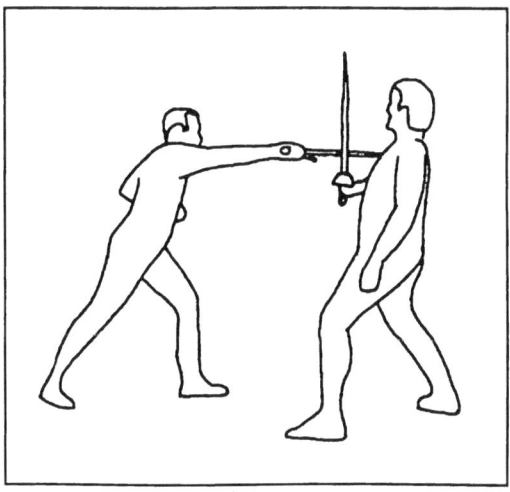

Fig. 434 Guiderius (left): pass forward onto left foot, cut right chest. Cloten: pass back onto right foot, parry three.

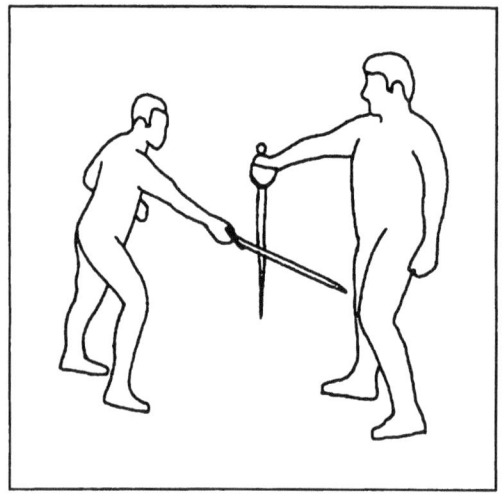

Fig. 435 Guiderius (left): pass forward onto right foot, cut left knee. Cloten: pass back onto left foot, parry one.

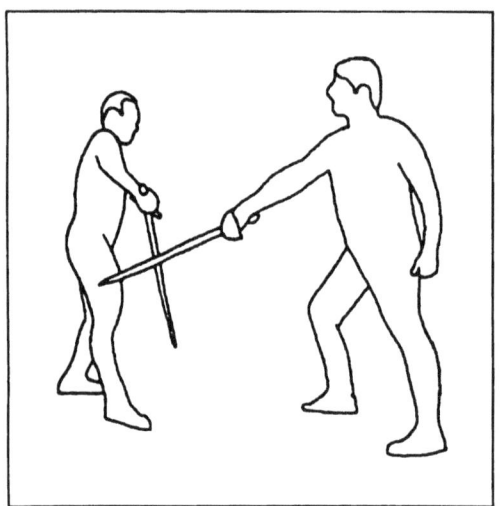

Fig. 436 Cloten (right): stationary, thrust right knee. Guiderius: stationary, parry two.

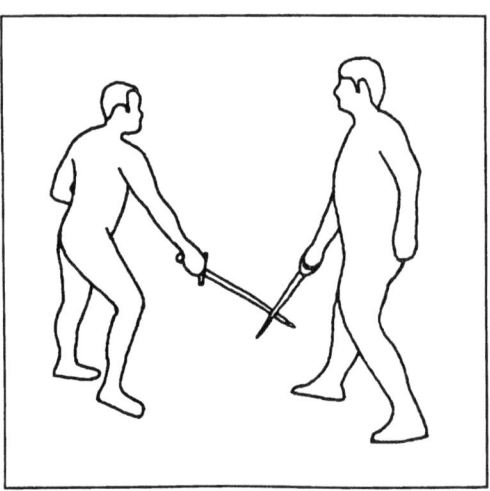

Fig. 437 Guiderius (left): stationary, envelopment to Cloten's low right side. Cloten exits offstage with Guiderius in pursuit.

Jachimo vs. Posthumus

The final duel in *Cymbeline* is the one that the audience has been waiting for. In Act V, Scene ii, the now bitter and self destructive British hero of the play faces the crafty and dishonest Italian. This wily Italian is responsible for our hero's and heroines' misfortunes.

The Britain, Posthumus, surely recognizes the Italian villain, Jachimo, whom Posthumus believes has seduced his wife. Conversely, Jachimo has no idea that Posthumus is his opponent in this duel; Posthumus is disguised as a peasant.

Enter Lucius, Jachimo, and the Roman army at one door, and the Britain army at another; Leonatus Post-humus following, like a poor soldier. They march over and go out. Then enter again, in skirmish, Jachimo and Posthumus: he vanquisheth and disarmeth Jachimo, and then leaves him.

The outline of the action is quite clear in the detailed stage directions, but the motives are not. Jachimo and Posthumus enter already fighting. Posthumus defeats and disarms Jachimo, but *he does not kill him*. Why not? Although he has reasons aplenty to kill Jachimo, Posthumus merely disarms him and leaves the stage. Perhaps Posthumus is beyond the pettiness of personal vendetta?

This duel is another wonderful example of Shakespeare's brilliance in intimately and consistently linking a character's psychological/emotional being with his actions. At this point in the play, Posthumus is almost aching for death to claim him. He believes that he is responsible for his wife's death (she's actually still living and all will end "happily ever after"). He is seeking redemption through valor, by pitting his life against the enemies of Britain. In his stirring monologue in Act V, Scene i, just prior to his duel with Jachimo, Posthumus painfully exposes his state of mind.

> I am brought hither
> Among th' Italian gentry, and to fight
> Against my lady's kingdom. 'Tis enough
> That, Britain, I have kill'd thy mistress; peace,
> I'll give no wound to thee. Therefore, good heavens,
> Hear patiently my purpose: I'll disrobe me
> Of these Italian weeds and suit myself
> As does a Britain peasant; so I'll fight
> Against the part I come with; so I'll die
> For thee, O Imogen, even for whom my life
> Is every breath a death; and thus, unknown,
> Pitied nor hated, to the face of peril
> Myself I'll dedicate.

The dual identity of Posthumus—i.e., a member of the aristocracy disguised as a peasant—argues the use of either the rapier and dagger, or the transition rapier. I believe it is more important to emphasize the aristocratic nature of this hero and not the flimsy peasant camouflage. Jachimo is unabashedly aristocratic and he would share the same choice of weapons.

Since *Cymbeline* was written in the first decade of the seventeenth century (1609-10), the transition rapier has been chosen for both combatants in this intense and complex duel. In this way the adversaries are evenly matched and the character's choices in the fight may be more dramatically revealed. Jachimo also has protective gauntlets, while Posthumus fights with bare hands.

These veteran warriors are already embroiled in physical conflict when they enter on stage. Jachimo, who is ignorant of the fact that he is fighting the noble Posthumus in disguise, merely sees his adversary as a "poor soldier." On their entrance, Jachimo is confident of the outcome of the fight and he is forcing Posthumus backwards with a series of well-executed cuts and thrusts to Posthumus' head and legs. He is shifting from high to low targets in order to induce an opening in his opponent's defense.

Posthumus is retreating and successfully parrying the cuts and thrusts. At the moment he is merely defending himself and refraining from any offensive moves against his enemy of old.

Jachimo suddenly alters the rhythm of his attack, and with a deep lunge, thrusts at Posthumus' chest. Posthumus passes back, dexterously parries Jachimo's thrust, and with a sweeping bind, drives Jachimo's sword to the ground. He follows with a swift deadly slash at Jachimo's head.

Jachimo scarcely has time to duck. Jachimo then resumes his guard. More cautious now, he warily begins to circle the motionless Posthumus. How did this peasant soldier learn to wield a blade so well?

Jachimo jumps in towards Posthumus with a shout, performs a false-thrust to the right leg, to draw a parry from Posthumus, and quickly disengages to thrust at Posthumus' left chest. Posthumus retreats and manages to parry the chest thrust, and immediately ripostes with a thrust of his own to Jachimo's chest. Jachimo parries the thrust with his gauntleted left hand.

A series of intricate thrusts, parries, slashes, avoidances and cuts are exchanged by the skillful warriors as they pivot around each other in a tight circle. Jachimo displays a growing resentment and anxiety as he recognizes the superiority of his opponent's skill. Posthumus fights almost without expression, as though he cares not whether he lives or dies.

In a stroke of luck, Jachimo manages to deflect a thrust, slide his blade up along Posthumus' blade and wound Posthumus' sword arm. Posthumus assumes a defensive guard, and Jachimo holds his ground searching for a new opening. Jachimo does not press his apparent advantage, because Posthumus does not react in pain to his wound. Although there is blood on his arm, he ignores the wound completely. Posthumus is beyond caring, beyond pain.

This time it is Posthumus who renews the attack. Posthumus thrusts low to the knee, and mounts a high cut to Jachimo's head, and continues his assault with another low cut to the leg. Jachimo manages to front the attacks and retorts with a thrust to Posthumus' chest.

Posthumus parries the chest thrust and with two powerful grinding circles, tearing Jachimo's sword from his grasp. Posthumus steps forward and with his left hand he violently pushes Jachimo backwards. Jachimo, defenseless, falls backwards to the stage floor.

For several long moments, Posthumus stands astride his fallen foe. Then Posthumus turns his head to listen to the sounds of battle which have been occurring off stage throughout this duel. After a second long glance at Jachimo, Posthumus abruptly wheels about and runs off stage, leaving the defeated and dejected Jachimo to curse himself.

Jachimo vs. Posthumus Choreography

Fig. 438 Jachimo (left): advance forward, right foot leading, cut head. Posthumus: retreat, left foot leading, parry five.

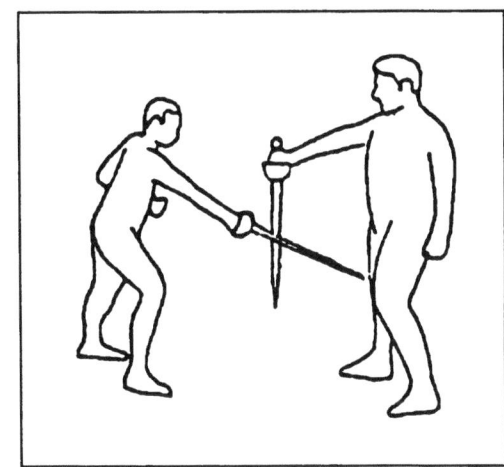

Fig. 439 Jachimo (left): advance forward, right foot leading, thrust right knee. Posthumus: retreat, left foot leading, parry one.

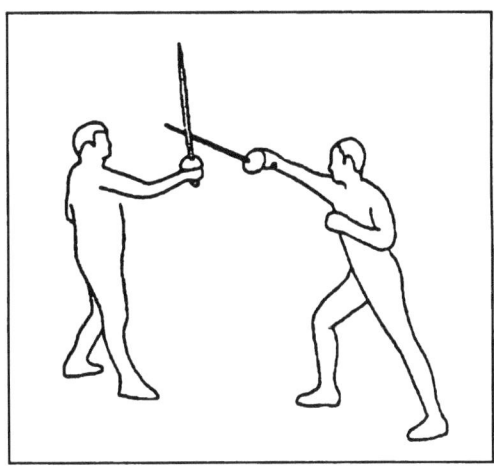

Fig. 440 Jachimo (right): advance forward, right foot leading, cut left shoulder. Posthumus: retreat, left foot leading, parry high four.

Fig. 441 Jachimo (right): pass forward into lunge onto left foot, cut right chest. Posthumus: pass back onto right foot, parry three.

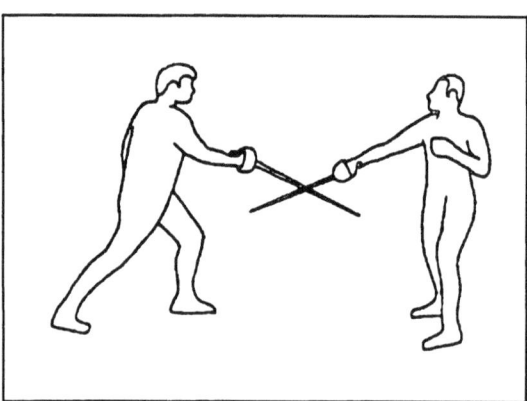

Fig. 442 Posthumus (left): stationary, bind to Jachimo's low right side.

Fig. 443 Posthumus (left): stationary, slash in pronation from left to right above head. Jachimo: duck head slash.

CYMBELINE

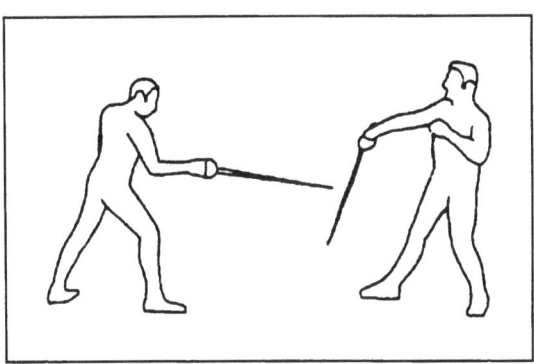

Fig. 444 Jachimo (left): circle counter-clockwise 180 degrees around Posthumus. Posthumus: pivot to face Jachimo. Jachimo: jump forward into distance, right foot forward, feint thrust in supination to left knee. Posthumus: parry two.

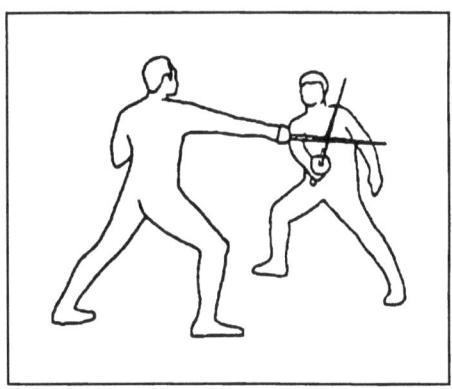

Fig. 445 Jachimo (left): disengage, lunge forward onto right foot, thrust left chest. Posthumus: retreat, parry four.

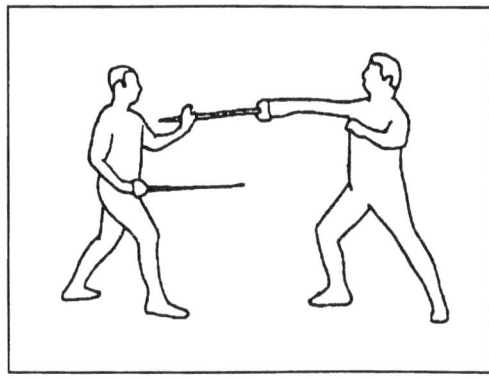

Fig. 446 Posthumus (right): advance forward, thrust left chest. Jachimo: stationary, left hand parry.

Fig. 447 Jachimo (left): advance diagonally to the right, right foot leading, thrust left chest. Posthumus: advance diagonally to the right, right foot leading, beat parry four.

Fig. 448 Posthumus (right): stationary, slash in pronation, from high inside to high outside above head. Jachimo: duck head slash.

Fig. 449 Jachimo (right): advance diagonally to right side, right foot leading, thrust right knee. Posthumus: advance diagonally to right side, right foot leading, parry one.

CYMBELINE

Fig. 450 Posthumus (left): stationary, cut right chest. Jachimo: stationary, circle parry three.

Fig. 451 Jachimo (left): pass forward onto left foot, slide blade along Posthumus' sword in a glissade and cut right sword forearm (control force of blade contact to arm). Posthumus: following blade contact with arm, pass back two steps.

Fig. 452 Posthumus (left): pass forward onto left foot, pass into lunge onto right foot, thrust left knee. Jachimo: stationary, parry two.

Fig. 453 Posthumus (left): stationary, head cut. Jachimo: stationary, parry five.

Fig. 454 Posthumus (left): pass forward onto left foot, cut to outside of Jachimo's left knee. Jachimo: pass back onto left foot, counter cut parry two.

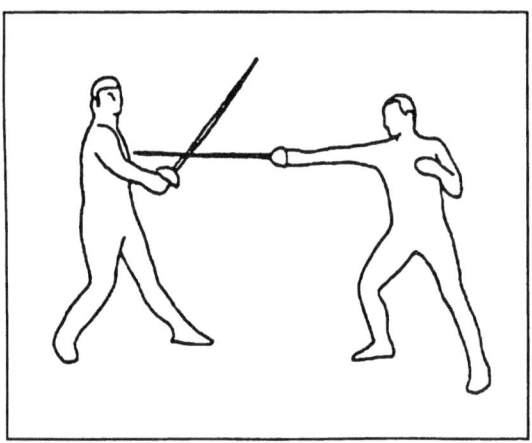

Fig. 455 Jachimo (right): stationary, thrust in supination to right chest. Posthumus: stationary, parry three.

Fig. 456 Posthumus (left): stationary, double envelopment and disarm to Jachimo's high left side. Jachimo: stationary, release rapier following second envelopment (control final stage position of rapier after release).

Fig. 457 Posthumus (left): stationary, left hand push to Jachimo's center chest (no force to be used on push, Jachimo controls re-action). Jachimo: backfall reaction to push.

THE TWO NOBLE KINSMEN

Lo, cousin, lo, our folly has undone us.

Palamon vs. Arcite

It is difficult to choose a favorite in this most genteel of Shakespeare's duels. The combatants indeed act like "noble kinsmen," and they treat each other with an almost comic deference as they prepare for battle.

From the entrance (Act III, Scene vi) of Arcite, "with armors and swords," to the actual fight is some 90 lines! A very long, nonetheless delightful exchange of courtesies and gentlemanly braggadocio. The combatants act as each other's squires and dutifully strap armor one upon the other. Finally, the martial preparations are complete and they amicably shake hands.

ARC.
Here, Palamon: this hand shall never more
Come near thee with such friendship.

PAL.
I commend thee.

ARC.
If I fall, curse me, and say I was a coward,
For none but such dare die in these just trials.
Once more farewell, my cousin.

PAL.
Farewell, Arcite.

Fight.

It is a stroke of luck for the fight choreographer that Shakespeare chose to precede this duel by having the combatants put on and name various pieces of sixteenth century jousting armor. There is less doubt as to what the combatants might be wearing and what weapons they would be using than in many of Shakespeare's enigmatic dueling scenes.

The pieces of jousting armor that Shakespeare names are the "casque"—an open helmet, "grand guard"—a large plate worn over the regular armor in tournaments in the sixteenth century, and "gauntlets"—armor for the hands. In addition, there are references to buckling on an un-named piece of armor, i.e., "I'll buckle't close and thrust the buckle Through far enough." The piece of armor referred to is probably a metal breastplate—a plate or plates covering the front of the body from the neck to a little below the waist and often accompanied by a backplate.

The armor that Arcite brings to the place of battle suggests that he would have preferred to joust on horseback. The sword most commonly used in a joust on horseback would be a single hand double-edged broadsword with a simple cross hilt. This is most likely the sword brought to the appointed duel by

Arcite. Ever the proper knight, Palamon carries a broadsword of similar design.

Palamon does not agree, however, with wearing complete body armor; hence, they discard the grand guard and much of the other traditional jousting armor. Instead they fight on foot clad in helmets, breast and backplates, and gauntlets.

As we can see, the combatants are fairly well protected on the head, chest and hands by their heavy armor. By not putting on the rest of the usual gear for a formal joust they remain, as Palamon points out, "the nimbler." The stage is now set for an honest, powerful, yet nimble duel between gentleman.

Arcite and Palamon stand motionless, their swords held out in front of their bodies, their hilts held low and their feet parallel in a classic wide stance. Simultaneously they shout and race toward each other, swinging their swords in a wide circle as they run; building up a powerful momentum for a mutually destructive blow.

They clash in the center as Arcite savagely cuts at Palamon's right shoulder. Palamon meets the blow with a powerful counter cut to the left and sweeps Arcite's sword aside. Standing his ground, Palamon swings his blade up and brings it down with all of his might at Arcite's head. Also holding his ground, Arcite lifts his sword and strongly blocks the head cut. Then with his gauntleted left hand, Arcite pushes Palamon's blade off to the left and smashes the pummel of his sword into his breastplate, driving Palamon backwards. Palamon attempts to regain his balance, but he stumbles and falls.

Arcite rushes forward, brandishing his sword, and stops above his compromised kinsman. For a moment there is silence. All this for the love of a woman? Or is it a question of honor? Arcite extends his hand toward Palamon. Palamon takes Arcite's offered hand, and Arcite helps Palamon to his feet. Arcite backs away from Palamon and there is another moment of stillness.

Bursting out of the stillness with a shout, Arcite rushes towards Palamon with his blade extended, as though to push his sword right through Palamon's body. Palamon avoids to the right and parries Arcite's thrust.

Palamon then passes forward toward Arcite and, with great speed, cuts at Arcite's right shoulder and left shoulder. Arcite passes backwards and parries the cuts. Arcite, stationary, returns a cut at Palamon's left chest. Palamon holds his ground and parries the chest cut and immediately binds Arcite's sword down to Palamon's lower right side. Palamon takes advantage of Arcite's momentary vulnerability, passes forward and strikes a heavy blow with his gauntleted left hand across Arcite's helmet.

This time it is Arcite who is struck to the ground. Palamon towers triumphant over the prostrate Arcite. Then slowly and simply, Palamon nods his head and without a word extends his hand to Arcite, helping him up from the ground. Who can resist the drama of a battle among equals?

The two noble kinsmen stand for a moment, motionless, their left hands clasped, their swords poised at their sides. At some passionate signal known only to themselves, they each take one step backwards and Palomon viciously attacks Arcite's shoulder. Arcite lifts his sword high to meet the attack.

Without hesitation, Arcite presses his familial adversary, passing forward and striking first at one exposed knee, then the other. Palamon gives ground and defends his legs. Growling, Palamon lashes out with a powerful decapitating slash at Arcite's head. Arcite ducks and wheels out of fighting distance.

At this moment the hunting horn is heard,

Horns within; they stand.

ARC.
Lo, cousin, lo, our folly has undone us.

PAL.
Why?

ARC.
This is the Duke, a-hunting as I told you.
If we be found, we are wretched. O, retire
For honor's sake, and safely presently
Into your bush again, sir. We shall find
Too many hours to die in, gentle cousin.
If you be seen, you perish instantly
For breaking prison, and I, if you reveal me,
For my contempt. Then all the world will
    scorn us,
And say we had a noble difference,
But base disposers of it.

PAL.
No, no cousin.
I will no more be hidden, nor put off
This great adventure to a second trial.
I know your cunning, and I know your cause.
He that faints now, shame take him! Put thy-
    self
Upon thy present guard-

ARC.
You are not mad?

PAL.
Or I will make th' advantage of this hour
Mine own; and what to come shall threaten
    me
I fear less than my fortune. Know, weak
    cousin,
I love Emilia, and in that I'll bury
Thee and all crosses else.

ARC.
Then come what can come,
Thou shalt know, Palamon, I dare as well
Die as discourse or sleep. Only this fears me,
The law will have the honor of our ends.
Have at thy life!

PAL.
Look to thine own well, Arcite.

Fight again.

    Palamon is desperate. He wants to end this conflict before they are stopped. He rushes Arcite, raining a flurry of savage blows at his rival. Arcite repels Palamon's fury and skillfully defends himself against Palamon's attack.
    In a sudden move, Arcite closes with Palamon and they begin to grapple, each trying to wrest the other's sword out of his grip. During this hand to hand struggle, the hunting horns sound once again and the combatants are discovered. Fortunately, their duel is never resolved in blood.

Horns.
Enter Theseus, Hippolyta, Emilia, Pirithous, *and* Train

THE.
What ignorant and mad malicious traitors
Are you, that 'gainst the tenor of my laws
Are making battle, thus like knights
    appointed,
Without my leave and officers of arms?
By Casor, both shall die.

PAL.
Hold thy word, Theseus.

Palamon vs. Arcite Choreography

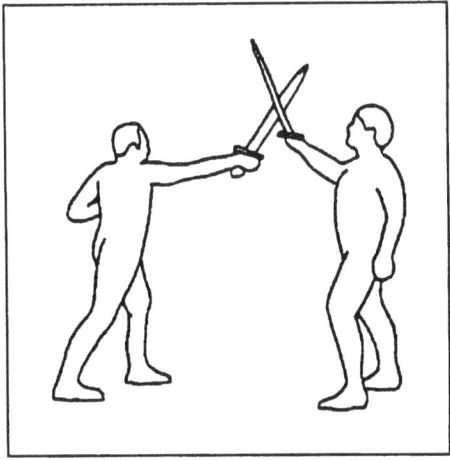

Fig. 458 Arcite and Palamon simultaneously close distance. Arcite (left): close distance, left side molinello, left foot forward, cut right shoulder. Palamon: close distance, left side molinello, left foot forward, counter cut high three.

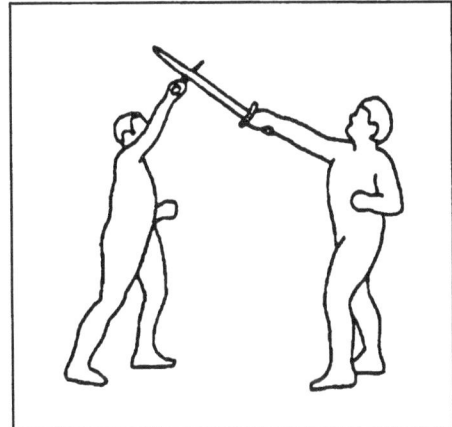

Fig. 459 Palamon (right): stationary, head cut. Arcite: stationary, parry five.

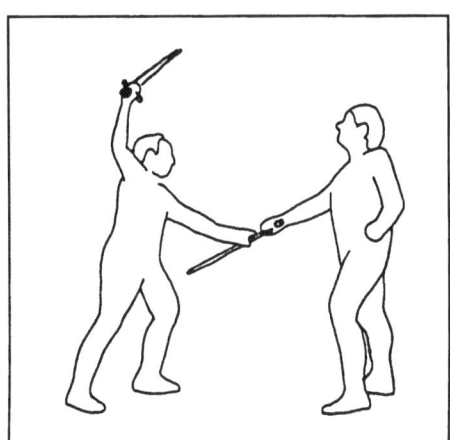

Fig. 460 Arcite (left): stationary, bind sword to Palamon's low right side with gauntleted left hand.

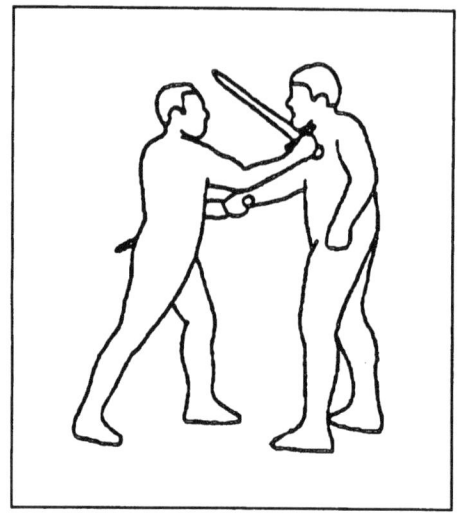

Fig. 461 Arcite (left): stationary, pommel blow to center chest.

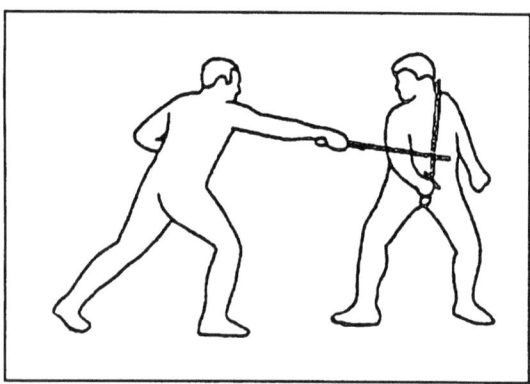

Fig. 462 Palamon falls backwards and Arcite helps him back to his feet and moves out of distance. Arcite (left): running attack with thrust to left outside of body outline. Palamon: sweep left foot behind right foot (demi volte), parry four.

Fig. 463 Arcite and Palamon pivot to face each other. Palamon (left): close distance, left foot forward, cut right shoulder. Arcite: pass back onto right foot, parry high three.

Fig. 464 Palamon (left): pass forward onto right foot, cut left shoulder. Arcite: pass back onto left foot, parry high four.

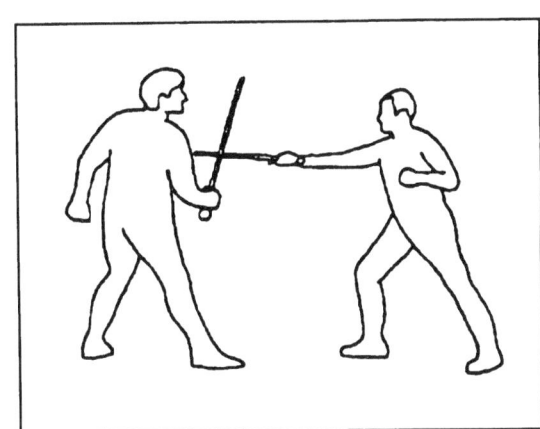

Fig. 465 Arcite (right): stationary, cut left chest. Palamon: stationary, parry four.

Fig. 466 Palamon (left): bind sword to Arcite's low right side, pass forward onto left foot, strike right side of helmet with left hand. Arcite: fall onto left side.

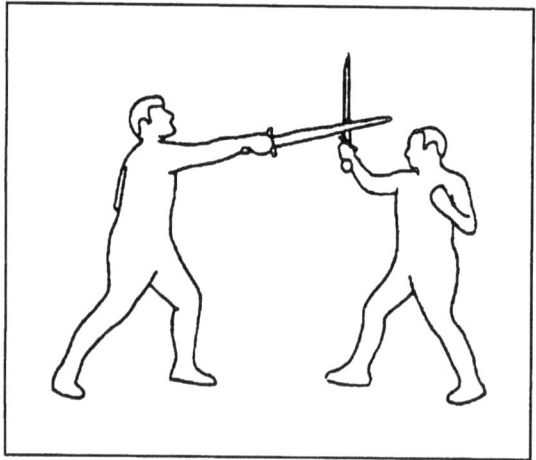

Fig. 467 Palamon helps Arcite to his feet. Holding left forearms, left foot forward, they are motionless for five counts. Palamon (left): on count six release arm, pass back onto right foot, cut left shoulder. Arcite: on count six, pass back onto left foot, counter cut parry high four.

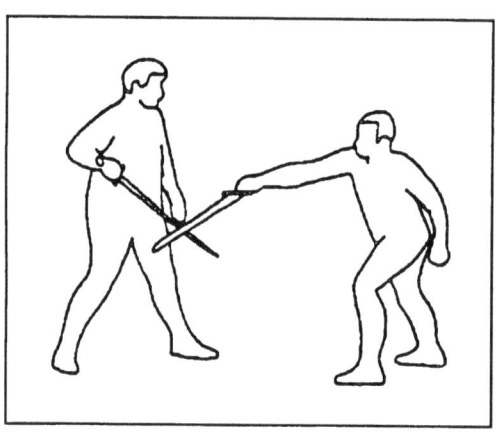

Fig. 468 Arcite (right): pass forward onto left foot, cut right knee. Palamon: stationary, parry two.

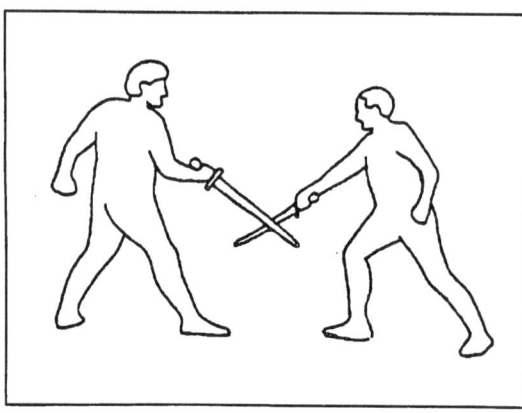

Fig. 469 Arcite (right): pass forward onto right foot, cut left knee. Palamon: pass back onto left foot, beat parry seven.

THE TWO NOBLE KINSMEN 261

Fig. 470 Palamon (left): stationary, sword slash in pronation from left to right above Arcite's head. Arcite: duck head slash, pass back two steps.

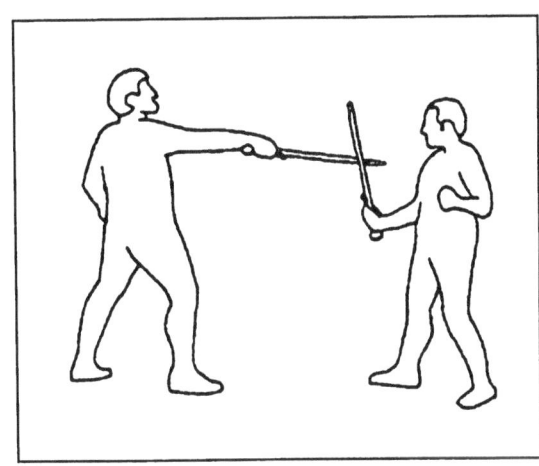

Fig. 471 Palamon (left): stationary, cut right chest. Arcite: stationary, parry three.

Fig. 472 Palamon (left): stationary, thrust in half pronation to left chest. Arcite: stationary, parry one.

Fig. 473 Arcite (right): pass forward onto left foot, grasp Palamon's right sword wrist with left hand. Palamon: pass forward onto left foot, grasp Arcite's right sword wrist with left hand. Arcite and Palamon struggle in a corps a corps until parted by Theseus.

GLOSSARY

Advance Sometimes referred to as "the fencing step." The leading foot steps forward, followed by the trailing foot.

Avoidance A movement intended to "dodge" an attack.

Balestra A combination of a jump forward and a lunge. There are two counts in this action; one-jump, two-lunge.

Beat Attack A sharp "tap" against the middle, or the foible of the opponent's blade, with the object of opening a line, or provoking an attack.

Beat Parry A parry which clears the line by striking an attacking blade, as opposed to blocking or redirecting the attacking blade.

Bind A blade taking action which carries the opposing weapon diagonally from high line to low line, or vice versa, across the body.

Butt End The trailing end of the staff in the En Garde position.

Centerline An imaginary line bisecting a body in equal halves, right and left.

Change Beat A change of engagement immediately followed by a beat attack.

Circle Parry A parry that begins in one line, travels in a position of a circle to meet the attacking blade in a different line.

Closed Said of a line of engagement, when the defender's weapon prevents an attack to that line of engagement.

Corps a Corps Means body to body. Describes the moment when the combatants come in close contact and the weapons are immobilized.

Counter Parry A parry that begins in one line, travels a full circle to meet the attacking blade in the original line.

Coupé A change of engagement that takes the blade around the opposing blade's point. Sometimes called a "cutover."

Croisé A blade taking action which carries the opposing weapon from a high line to a low line, or vice versa, but on the same side as the engagement, not diagonally across like a bind.

Cross Parry A parry using both rapier and dagger held forte to forte so that the blades cross. forming an open "V" to catch the attacking blade.

Cut An attack made with the edge of the blade.

Demi Volte A method of effacing the target by swinging the rear leg backward and sideways, so that the trunk is brought 90 degrees in relation to the attack.

Disarm The act of removing a combatant's weapon from their hand.

Disengage Passing the blade under that of the opponent and terminating on the side opposite to the original engagement.

Engagement When the blades are in contact with each other, they are said to be engaged.

En Garde The basic "ready" position of skilled fighters.

Envelopment An attack on the blade that, by describing a circle, picks up the opposing blade and brings it back to the original line of engagement.

Eye Contact The technique of cueing a partner by looking into his/her eyes prior to executing an action.

False Edge Historically, a term used for the back edge of the foible on a single-edged sword; in stage fighting—the left edge of a blade when a sword is held in pronation in the right hand.

Fighting Distance The correct linear measure to create the illusion of possible body contact when engaged in stage combat.

Fore End The leading end of the staff in the En Garde position.

Glissade An offensive action against an opponent's blade that applies lateral pressure while moving forward.

High Line The possible engagements above the waist.

Inside Line The possible engagements on the left side of the centerline in relation to a right-handed combatant.

Invitation Any movement of the weapon or body intended to tempt the opponent into an attack.

Knap A sound safely created by one of the combatants which mimics a sound of impact.

Line An imaginary path from the attacker's weapon to a quadrant of the defender's body (*see* Inside line, Outside Line, Low Line, High Line).

Low Line The possible engagements below the waist.

Lunge The "extended" leg position used as a method of reaching the opponent on an attack. To lunge, the leading leg extends forward in a long step, while the trailing leg remains in place.

Molinello Means "little windmill" and describes the action of pivoting the blade in circles in a diagonal, vertical, or horizontal plane.

Outside Line The possible engagements on the right side of the centerline in relation to a right-handed combatant.

Parry The defensive action of deflecting or blocking an attack.

Pronation The position of the sword hand with the palm facing down.

Punto Reverso A point attack delivered from the attacker's inside line to the partner's outside line with the hand often in supination.

Recover To return to an En Garde foot position following a lunge.

Retreat The rear foot steps backward, followed by the front foot.

Riposte An attack immediately following a successful parry.

Supination The position of the sword hand with the palm facing up.

Thrust An attack made with the point of the weapon.

APPENDIX I: THE SOCIETY OF AMERICAN FIGHT DIRECTORS

The Society of American Fight Directors (SAFD) is a nonprofit organization devoted to providing training in the Stage Combat Arts and to improving the quality of stage combat choreography since 1977. The SAFD is committed to the highest standards of safety in the theatrical, film and television industries. The SAFD offers educational opportunities at universities, in schools, through personal tutorials, and at the annual National Stage Combat Workshop. In addition, the SAFD tests individuals in three categories: Actor/Combatant, Teacher, Fight Master.

One need not take any sort of test in order to be a member of the SAFD. Anyone interested in the art of stage fight choreography and stage fighting can join as a Friend. Members of the SAFD receive *The Fight Master,* a journal published twice yearly containing in-depth articles on the history and practice of stage combat, the latest equipment, staging practices, etc. SAFD members also receive *The Cutting Edge,* a bi-monthly newsletter updating SAFD activities, policies and member news.

APPENDIX II: SUPPLIERS OF STAGE WEAPONS

The Armory, American Fencers Supply, 1180 Folsom St., San Francisco, CA 94103

Arms and Armor, 1101 Stinson Blvd. NE, Minneapolis, MN 55413

Art of the Sword, 761 Calusa, El Cerrito, CA 94530

Rod Casteel, Colonial Armory, 106 Lynnbrook, Eugene, OR 97404

Center Firearms Co., 10 West 37th St., New York, NY 10018

Eiler Robert Cook, P.O. Box 188, Etowah, NC 28729

Gratzner Period Accoutrements, P.O. Box 12023, Marina Del Ray, CA 90295

Dennis Graves, Swordcutler, 255 S. 41st St., Boulder, CO 80303

Mark Haney, 6000 J. Street, Sacramento, CA 95819

Lundegaard Armoury, P.O. Box 287, Crompond, NY 10517

Museum Replicas Limited, 2143 Gees Mill Road, Box 840, Conyers, GA 30207

Lewis Shaw, 3013 Shannon Dr., Baltimore, MD 21213

Triplette Competition Arms, 162 West Pine Street, Mount Airy, NC 27030

Steve Vaughn, 800 Vernal Road, Attica, NY 14011

BIBLIOGRAPHY

Anderson, Bob. *Stretching*. California: Shelter Publications, Inc., 1980.
Anglin, Jay P. "The School of Defence in Elizabethan London." *Renaissance Quarterly*, 37 (3), (1984): 393–410.
Ascham, Roger. *Toxophilus*, ed. Edward Arber. Westminster: A. Constable and Company, 1985.
Aylward, J.D. *The English Master of Arms, from the Twelfth to the Twentieth Century*. London: Routledge and Kegan Paul, 1956.
Baldick, Robert. *The Duel: A History of Duelling*. New York: Clarkson N. Potter, Inc., 1965.
Bartlett, John. *A New and Complete Concordance or Verbal Index to Words, Phrases, & Passages in the Dramatic Works of Shakespeare*. New York: The Macmillan Co., 1896.
Bartow, Arthur. *The Director's Voice: Twenty-One Interviews*. New York: Theatre Communications Group, 1988.
Bentley, Gerald Eades. *The Profession of Player in Shakespeare's Time, 1590–1642*. Princeton: Princeton University Press, 1984.
Berry, Herbert. *The Nobel Science: A Study and Transcription of Sloane Ms. 2530, Papers of the Masters of Defence of London, Temp. Henry VIII to 1590*. Newark: University of Delaware Press, 1991.
Blackmore, Howard L. *Arms and Armour*. London: Studio Vista, 1965; NYC: E.P. Dutton and Company.
Brown, Ivor. *Shakespeare and the Actors*. London: The Bodley Head, 1970.
____. *Shakespeare in His Time*. Edinburgh: Thomas Nelson and Sons Ltd., 1960.
Burton, Richard P. *The Book of the Sword*. London: Chatto and Windus, Piccadilly, 1884.
Castle, Egerton. *Schools and Masters of Fence*. London: George Bell, 1885; George Shumway, R.D. 7, York, Pennsylvania.
Chambers, Edmund K. *The Elizabethan Stage*. 4 vols, Oxford: The Clarendon Press, 1923.
Craig, Horace S. "Duelling Scenes and Terms in Shakespeare's Plays." *University of California Publications in English 9*, No. 1. 1940.
Creizenach, Horace S. *The English Drama in the Age of Shakespeare*. London: Sedgwick & Jackson, 1916.
De Loque, Bertrand. *Discourses of Warre and Single Combat, Translated out of French by J. Eliot*. London: John Wolfe, 1591.
Desson, Alan C. *Elizabethan Stage Conventions and Modern Interpreters*. Cambridge: Cambridge University Press, 1984.
Di Grassi, Giacomo. *Giacomo Di Grassi, His True Arte of Defence, Plainlie Teaching by Infallable Demonstrations, Apt Figures, and Perfect Rules the Manner and Forme How a Man, Without Other Teacher or Master May Safelie Handle All Sortes of Weapons as Well Offensive as Defensive with a Treatise of Disceit or Falsinge*. London: Hand and Starre, 1594.
Edelman, Charles. *Brawl Ridiculous: Swordfighting in Shakespeare's Plays*. Manchester and New York: Manchester University Press, 1992.
Gordon, Gilbert. *Stage Fights*. New York: Theatre Arts Books, 1973.
Harrison, George B. *An Elizabethan Journal, Being a Record of Those Things Most Talked of During the Years 1592–1594*. London: Constable & Co., 1928.

_____. *Elizabethan Plays and Players.* London: George Routledge and Sons, 1940.

_____. *A Last Elizabethan Journal, Being a Record of Those Things Most Talked of During the Years 1599–1603.* London: Constable & Co., 1933.

_____. *A Second Elizabethan Journal, Being a Record of Those Things Most Talked of During the Years 1595–1598.* New York: Richard R. Smith, 1931.

_____. *Shakespeare's Fellows, Being a Brief Chronicle of the Shakespearean Age.* London: John Lane, 1923.

Hewitt, John. *Ancient Armour and Weapons in Europe: From the Iron Period of the Northern Nations to the End of the Seventeenth Century.* Oxford and London: John Henry and James Parker, MDCCCLX. Vol. 3.

Hobbs, William. *Stage Fight.* New York: Theatre Arts Books, 1967.

Honigmann, E.A.J. *Shakespeare: The 'Lost Years.'* New Jersey: Barnes & Noble, 1985.

Hussey, Jeannette. *The Code Duello in America.* Washington, D.C.: Smithsonian Institution Press, 1980.

Hutton, Alfred. *Cold Steel.* London: Clowes, 1889.

_____. *Old Sword-Play: The Systems of Fence in Vogue During the XVIth, XVIIth, and XVIIIth Centuries with Lessons Arranged from the Works of Various Ancient Masters.* London: H. Grevel and Co., 1892.

_____. *The Sword and the Centuries: Or, Old Sword Days and Old Sword Ways.* Vermont: Charles E. Tuttle Co., 1980.

Jackson, James L. "They Catch One Another's Rapiers: The Exhange of Weapons in Hamlet." *The Shakespeare Quarterly Fall 1990,* Volume 41, Number 3.

Knight, George Wilson. *Principles of Shakespearean Production.* New York: Macmillan, 1937.

McElroy, Mary, and Kent Cartwright. "Public Fencing Contests on the Elizabethan Stage." *Journal of Sport History,* 1986, 13 (3): 193–211.

MacIntyre, Jean. *Shakespeare and the Battlefields: Tradition and Innovation in Battle Scenes.*

Marshall, Henry. *Stage Swordplay.* Tarrytown, New York: Marymount College, 1977.

Martin, Michael R., and Richard C. Harrier. *The Concise Encyclopedic Guide to Shakespeare.* New York: Horizon Press, 1971.

Martinez, J. D. *Combat Mime: A Non-Violent Approach to Stage Violence.* Chicago: Nelson-Hall Publishers, 1982.

Mitchell, Lee. "The Fencing Scene in Hamlet." *Philological Quarterly.* 16 (January, 1937), 71–73.

Morseberger, Robert E. "Of Opposition to the New Schools of Fence and Satires Upon Them," "Of Duelling and Honorable Quarrels," "Of Fencing Matches in the Theatres," "Of the Swordplay of Actors and of Techniques of Elizabethan and Jacobean Fence," "Of the Performance of Stage Fights," "Of the Duel in *Hamlet.*" *Swordplay and the Elizabethan and Jacobean Stage.* Ed. James Hogg. Salzburg Studies in Elizabethan Literature. 37 (1974). 10–129.

Musashi, Miyamoto. *A Book of Five Rings.* Trans. Victor Harris. New York: The Overlook Press, 1974.

Norman, A.V.B. *The Rapier and Small-Sword, 1460–1820.* London: Arms and Armour Press; New York: Arno Press, 1980.

Oakeshott, R. Ewart. *European Weapons and Armour: From the Renaissance to the Industrial Revolution.* Guilford: Lutterworth Press, 1980.

_____. *The Sword and the Age of Chivalry.* London: Lutterworth Press, 1964.

Palffy-Alpar, Julius. *Sword and Masque.* Philadelphia: F.A. Davis Co., 1967.

Pollock, Frederick. *Oxford Lectures and Other Discourses.* London: Macmillan and Co., 1890.

Powell, George H. *Duelling Stories of the Sixteenth Century: From the French of Brantome.* London: A. H. Bullen, 1904.

Reynolds, George Fullmer. *The Staging of Elizabethan Plays At the Red Bull Theatre 1605–1625.* New York: Modern Language Association of America, 1940.

Saviolo, Vincentio. *Vincentio Saviolo His Practice. In Two Books. The First Intreating of the Use of the Rapier and Dagger. The Second, of Honor and Honorable Quarrels, Both Interlaced with Sundrie Pleasant Discourses, Not Unfit for All Gentlemen and Captaines That Professe Armes.* London: William Mattes, 1595.

Schoenbaum, S. *William Shakespeare: A Compact Documentary Life.* Oxford: Oxford University Press, 1977.

Segar, William. *The Book of Honor and Armes*. London: Richard Thones, 1590.
Seldon, John. *The Duello, or, Single Combat: From Antiquity Derived Into This Kingdom of England: With Several Kinds of Ceremonies Forms Thereof From Good Authority Described*. London: William Bzay, 1610. Reprint 1711.
Shakespeare, William. *The Riverside Shakespeare*. Ed. G. B. Evans. Boston: Houghton Mifflin Co., 1974.
Silver, George. *Paradoxes of Defence*. Shakespeare Association Facsimiles, No. 6, London: Oxford University Press, 1933.
____. *The Works of*, Comprising "Paradoxes of Defence" (printed in 1559 and now reprinted) and "Brief Instructions Upon My Paradoxes of Defence" (printed for the first time from the MS. in the British Museum. ed. Cyril G.R. Matthew) London: George Bell and Sons, 1898.
____. Smith, Raymond Gaston. *The Art of the Sword in the Late Middle Ages*. Washington, D.C.: Catholic University of America, 1992.
Sprague, Arthur Colby. *Shakespeare—The Actors, The Stage Business in His Plays (1660–1905)*. The Harvard University Press, 1944.
Steinmetz, Andrew. *The Romance of Duelling in All Times and Countries*. Volume II. London: Chapman and Hall, 193, Piccadilly, 1868. 2 vols.
Stone, George Cameron. *A Glossary of the Construction, Decoration, and Use of Arms and Armor in All Countries and in All Times*. New York: Jack Brussel, 1961.
Sun-Tzu. *The Art of Strategy*. New York: Doubleday, 1988.
Sweigard, Lulu E. *Human Movement Potential: Its Ideokinetic Facilitation*. New York: Harper & Row, 1974.
Swetnam, Joseph. *The School of the Noble and Worthy Science of Defence*. London: Nicholas Okes, 1617.
Thimm, Carl A. *A Complete Bibliography of Fencing & Duelling*. New York: Benjamin Blom Inc., 1968.
Turner, Craig, and Tony Soper. *Methods and Practice of Elizabethan Swordplay*. Carbondale: Southern Illinois University Press, 1990.
Wise, Arthur. *Weapons in the Theatre*. New York: Barnes & Noble, Inc., 1969.
Wise, Terence. *Medieval Warfare*. New York: Hastings House, 1976.
Wright, Louis B. "Elizabethan Sea Drama and Its Staging." *Anglia*, 51 (1927), 104–118.

INDEX

abdominal breathing rhythms 14
Achilles 163, 180, 181, 182, 183, 184
acrobatics 3
acting 3
action 1, 3, 4, 7, 9, 17, 18, 23, 25, 27, 28, 29, 37, 51, 52, 92, 93, 100, 113, 114, 122, 129, 138, 140, 141, 162, 164, 192, 210, 219, 223, 229, 230, 236, 245, 253
actor 1, 2, 3, 4, 6, 7, 8, 9, 13, 14, 17, 18, 21, 22, 23, 25, 27, 32, 41, 93, 99, 113, 122, 123, 131, 163, 180, 220
actor-combatant 4, 8, 10, 11, 12, 14, 15, 16, 18, 21, 24
actresses 2
actual fighting 13
advance 4, 7, 9, 13, 30, 31, 55, 58, 59, 61, 83, 84, 85, 88, 100, 114, 122, 127, 137, 143, 144, 147, 150, 153, 154, 164, 165, 197, 202, 209, 227, 234, 235, 236, 241, 242, 247, 249, 250
advantageous position of strength 5
adversary 5, 17, 43, 60, 61, 82, 87, 111, 113, 213, 245, 255
Aeneas 165, 168
aerobic training 14
Agamemnon 164
agility 6, 23
Ajax 163, 164, 165, 166, 167, 168, 174, 175, 176, 177, 179, 180
alarms 214
alarum 61, 62, 71, 93, 99, 164, 193, 231
Alexander Iden 75
amount of force 7
ancient masters 1, 5, 11
angle of approach 16, 30
apprentice 11, 21, 23, 70, 71
archaic techniques of self defense 10
Arcite 254, 255, 256, 257, 258, 259, 260, 261, 262
aristocracy 24, 99, 112, 214, 245
armed conflicts 1
armor 22, 23, 25, 29, 37, 55, 60, 61, 62, 70, 75, 82, 83, 93, 142, 162, 164, 169, 180, 181, 185, 208, 214, 215, 254, 255
armorer 70
arm(s) 1, 2, 4, 5, 9, 17, 22, 25, 37, 41, 52, 99, 114, 162, 164, 204, 215, 256
art 3, 7
Arviragus 239
attack 4, 5, 6, 9, 13, 15, 16, 17, 18, 23, 24, 25, 30, 33, 37, 42, 55, 60, 61, 62, 71, 75, 82, 93, 94, 100, 113, 114, 121, 122, 135, 140, 142, 143, 144, 145, 146, 160, 163, 164, 169, 170, 175, 181, 184, 185, 192, 193, 200, 204, 215, 224, 232, 241, 246, 255, 256, 258
attack/defense combinations 11
attacker 9, 10, 13, 15, 16, 17
attitude 4
audience 1, 3, 4, 6, 7, 8, 9, 10, 13, 15, 16, 17, 18, 24, 25, 27, 29, 32, 42, 43, 50, 51, 65, 70, 81, 108, 111, 128, 129, 131, 132, 134, 138, 139, 140, 141, 142, 145, 163, 184, 193, 203, 207, 213, 219, 220, 223, 231, 239, 245
Aufidius 230, 231, 232, 233, 234, 235, 236, 237, 238
auncient 22
avoidance 35, 38, 43, 45, 48, 49, 58, 66, 67, 69, 72, 81, 85, 90, 102, 103, 104, 115, 116, 119, 122, 126, 131, 132, 136, 158, 170, 173, 176, 177, 188, 190, 194, 196, 202, 210, 211, 212, 216, 227, 241, 242, 246

backe sword 22, 240
backfall 91, 253
backplate 82, 254, 255
backward fall 60, 120
balance 3, 5, 6, 10, 12, 14, 16, 19, 20, 33, 42, 61, 62, 93, 100, 122, 164, 168, 183, 200, 215, 219, 223, 241, 255
balancing tactics 6
balestra 123, 158

ballow 208
Bardolph 51, 52
basic principles 4, 5, 6, 19
bastard sword 21, 22, 37, 61, 75, 86
battle 4, 6, 8, 10, 20, 22, 25, 27, 28, 29, 32, 37, 41, 42, 43, 51, 62, 71, 75, 82, 92, 93, 94, 99, 100, 109, 111, 112, 114, 140, 163, 164, 168, 180, 184, 185, 204, 208, 213, 214, 215, 220, 221, 224, 230, 231, 232, 240, 246, 254, 255, 256
battle plan 6
bear garden 185, 220
beat parry 36, 38, 47, 77, 88, 115, 222, 225, 226, 227, 243, 250, 261
Belarius 239
Benvolio 109, 110, 111, 112, 113, 114, 115, 116, 117, 118, 119, 120, 121, 122, 129, 130
bills 113
bind 37, 41, 63, 74, 79, 89, 94, 97, 98, 100, 106, 114, 118, 123, 127, 144, 145, 147, 155, 156, 193, 204, 225, 236, 246, 248, 255, 258, 260
Blackfriars Theatre 1
blade 9, 10, 12, 20, 22, 23, 25, 31, 32, 35, 43, 46, 47, 50, 52, 53, 55, 59, 60, 61, 62, 64, 65, 75, 81, 86, 87, 91, 93, 94, 95, 97, 108, 110, 111, 112, 113, 114, 116, 134, 143, 145, 158, 161, 193, 196, 198, 200, 203, 208, 209, 223, 224, 237, 240, 241, 242, 246, 251, 255; replacement 12
blueprint 7
Blunt, Sir Walter 29, 30, 31, 32, 37
Boar's Head Tavern 51
body outline 10, 32, 53, 138, 146, 158, 161, 170, 173, 200, 202, 203, 212, 213, 219, 223, 258
botte secrete 5
breastplate 30, 32, 40, 75, 83, 86, 163, 169, 181, 254, 255
breath control 12, 13, 14, 16
breathing rhythmically 14
breathing rhythms 13, 14
broadsword 19, 20, 52, 55, 61, 82, 86, 87, 93, 113, 121, 134, 163, 169, 192, 204, 221, 224, 231, 241, 254
buckler 21, 23, 24, 52, 112, 140, 163, 231
Burbage, Richard 21, 25
butt end 72, 73

Cade 75, 76, 77, 78, 79, 80, 81, 82
Cade's rebellion 75
Caius 204
Caius Martius Coriolanus 230
Capulet 22, 109, 112, 113, 120, 129, 134
casque 254
Cassio 191, 192, 193, 194, 195, 196, 197, 198
Catesby 99

center chest 16, 35, 39, 87, 90, 95, 123, 158, 172, 179, 182, 195, 196, 218, 235, 253, 258
center head 30, 34, 39, 44, 45, 47, 50, 56, 57, 59, 63, 67, 71, 77, 78, 80, 83, 84, 85, 167, 172, 177, 179, 182, 183
centering 14
centerline 121, 136
certified teacher 2, 3, 10, 11, 12, 14, 15, 28
chain mail 22
chairs 5
character 4, 5, 6, 18, 27, 28, 29, 42, 43, 86, 87, 92, 109, 111, 112, 139, 142, 145, 162, 203, 245
characterization 18
Charles 54, 55, 56, 57, 58, 59, 60
choke 106, 107, 108, 132
choreographer 1, 3, 4, 5, 6, 7, 8, 10, 11, 12, 14, 15, 16, 20, 29, 99, 100, 109, 254
choreographic phrase 14, 15, 16
choreography 1, 3, 5, 13, 14, 15, 27, 28, 30, 33, 38, 44, 56, 62, 71, 76, 83, 87, 94, 101, 114, 124, 131, 135, 140, 146, 165, 170, 175, 182, 186, 193, 200, 203, 205, 209, 216, 221, 225, 233, 241, 247, 257
circle 30, 31, 33, 37, 38, 39, 42, 47, 52, 55, 56, 61, 62, 64, 66, 69, 71, 72, 75, 77, 80, 87, 89, 93, 94, 97, 100, 103, 105, 115, 117, 122, 125, 132, 143, 144, 146, 151, 166, 169, 170, 200, 215, 216, 218, 225, 227, 228, 246, 249
circle parry 159, 200, 201, 251
civilian peace keepers 22
civilized man 3
Claudius 10, 140, 141, 142, 143, 144
Clifford 82, 83, 84, 85, 86, 87, 92, 93, 94, 95, 96, 97, 98
climax 7, 100
cloak 140
clockwise motion 39, 48, 56, 64, 77, 89, 97, 105, 127, 132, 218, 225,
close measure 5
Cloten 239, 240, 241, 242, 243, 244, 245
clubs 112
code duello 28
cohesive images 6
combat 1, 3, 4, 5, 6, 7, 8, 11, 12, 13, 15, 16, 19, 20, 25, 28, 54, 70, 123, 141, 163, 164, 166, 191, 207, 214, 215, 254
combat arts 109
combat studio 12
combatants 3, 4, 5, 6, 7, 11, 12, 13, 14, 15, 16, 17, 28, 43, 70, 99, 100, 111, 112, 123, 130, 140, 141, 142, 143, 145, 163, 192, 193, 207, 214, 215, 245, 254, 255, 256
combative skills 4
common people 22, 24
competitive foil 19
conceptual framework 27, 121, 139

INDEX

conflict 1, 3, 4, 7, 10, 27, 29, 41, 55, 70, 100, 111, 120, 163, 184, 245, 256
control 3
co-operation 11
coordination 6
Cordelia 203
Coriolanus 230–238
Corioles 231
Cornwall 199, 200, 201, 202, 203, 204, 207
corps a corps 35, 114, 120, 130, 145, 158, 204, 207, 219, 262
costumes 12
counter-attack 4, 6, 23, 24, 25, 143
counter clockwise motion 45, 66, 72, 77, 80, 103, 117, 125, 151, 170, 216, 227, 242, 249
counter cut 33, 38, 40, 45, 56, 62, 65, 68, 76, 97, 226, 252, 255, 260
counter parry 149, 151
coup de grâce 165
craft 3
Crean, Patrick 12
Cressida 162, 168
crippling and grappling maneuvers 8
criticism 3, 12, 13, 27
croisé 149, 152, 212
cross hilt 22, 23, 254
cross parry 113, 114, 116, 119, 122, 125, 126, 143, 145, 147, 160, 194
cross section 20
cudgel 208, 209
cue-reaction-action 9
cueing 9, 15, 16, 80, 99, 102, 158, 164, 185
cuirass 87
cuisse 82
cut 5, 8, 9, 10, 13, 15, 17, 18, 22, 23, 25, 30, 31, 33, 34, 36, 37, 38, 39, 40, 42, 43, 44, 45, 46, 47, 48, 50, 52, 53, 55, 56, 57, 58, 59, 61, 62, 63, 64, 65, 67, 68, 71, 75, 76, 77, 78, 79, 80, 82, 83, 84, 85, 86, 87, 88, 89, 92, 93, 94, 95, 96, 97, 100, 101, 102, 103, 105, 111, 113, 114, 119, 122, 130, 131, 132, 133, 134, 135, 136, 143, 144, 145, 146, 147, 148, 149, 150, 151, 152, 153, 154, 155, 156, 157, 158, 164, 165, 166, 167, 168, 169, 170, 171, 172, 175, 177, 178, 179, 181, 182, 183, 185, 186, 187, 188, 192, 193, 194, 196, 197, 202, 204, 206, 207, 215, 216, 217, 218, 221, 222, 223, 224, 225, 227, 228, 229, 231, 232, 233, 234, 237, 240, 241, 243, 244, 245, 246, 247, 248, 251, 252, 255, 257, 259, 260, 261
cutting the body 8
Cymbeline 239–253

dagger 17, 20, 21, 22, 23, 24, 25, 113, 114, 115, 117, 120, 121, 122, 123, 124, 125, 127, 134, 139, 140, 141, 142, 143, 144, 145, 146, 148, 149, 151, 152, 153, 154, 155, 156, 157, 159, 160, 192, 193, 195, 197, 198, 214, 215, 219, 240, 245
dance 1, 3
Dauphin 60
Davy vs. John Catour Combat of 1446 70
defender 9, 13, 15, 16, 122, 230
defense 3, 6, 9, 10, 15, 20, 22, 24, 25, 33, 37, 93, 99, 121, 129, 134, 140, 208, 213, 215, 246; ancient systems of 5; manuals of 10, 24, 25, 121, 130, 140
defensive 4, 5, 6, 7, 14, 22, 23, 24, 25, 55, 140, 246
defensive positions 5, 25
defensive space 6
defensive spatial advantage 4
deltoid 107
demi volte 125, 146, 258
de Sainct-Didier, Henri 143
design 10
designers 7
diagonal slash 49, 55, 62, 66, 67, 72, 102, 113, 114, 200, 202, 209, 210
dialogue 1, 7, 14, 20, 28, 61, 82, 100, 112, 113, 170, 185, 193
Di Grassi, Giacomo 22
dilettante 8
Diomedes 165, 168, 169, 170, 171, 172, 173, 174, 175, 176, 178, 179, 180
directed energy 7
directing 3
director 4, 7, 8, 17, 43, 99, 140, 142
disarming 6, 23, 25, 50, 60, 100, 106, 145, 160, 174, 200, 223, 245, 253
disengagement 131, 134, 149, 246, 249
distance 9, 17, 25, 33, 35, 37, 39, 44, 47, 48, 60, 62, 66, 75, 89, 94, 96, 100, 104, 108, 110, 121, 122, 125, 126, 128, 131, 132, 144, 146, 151, 160, 166, 170, 175, 179, 180, 182, 183, 184, 188, 193, 195, 197, 200, 201, 205, 209, 213, 215, 216, 218, 221, 225, 226, 232, 234, 241, 249, 257, 258, 259
Docciolini, Marco 5
Doll Tearsheet 51, 52
Douglas 29, 30, 31, 32, 33, 34, 35, 36, 37, 38, 39, 40, 41, 42, 43
dramatic action 8, 18, 93, 109, 141
dramatic character 4
dramatic conflict 3
dramatic effect 4
dramatic intentions 7
dramatic literature 3
dramatic production 3
dramatic purpose 4
dramatic tension 29, 100, 140
drill 11, 15, 17, 18
drums 143, 213

dubble 122
duck 13, 42, 52, 55, 59, 61, 62, 64, 66, 71, 72, 75, 94, 100, 114, 117, 130, 164, 165, 185, 208, 209, 215, 228, 246, 248, 255
duel 1, 20, 25, 28, 29, 32, 41, 43, 60, 82, 86, 99, 100, 109, 110, 111, 112, 114, 120, 121, 122, 123, 129, 130, 134, 139, 140, 141, 162, 163, 174, 180, 184, 185, 191, 192, 199, 204, 213, 220, 230, 231, 239, 241, 245, 246, 254, 255, 256
Duke of Albany 213
Duke of Cornwall 199, 204
Duke of Gloucester 92
Duke of York 82, 92
durability 10
dynamic energy 7

Earl of Gloucester 199, 208, 213
Earl of Kent 203, 204
economy 4, 6, 61
Edgar 207, 208, 209, 210, 211, 212, 213, 214, 215, 216, 217, 218, 219
edge 3, 9, 10, 16, 19, 22, 23, 24, 25, 36, 49, 53, 61, 62, 75, 86, 87, 130, 133, 134, 138, 141, 143, 148, 149, 153, 163, 164, 166, 167, 180, 181, 184, 192, 203, 213, 223, 231; false 9, 10, 31, 134, 143, 148, 159, 161, 203, 213
Edmund 203, 204, 205, 206, 207, 208, 213, 214, 215, 216, 217, 218, 219
Edward III 214
eighteenth century 19, 22
elbow blow 126
element of surprise 4
Elizabethan period 1, 8, 9, 20, 21, 22, 24, 27, 109, 120, 140, 141, 163, 185, 192, 220, 231, 240
Emilia 256
emotional responses 4
endurance 6, 142
enemy 5, 13, 29, 70, 82, 87, 143, 168, 224, 230, 246
England 1, 21, 22, 23, 24, 25, 41, 60, 75, 92, 93, 109, 120, 130, 141, 163, 240
English 9, 21, 22, 23, 24, 25, 54, 60, 109, 110, 111, 113, 120, 121, 130, 134, 141, 163, 203, 204, 208, 231, 241
envelopment 61, 64, 69, 106, 144, 150, 154, 241, 244, 253
epee 19
espauliere 82
etiquette 109
Europe 1
event theatrical 8
exhalation 14
explosives 3
extraneous tensions 14
eye-contact 16

Fabris, Salvator 5
facsimile weaponry 9
false edge 9, 10, 31, 134, 143, 148, 159, 161, 203, 213
Falstaff 22, 42, 43, 51, 52, 53
fashion 4, 19, 20, 21, 24, 75, 109, 110, 112, 180
feint 23, 25, 86, 87, 104, 135, 137, 144, 152, 153, 249
fencing 19, 52, 140, 143; manual 22; masks 12; matches 139, 140, 141, 142; "measure" 4; teachers 21
feud 109
fights 1, 2, 3, 4, 5, 6, 7, 8, 9, 10, 11, 12, 13, 14, 15, 16, 17, 20, 22, 23, 24, 25, 28, 29, 30, 32, 37, 41, 42, 43, 51, 52, 54, 55, 61, 71, 75, 82, 86, 89, 93, 99, 104, 110, 111, 112, 113, 114, 121, 122, 129, 130, 134, 139, 140, 163, 164, 165, 166, 168, 169, 174, 175, 180, 181, 184, 185, 191, 192, 199, 203, 204, 207, 208, 214, 220, 224, 230, 231, 240, 241, 245, 246, 254, 255, 256
fight director 17
fight master 1, 2, 3, 8, 10, 11, 12, 14, 15, 16, 21, 22, 28
"fight or flight" syndrome 14
fighting distance 10, 12, 17, 23, 25, 33, 57, 62, 81, 84, 85, 87, 90, 101, 105, 106, 119, 124, 126, 131, 132, 158, 160, 176, 182, 183, 187, 189, 190, 194, 195, 196, 211, 226, 227, 229, 232, 235, 255
fighting styles 20, 21, 140, 141
film 4
firearms 3, 110
first aid 3
flank 6, 32, 33, 37, 42, 87, 93, 108, 128, 143, 144, 145, 149, 153, 161, 167, 203, 213, 215, 219
flat of blade 23, 32, 35, 46, 50, 81, 86, 91, 108, 134, 139, 143, 184, 223, 237, 241, 242
fleche 146, 170
flexibility 14, 93
Flynn, Errol 12
foible 44, 153
foil 19, 139, 142
foins 208, 210
Folio 140
follow-through 10, 223
foot soldiers 22
footwork 6, 16, 17, 18, 23, 25
footwork patterns 11
force 7, 15
fore end 71, 72, 73, 74
forehand guard 122
forehand ward 134
forte 159
France 54, 139, 141
French 21, 24, 54, 60, 141
frontal attacks 6

INDEX

gaining ground 5
gaining the high ground 5
gauntlet 22, 23, 37, 39, 43, 44, 49, 61, 82, 134, 245, 246, 254, 255, 258
Gawsey, Sir Nicholas 41
geometric patterns 7
Georgian 9
Gertrude 140, 144
gestural conversation 13
glissade 90, 251
Globe Theatre 1
Gloucester 86, 92, 199, 200, 203, 204, 207, 208, 213, 214
gloves 12
Goneril 207, 208, 214, 215
grand guard 254
grappling 8, 23
gravity 7
greaves 163, 169, 181
Greeks 162, 163, 164, 165, 168, 169, 175, 180, 184
Gregory 112
grip 16, 37, 105, 108, 123, 165, 209, 215
guard 16, 22, 23, 30, 87, 100, 114, 135, 145, 163, 181, 214, 232, 246, 256
guidelines 4
Guiderius 239, 240, 241, 242, 243, 244, 245

Hal 37, 41, 42, 43, 46, 48, 99
halberd 114
half-pronated 50, 76, 77
half-pronation 32, 56, 58, 81, 84, 85, 137
Hamlet 1, 8, 10, 25, 139, 140, 141, 142, 143, 144, 145, 146, 147, 148, 149, 150, 151, 152, 153, 154, 155, 156, 157, 158, 159, 160, 161
hand-eye coordination 15
Harry 30, 37, 41, 42
Harry Monmouth 41
Harry Percy 41
head cut 16, 122, 124
head slash 13, 55, 59, 61, 62, 64, 66, 72, 75, 76, 79, 81, 97, 104, 117, 131, 165, 209, 216, 248, 250, 261
Hector 162, 163, 164, 165, 166, 167, 168, 180, 181, 182, 183, 184, 231
Helen of Troy 184
helmet 41, 61, 82, 93, 163, 164, 165, 168, 169, 174, 181, 184, 208, 214, 215, 221, 254, 255, 260
Henry IV, Part 1 29–50, 52
Henry IV, Part 2 22, 51–53
Henry VI, Part 1 54–69
Henry VI, Part 2 22, 70–91, 99
Henry VI, Part 3 92–97
high ground 5, 23
hilt 22, 23, 29, 32, 44, 114, 121, 134, 137, 145, 149, 160, 161, 168, 173, 208, 209, 212, 254, 255
Hippolyta 256

historical authenticity 8; technique 9; weapons 1, 3
history play 1
honor 11, 20, 29, 41, 42, 43, 129, 144, 191, 213, 215, 230, 255, 256
Horner 70, 71, 72, 73, 74
Hostess Quickly 51, 52
Hotspur 29, 32, 41, 42, 43, 44, 45, 46, 47, 48, 49, 50
hunting sword 240

Iago 191, 192, 193
Iden 75, 76, 77, 78, 79, 80, 81, 82
idiosyncratic tendencies 4
illusion 8, 9, 10, 13, 17, 74, 80, 93, 116, 120, 122, 123, 138, 158, 174, 210; of violence 10, 13
image 4
imbalance 14
imbrocata 123
incartata 122
inhalation 14
injury 4, 11, 13, 52, 129, 168
instinctual aggressive response 14
intention 7, 12, 13, 15, 16, 17, 18
intrinsic strategy 4
invitational positions 5
Italian 5, 21, 24, 109, 111, 120, 121, 130, 134, 141, 245
Italian fencing master 5
Italian Masters of Defence 21

Jachimo 245, 246, 247, 248, 249, 250, 251, 252, 253
Jacobean period 9, 20, 27, 240
Jamb 82
Joan De Pucelle 54–69
Joan of Arc 54
John of Lancaster 43
jousting armor 254
Juliet 1, 22, 24, 109, 110, 120, 129, 134, 135, 140, 162
justice 2

Kelly, Colleen 15
Kent 203, 204, 205, 206, 207
King Henry 2, 28, 32, 30, 33, 70
King Henry the Fifth 2
King Lear 199–219
knife 17, 240

Lady Capulet 113
Lady Montague 113
Laertes 139, 140, 141, 143, 144, 145, 146, 147,

148, 149, 150, 151, 152, 153, 154, 155, 156, 157, 158, 159, 160, 161
"lasie or careless guard" 121
Lear 199, 203, 207
levels 5, 7
lighting design 3
limitations 4
lines of attack 143
lines of force 7
lists 163, 214, 215
logical sequence of events 4
London 1, 21, 22, 24, 25, 109, 110, 140, 141
London Masters of Defence 1, 21, 22
long sword 21, 22, 214
Lord Clifford 82
Lord of Stafford 30
lunge 33, 66, 87, 113, 116, 117, 118, 126, 128, 133, 143, 149, 152, 158, 173, 193, 195, 196, 200, 201, 202, 203, 204, 205, 206, 208, 210, 246, 248, 249, 251

Macbeth 1, 220–229
Macduff 224, 225, 226, 227, 228, 229
Marozzo, Achille 123
Martius 230, 231
Masters of Defence 1, 8, 9, 21, 22, 23, 24, 23, 109, 110, 120, 121, 130, 134, 141; ancient 1, 5, 11
maximum effect 4
measure 4, 5, 6, 185
medieval 9, 22, 24, 70, 163
Menelaus 184, 185, 186, 187, 188, 189, 190
mercenaries 163, 181
merchant class 24, 109
Mercutio 109, 110, 111, 120, 121, 122, 123, 124, 125, 126, 128, 129, 130
The Merry Wives of Windsor 22
military 22, 23, 24, 204
mime 3
minimum effort 4
minute book 22, 141
misericorde 214
Mistress Quickly 52
misura larga 5
misura stretta 5
mobile defense 6
molinello 30, 34, 35, 38, 39, 45, 48, 49, 50, 56, 57, 59, 62, 63, 65, 66, 67, 77, 81, 85, 88, 94, 96, 97, 101, 113, 114, 119, 131, 133, 154, 194, 216, 218, 221, 227, 228, 257
Montague 22, 109, 112, 113, 120, 129
Montano 191, 192, 193, 194, 195, 196, 197, 198
montante 123
motivation 18

Nestor 180
nobility 24, 30, 109, 111, 120, 141, 199, 240

nonviolent relationship 13
novices 1

obstacles 4, 5
off stage 62, 163, 184, 220, 245
offense 6, 20, 22, 93, 99
offensive 4, 5, 6, 7, 9, 13, 14, 22, 23, 24, 25, 37, 122, 140, 230, 232, 246
offensive spaces 4
offensive spatial advantage 4
on stage 111, 169, 184
opponent 4, 5, 6, 17, 20, 22, 23, 24, 25, 62, 83, 86, 87, 92, 94, 100, 112, 122, 134, 139, 143, 144, 145, 204, 245, 246; mobility of 6
Osric 140, 141, 142, 143, 145, 158
Oswald 203, 207, 208, 209, 210, 211, 212, 213
Othello 191–198
overthwarting 121, 123

pain reaction 10, 32, 133, 183, 223, 236
Palamon 254, 255, 256, 257, 258, 259, 260, 261, 262
Parallel Parry 124, 127
Paris 134, 135, 136, 137, 138, 184, 185, 186, 187, 188, 189, 190
parries 32, 33, 37, 42, 43, 52, 55, 61, 62, 71, 75, 86, 87, 93, 100, 113, 114, 122, 123, 130, 131, 134, 135, 143, 144, 145, 169, 181, 185, 192, 193, 200, 204, 215, 221, 224, 232, 241, 246, 255
parrying 5, 13, 15, 22, 23, 30, 31, 33, 34, 36, 37, 38, 39, 40, 44, 45, 46, 47, 48, 49, 50, 53, 55, 56, 57, 58, 59, 62, 63, 64, 65, 67, 68, 71, 72, 73, 76, 77, 78, 79, 80, 82, 83, 84, 85, 86, 87, 88, 89, 90, 93, 94, 95, 96, 97, 100, 101, 102, 103, 104, 105, 113, 114, 115, 116, 117, 118, 119, 120, 122, 124, 125, 126, 127, 130, 132, 133, 134, 135, 136, 137, 141, 143, 144, 145, 146, 147, 148, 149, 150, 151, 152, 153, 154, 155, 156, 157, 158, 159, 160, 165, 166, 167, 170, 171, 172, 175, 176, 177, 178, 179, 180, 182, 183, 184, 186, 187, 188, 189, 193, 194, 195, 196, 197, 198, 200, 201, 202, 204, 205, 206, 207, 210, 216, 217, 218, 221, 222, 223, 225, 226, 227, 228, 232, 233, 234, 235, 236, 237, 241, 242, 243, 244, 246, 247, 248, 249, 250, 251, 252, 257, 258, 259, 260, 261, 262
partizan 112
partner 9, 13, 15, 16, 17
partnering 12
pass 31, 32, 34, 35, 36, 38, 39, 40, 44, 45, 47, 48, 49, 50, 55, 56, 57, 58, 59, 62, 63, 64, 65, 67, 68, 71, 72, 76, 77, 78, 79, 85, 88, 89, 90, 91, 94, 95, 96, 98, 101, 102, 103, 104, 105, 108, 114, 115, 116, 117, 118, 119, 124, 125, 126, 127, 135, 136, 137, 144, 145, 146, 147, 148, 149, 151,

152, 154, 156, 157, 158, 160, 165, 166, 167, 170, 171, 175, 176, 177, 178, 179, 180, 182, 183, 184, 186, 187, 188, 189, 190, 195, 196, 197, 201, 202, 203, 205, 206, 207, 210, 211, 212, 217, 218, 222, 226, 227, 228, 229, 235, 236, 237, 243, 244, 248, 251, 252, 259, 260, 261, 262
passado 110, 121, 122
Patrocles 181
patterns 7
performance theory 7, 11
performance training 14
performers 3
period plays 8, 9
period style 5
personal warfare 6
Peter 70, 71, 72, 73, 74
Petruchio 129
physical advantage 6
physical history 12
physical type 4, 6
physiology 3, 17
physique 5, 17
pike 22
Pirithous 256
Pistol 20, 51, 52, 53
plan of action 4
playhouse 21
playing a prize 21, 141
playing area 142
plot 4, 7, 27, 120, 139, 142
point 1, 5, 8, 10, 15, 16, 43, 55, 75, 87, 114, 121, 122, 130, 137, 140, 141, 143, 144, 145, 146, 162, 168, 192, 209, 215, 231, 255
point of view 17
pole arms 22
poniard 21, 113, 114, 116, 120, 121, 122, 124, 125, 126, 130, 131, 132, 140, 141, 142, 143, 144, 145, 146, 147, 152, 155, 156, 157, 160
position 5, 6, 12, 14, 25, 62, 81, 91, 106, 112, 126, 130, 137, 144, 173, 216, 217, 223
positional advantages 5
positions of balance 14
Posthumus 239, 245, 246, 247, 248, 249, 250, 251, 252, 253
preparatory movement 16
pretending to fight 13
Prince Escalus 113
Prince Hal 37, 41, 42, 43
Prince Henry 37, 38, 39, 40, 41, 43, 44, 45, 46, 47, 48, 49, 50
Prince of Wales 29, 37, 41, 42
principles 3
prize-fight 163
pronation 32, 49, 53, 57, 69, 76, 81, 117, 125, 135, 137, 146, 165, 173, 174, 176, 180, 188, 189, 196, 203, 209, 211, 212, 213, 216, 227, 235, 242, 248, 250, 261, 262

property design 3
proportion 121, 122
psycho/physical preparation 14
psychological condition 4
Pucelle 54, 55, 56, 60, 61, 62
pummel 22, 23, 55, 59, 60, 107, 111, 113, 116, 135, 138, 169, 174, 219, 255, 258
punta riversa 123
punto reverso 110, 121
puts by 122

quarterstaff 20, 70, 71, 74
quarto 139
Queen Elizabeth 9, 22

rapier 20, 21, 22, 24, 25, 51, 52, 111, 112, 113, 114, 115, 116, 117, 118, 120, 121, 122, 123, 124, 125, 126, 127, 128, 130, 131, 132, 133, 134, 135, 137, 138, 139, 140, 141, 142, 143, 144, 145, 146, 147, 148, 149, 150, 151, 152, 153, 154, 155, 156, 157, 158, 159, 160, 161, 192, 193, 194, 195, 196, 197, 198, 199, 200, 203, 204, 208, 209, 212, 213, 231, 240, 241, 242, 245, 253
rapier and dagger 20, 21, 22, 24, 25, 114, 140, 141, 240, 245
Regan 199, 200, 203, 204, 208
rehearsal 9, 12, 13, 14, 15, 16, 17, 27
rehearsal room 12
release 14, 41, 53, 55, 69, 74, 108, 138, 173, 174, 209, 223, 260
Renaissance 9
replacement blades 12
resistance 7
rest periods 12
retreat 4, 13, 30, 31, 42, 55, 56, 57, 60, 62, 75, 83, 84, 85, 87, 88, 117, 118, 122, 141, 143, 144, 147, 153, 154, 158, 181, 184, 185, 200, 215, 232, 242, 246, 247, 249
reverse cut 9, 10, 122
reverse edge 9
rhythm 5, 7, 13, 14, 15, 246
Richard 1, 21, 25, 86, 87, 88, 89, 90, 91, 92, 93, 94, 95, 96, 97, 98, 99, 100, 101, 102, 103, 104, 105, 106, 107, 108
Richard Gloucester 86
Richard Tarleton 1
Richard III 99–108
Richard the Third 1, 86, 99
Richmond 86, 99, 100, 101, 102, 103, 104, 105, 106, 107, 108
rifle 20
Roderigo 191, 192
Roman period 163
Romans 163, 230, 231, 245
Romeo 1, 22, 24, 109, 110, 111, 120, 121, 122, 123,

126, 128, 129, 130, 131, 132, 133, 134, 135, 136, 137, 138, 140, 162
Romeo and Juliet 1, 22, 24, 109–138, 140

sabre 19
SAFD 3
safety 3, 4, 9, 11, 12, 13, 14, 16, 17, 25, 27, 28, 130, 139
safety sequence 9
Saviolo,Vincentio 121, 123, 134, 143
scene partner 13
scenes of violence 1
schools of fence 21, 25
"the Scottish play" 220
scuffling 145
second guard 134
self defense 8, 9, 10, 27, 192
sensory awareness 12, 16
sequence of techniques 5
sequential movements 9
servants 24, 75, 109, 111, 112, 199 200, 201, 202, 203, 204
seventeenth century 5, 121, 140, 141, 163, 192, 204, 240, 241, 245
Shakespeare 1, 3, 5, 8, 10, 20, 21, 22, 23, 24, 25, 27, 28, 29, 32, 51, 54, 62, 70, 75, 82, 86, 109, 110, 111, 112, 120, 121, 129, 130, 139, 140, 141, 162, 163, 168, 175, 184, 192, 203, 208, 213, 220, 230, 231, 240, 245, 254
shape 6, 19, 92, 180
shield 15, 22, 24, 29, 30, 31, 32, 33, 34, 35, 36, 37, 38, 39, 42, 43, 44, 46, 49, 82, 83, 84, 85, 86, 87, 90, 91, 93, 94, 95, 99, 100, 112, 163, 164, 165, 166, 167, 168, 169, 170, 172, 173, 174, 175, 176, 177, 178, 179, 181, 182, 183, 184, 185, 186, 187, 188, 189, 214, 215, 216, 217, 218, 219, 221, 222, 223, 224, 225, 226, 227, 228, 229, 231, 232, 233, 234, 235, 236, 237
short sword 20, 21, 22, 23, 24, 214
signals 12
Signor Rocco 121
Silver, George 122, 123, 134, 143
simulated cut 10
simultaneous attack and defence 8
single handed sword 29
single-stick 22
sixteenth century 9, 20, 21, 22, 23, 24, 109, 110, 111, 112, 121, 140, 141, 142, 143, 163, 168, 199, 254
size 6
slapstick 203
slash 7, 13, 33, 42, 43, 48, 49, 55, 57, 59, 61, 62, 64, 66, 67, 69, 71, 72, 75, 76, 79, 81, 83, 87, 90, 94, 97, 100, 102, 103, 104, 105, 106, 111, 113, 114, 115, 117, 119, 122, 123, 124, 126, 128, 130, 131, 132, 145, 158, 165, 169, 170, 176, 177, 180, 185, 187, 190, 193, 194, 196, 200, 202, 208, 209, 210, 211, 215, 216, 224, 227, 229, 235, 241, 242, 246, 248, 250, 255, 261
slip 122, 123, 135
slow motion 7, 12
small sword 19, 20, 140
social class 24
Society of American Fight Directors 1, 2, 3, 8, 10, 11, 15, 16
soft-soled shoes 12
soldier 22, 23, 32, 43, 61, 62, 100, 162, 163, 184, 204, 208, 215, 230, 231, 232, 238, 245, 246
Somerset 86, 87, 88, 89, 90, 91, 97
sounds of conflict 7
space 4, 5, 6, 7, 12, 16, 33, 100, 112, 134
Spanish 21, 24, 109, 111, 121, 134, 141
spatial advantage 4, 6
specialist 3
spectacle 1
speed 5, 6, 9, 12, 14, 15, 16, 100, 113, 114, 134, 255
sport 8, 19, 22, 23, 25, 70, 185
sport fencing 19
staff 20, 21
Stafford, Sir Humphrey 75
stage 1, 2, 3, 4, 5, 6, 7, 8, 9, 10, 11, 12, 14, 16, 17, 20, 24, 25, 27, 29, 32, 41, 42, 43, 52, 55, 62, 75, 80, 87, 99, 100, 106, 108, 111, 112, 113, 114, 129, 139, 140, 141, 142, 162, 163, 164, 169, 175, 180, 184, 185, 190, 193, 204, 213, 220, 223, 224, 229, 231, 232, 241, 245, 246, 253, 255
stage fights 1, 2, 3, 4, 5, 6, 7, 8, 9, 10, 11, 12, 13, 14, 15, 16, 17, 18, 20, 27, 28, 29, 99, 109, 121, 122, 131, 135, 139; choreography 1, 3; director 4
stage movement 3
stage setting 3, 7, 27
stage worthy weaponry 11
stance 5, 6, 9, 14, 25, 47, 66, 83, 89, 96, 104, 121, 162, 166, 170, 180, 213, 234, 255
standard bearer 22
standardization 23
Stanislavsky, Konstantin 17
stationary 30, 33, 35, 36, 38, 41, 44, 45, 46, 47, 48, 49, 50, 53, 56, 57, 59, 60, 62, 63, 64, 65, 66, 67, 68, 69, 71, 72, 73, 74, 76, 77, 78, 79, 80, 81, 85, 86, 87, 89, 90, 91, 95, 96, 97, 98, 103, 104, 105, 106, 107, 108, 115, 116, 117, 118, 119, 120, 124, 125, 126, 128, 131, 132, 133, 134, 135, 136, 137, 138, 143, 146, 147, 149, 150, 151, 152, 153, 154, 155, 156, 157, 158, 159, 160, 161, 165, 167, 168, 170, 172, 173, 174, 175, 176, 177, 179, 180, 183, 188, 193, 194, 195, 196, 197, 198, 201, 202, 203, 205, 206, 207, 209, 210, 212, 213, 216, 217, 218, 221, 222, 223, 225, 226, 227, 228, 233, 234, 236, 237, 238, 242, 244, 248, 249, 250, 251, 252, 253, 257, 258, 259, 260, 261, 262

stealing ground 123
steel plate 22
steps 5
stoccata 122, 123
stomach punch 78
storyline 4, 7, 121
stramazone 123
strategic drama 9
strategy 4, 7, 9, 16, 19, 20, 23, 25, 87
Stratford Shakespeare Festival 12
strength 4, 5, 6, 33, 37, 60, 61, 100, 142, 204, 208, 213, 215
styles of technique 20
Suddeth, Allen 16
supination 35, 40, 48, 57, 58, 59, 67, 83, 86, 90, 119, 124, 126, 127, 131, 153, 159, 184, 186, 189, 190, 194, 201, 210, 211, 216, 229, 249, 252
suspension of disbelief 3, 17
swashbuckler 112
Swetnam, Joseph 121
sword 1, 2, 4, 5, 8, 9, 10, 11, 12, 13, 16, 17, 19, 20, 21, 22, 23, 24, 25, 29, 30, 32, 33, 35, 36, 37, 38, 41, 42, 43, 44, 50, 51, 52, 53, 54, 55, 59, 61, 62, 63, 69, 75, 79, 80, 81, 82, 83, 86, 87, 89, 91, 93, 94, 97, 98, 99, 100, 102, 108, 110, 111, 112, 113, 114, 118, 119, 120, 121, 122, 123, 124, 125, 127, 128, 130, 131, 132, 133, 134, 135, 137, 138, 139, 140, 145, 146, 147, 161, 163, 164, 165, 168, 169, 172, 173, 174, 175, 180, 181, 185, 187, 190, 192, 193, 196, 199, 200, 201, 203, 204, 208, 209, 213, 214, 215, 216, 217, 218, 219, 220, 221, 223, 224, 225, 226, 227, 228, 229, 230, 231, 232, 233, 234, 235, 236, 237, 240, 241, 246, 251, 254, 255, 256, 258, 260, 261, 262
sword and buckler 24, 52, 112, 163, 231
sword and dagger 22, 124, 127
sword fighting 1, 11, 12, 19, 20, 21, 25, 109, 111, 120, 121, 134, 141, 163
swordplay 1, 9, 10, 19, 20, 21, 25, 109, 120, 121, 130, 139, 141; systems of 8
swordsmen 19, 20, 21, 111, 141
swordsmiths 10, 11, 19, 20
synthesizer 15

tactical elements 6
tactics 6, 7, 17, 87
Talbot 60, 61, 62, 63, 64, 65, 66, 67, 68, 69
target 4, 5, 7, 9, 12, 13, 15, 16, 17, 18, 21, 23, 24, 37, 43, 52, 122, 123, 130, 141, 142, 163, 241, 246
targeting 8, 15, 16
targeting & cueing 12
targeting the face 8
targets 4, 5, 16, 23, 37, 241, 246
Tarleton, Richard 21

teaching 1
techniques 1, 2
temperament 4
tempo 5, 11, 12, 14, 15, 16, 52, 55, 113, 121, 140, 145, 175
tension 14, 16, 140
textual references 1
Thalhoffer, Hans 22
theatre 1, 3, 8, 10, 21, 28, 141, 240
theatrical distance 17
theatrical effect 8, 37
theatrical flow 6
theatrical illusion 8
theatrical manipulation 5
theatrical tradition 7
theme 4
Thersites 168, 184, 185
Theseus 256, 262
Thomas of Woodstock 163, 214
thrust 8, 16, 17, 18, 22, 23, 24, 25, 30, 32, 33, 35, 37, 40, 43, 48, 49, 50, 51, 52, 53, 55, 56, 58, 61, 62, 68, 73, 74, 75, 76, 77, 81, 82, 83, 84, 85, 86, 87, 90, 91, 93, 94, 95, 96, 100, 101, 104, 108, 111, 113, 114, 115, 116, 117, 118, 120, 121, 122, 123, 124, 126, 127, 128, 130, 131, 134, 135, 136, 137, 138, 141, 143, 144, 145, 146, 148, 149, 150, 151, 152, 153, 156, 157, 158, 159, 160, 161, 164, 165, 167, 169, 170, 171, 173, 176, 181, 182, 183, 184, 185, 186, 187, 189, 192, 193, 195, 196, 198, 200, 201, 202, 203, 204, 205, 206, 208, 209, 210, 212, 213, 215, 219, 221, 223, 226, 227, 231, 232, 235, 236, 240, 241, 242, 243, 244, 245, 246, 247, 249, 250, 251, 252, 255, 258, 262
tierce 123
time 1, 4, 5, 7, 8, 10, 13, 15, 24, 28, 41, 55, 110, 121, 122, 140, 144, 145, 164, 220, 230, 241
time-lengths 5
timing 9, 15, 23, 80, 86, 100, 113
Titus Andronicus 27, 163
Titus Lartius 230
torso 45, 67, 100, 105, 114, 116, 141, 202, 210, 212
traditional technique 9
training 1, 3, 9, 10, 11, 12, 13, 15, 16, 17, 18, 20, 21, 23, 130, 143, 144
transition rapier 140, 240, 245
trapezius 107
trapping an opponent 4
traverse 122, 123
trial by combat 70, 163, 214, 215
triangular cross-section 141
triangular shield 29
triple intention attack 18
tripping 22
Troilus 162, 164, 168, 169, 170, 171, 172, 173, 174, 175, 176, 177, 178, 179, 180, 181
Troilus and Cressida 162–190

Trojan War 162, 163, 184, 185
Trojans 162, 163, 164, 165, 169, 174, 175, 184, 185
true edge 122
trumpet 29, 61, 71, 143, 164, 165, 180, 184, 213
Tudor 27
Tullus 231
Tullus Aufidius 230
Twelfth Night 28
The Two Noble Kinsmen 254–262
two-weapon techniques 24
Tybalt 109, 110, 111, 112, 113, 114, 115, 116, 117, 118, 119, 120, 121, 122, 123, 124, 125, 126, 127, 128, 129, 130, 131, 132, 133, 134, 140

Ulysses 174
uneven ground 5
unifying elements in basic training 14
United States 1
unsafe techniques 8

vault 196, 211
verisimilitude 8
victim 9, 10, 17, 92, 134, 221
violence 1, 3, 4, 13, 25, 27, 29, 110, 111, 134, 140, 144, 145, 191, 192, 204, 209; illusion of 10, 13
visor 215
visualization 6, 7, 21
vocal reaction 138, 210, 229
vocalizations 14

Volsces 231
Volscian 232
Volscian Army 231
vulnerability 4, 5

Wagner, Eduard 23
Wales 239
warm-ups 14
weapon(s) 1, 3, 4, 5, 7, 9, 10, 11, 12, 13, 16, 17, 19, 20, 21, 22, 23, 24, 25, 51, 52, 62, 70, 71, 87, 93, 99, 109, 110, 112, 113, 115, 121, 122, 123, 134, 138, 139, 140, 141, 142, 144, 145, 146, 161, 163, 164, 166, 169, 192, 193, 199, 204, 214, 215, 221, 232, 240, 245, 254; facsimile 9
weight 14, 15, 16, 17, 19, 20, 45, 48, 174, 215
Whithall 25
wide measure 5
wide stance 5
Woodstock Code 214
wounds 10, 17, 37, 42, 43, 51, 61, 83, 91, 100, 106, 114, 129, 131, 134, 140, 143, 145, 181, 193, 196, 199, 200, 203, 204, 213, 219, 220, 221, 229, 231, 232, 235, 236, 245, 246
wrestling 6
wrist guard 181

York 71, 82, 83, 84, 85, 86, 92
Young Clifford 82, 87
Young Siward 223, 220, 221

www.ingramcontent.com/pod-product-compliance
Ingram Content Group UK Ltd.
Pitfield, Milton Keynes, MK11 3LW, UK
UKHW050540150426
5217IPUK00026B/2007